David Janssen
Our Conversations

The Final Years
(1973-1980)

Michael Phelps

David Janssen – Our Conversations
Volume Two – The Final Years
1973 – 1980

Cover design: Bradleigh S. Stockwell
Editor/Interior Design: Norma Budden

ISBN: 978-0-9887778-1-1

Blue Line Publishing House, Inc.
New York, NY * Miami, FL

"My former lover, David Janssen, was the most sensitive, passionate man I knew. Michael Phelps, in his book 'David Janssen - Our Conversations' shares David's passions and sensitivity with the world."

Carol Connors – May, 2013

1976 - Award Winning Singer/Songwriter Carol Connors & David Janssen celebrate, *My Sensitive, Passionate Man.*

Award Winning Singer/Songwriter Carol Connors & Author Michael Phelps. Carol was David's last true love. Michael Phelps was one of his true friends. (Photo by Moises Raudez)

David Janssen at the start of his fourth television series, *Harry O,* in July of 1974. The first two episodes were filmed in Los Angeles, but the idea of filming on location in San Diego came from ABC Television and Dave loved the idea.

FOREWORD

Michael Phelps, whom I affectionately call Mike, has become a dear friend over the past few years; he is quick to point out that he is not the Olympic swimmer whom most people think of when they first hear his name.

Throughout the past couple of years, I've read bits and pieces of *David Janssen – Our Conversations*. From the onset, I became absorbed in the story, often feeling I was an unseen party witnessing private conversations between David and Mike.

I feel as though I've gotten to know David Janssen, though I had never heard his name until Mike brought him up in conversation. Since that time, I've watched a few episodes of *The Fugitive* and fully understand why, even after three decades since he has passed, fans still think about him, even miss him.

David Janssen came across, to me, as a man who possessed more than charm and good looks; he had a magnetic personality which, instinctively, drew people towards him. His calm manner, confidence in himself and his 'down-to-earth' nature were tell-tale signs that he possessed this characteristic.

Between the pages of *David Janssen – Our Conversations*, I watched a friendship grow, even blossom. Mike and David were two blessed men in that they discovered a rare and lasting friendship with each other; they loved each other like brothers and trusted each other with their lives.

After embarking on such a journey into the life of one of the most beloved actors the world has known, imagine how I felt when Mike passed the reigns over to me, asking me to prepare his memoir for publication! I was beyond delighted – thrilled to be part of such an endeavor, even though it would take numerous days to complete the task.

Throughout my journey, I've discovered that David Janssen was a rich man in terms of the wealth he possessed. He was rich in that he had a handful of close friends like Michael Phelps to brighten the darkest days of his life. In other areas, however, I am richer than David Janssen ever was.

I might not have the balance that was in his bank account, in relation to what it would be worth today, but I do count Mike as one of my closest friends. I also live a relatively simple life, surrounded by people who love and care about me – never feeling forced to have to surround myself with people who don't enhance my life in any way.

By the time you finish reading *David Janssen – Our Conversations*, I hope you will feel as I do. I hope you will count your blessings, those which do not relate to the number of dollars in your bank account. I pray you will be thankful for your friends who have been true to you – friends you will hold dear for the remainder of your life, knowing they love you - for you - not for the material wealth you possess.

Author,
Norma Budden of Norma's Books
www.normasbooks.com

David Janssen
Our Conversations

The Final Years
(1973-1980)

Michael Phelps

1

~1973~

The holidays came and went. I relaxed at home with Baron. I took Rose Marie out for Christmas Eve dinner and, of course, for New Year's Eve.

After dinner, we made our way to Times Square to join the festivities of watching the ball drop at the stroke of midnight. I had Rose Marie home by 1:30 and I made it home by two o'clock.

Dave called me Friday morning, January 12, at 5:30.

"Good morning, Mike. It's me. Happy New Year! How were your holidays?"

"Happy New Year to you and Dani, too. I had a very relaxing holiday season ... glad they're over and I'm back at work."

"What did you do to celebrate? Did you celebrate with Rose Marie?"

"Yes, of course. I took her to the Rainbow Room for dinner; she loves the place. That was Christmas Eve, and then we went to Joe Allen's for New Year's Eve. She talked all about when you and Rosemary invited us to Joe Allen's and she loved the food. I had a nice holiday. What did you and Dani do?"

"We went to several parties and then just relaxed at home. It was good. I just wanted to give you a call and tell you I will be doing the pilot for a new television series."

"A new series? GOOD ... but I thought you didn't want to do another series. What is it about?"

"You will love it! It's about a cop wounded in the line of duty ... has to retire and becomes a private detective."

"That sounds like it will be another 'hit' for you! Where were you wounded ... how long had you been on LAPD? Are you married ... have kids?" I peppered him with rapid fire questions.

"Okay ... slow down. I had been shot in the back - bullet too close to my spine for them to take it out. I had been a cop for several years - a patrol officer. I'm divorced, no kids ... and it's the San Diego Police Department, not LAPD," he said.

"San Diego? Why not LAPD? You're going to film it in LA, right?"

"San Diego is where the writer, Howard Rodman, set it. He's a damn good writer! I love the script for the pilot; otherwise, I would not have agreed to do the pilot. We'll be filming it here in Burbank, not San Diego."

"Is Quinn Martin going to be the producer?" I asked.

"No, it's being produced and directed by Jerry Thorpe and it's commissioned by ABC. If the pilot is well received, there is a good chance it will be on the ABC fall line up."

"So that would mean you will be back to the 14 to 16 hours a day schedule ... the grueling schedule you vowed never to be trapped in again ... right?"

"Yeah ... you are right, that's what it would mean - but I like the potential of this series. I think it will be worth it."

"Does Dani know about it? Is she okay with it? Will she be appearing in the show as a guest star?"

"Of course, she knows ... and I think she's as excited as I am. If it goes ahead then I'd have to cut back on the party circuit, which Dani seems to live for; she loves parties but I'll not be able to keep up that kind of schedule if I'm doing the series."

"I remember when we first met you told me you liked playing a cop and, from what I've seen, starting with *Richard Diamond*, *Warning Shot*, even *O'Hara*, you are damn good at it. I'm glad they did not cast you as Lieutenant Gerard, though; everyone hated him and, for four years on the run, you made him look like an inept, incompetent cop."

Dave laughed. "Yeah, I would not have taken Morse's role but, then again, he was from Indiana, a small town. Of course, I'm not saying all Indiana cops are incompetent." He laughed again.

"Yeah ... right ... you're not saying all Indiana cops are incompetent, but I have a surprise for you: some of them are." We both laughed.

"I was just kidding, Mike."

"I know. So tell me, what is the pilot story? What is the title?"

"It's called *Harry O;* my character's name is Harry Orwell but he's called *Harry O* for short by his friends. The plot is: a member of the robbery crew who shot me four years ago hires me to find his partners in crime. It's called *Such Dust As Dreams Are Made On;* I think you will like it."

"I'm sure I will, but wait a minute! The guy who shot you comes back and hires you to find his cohorts ... that doesn't sound too plausible. Who else will be in the pilot?"

"He's the one who pulled the trigger so I have good reason to lock him up, but more reason to take the case and find the other guy who shot and killed my partner. This guy has remorse; he turned his life around, saved up money for me to have an operation.

"Mel Stewart plays Sergeant Granger, a cop, my old boss; Martin Sheen, the bad guy who shot me; Sal Mineo as the bad guy who shot my partner; Will Geer plays a chemist friend of mine and there's a female cop who keeps hitting on me. That's the main line up. I'll let you know who else when I find out who they cast."

"Thanks. Does this Sergeant Granger have a recurring role, if the series moves forward?"

"Yeah, at least, I think he will. He'll be my main contact in the San Diego PD and I use him to get into police files I no longer can and, of course, I use him in other ways. He knows it - doesn't really like it, but we're friends, and I solve cases. He gets the credit."

"Dave, it all sounds really exciting. I'm sure it will turn into a good series; I can't wait to see it. Do you have any idea when it will be aired?"

"No, we haven't started filming yet so it will take a couple of weeks of filming, then they have to do the editing, music and all that stuff ... so it won't be anytime soon. Don't worry, Mike! I'll be sure to call you when I know."

"Well, I'm pretty sure it will be a hit ... and I, for one, will like seeing you at least once a week, even if it is only on television," I said, joking.

"I'll keep you up-to-date on it. I'm looking forward to getting back into something steady. I just wanted to give you a call and touch base with you so I'll run for now and call you later."

"Thanks, Dave ... let me know for sure when you start, or when you finish, filming this one. Talk later."

I was glad to hear from Dave and especially the news about his prospective new series. The way Dave explained the series, I felt certain it would garner good ratings and make ABC and Dave a lot of money.

Several weeks passed and I saw nothing in the New York newspapers, *TV Guide* or the fan magazines about Dave or *Harry O*. I was beginning to think that maybe it did not work out and there would be no series to look forward to. Dave had not called since the 12th of January so I assumed he was very busy, could even be filming the pilot for all I knew.

Sunday morning, February 25, 1973, Dave called me at 6:15. I had just fixed my first cup of coffee and Baron was anxiously awaiting his run in Riverside Park.

"Good morning, Mike ... hope I didn't wake you."

"Not at all, Dave - just having my first cup of coffee then I'll take Baron to his park. How are you? Haven't heard from you for over a month ... you had me worried."

"Don't worry! I have just been very busy. A good friend of mine passed away, went to his services ... finished the pilot for *Harry O* and now I'm taking it easy."

"I wasn't really worried, Dave. I knew you must be very busy. Sorry about your friend ... was he a TV or movie star?"

"No, he was a businessman ... Ralph Stolkin - a really nice guy, a good friend. I stayed at his home for a couple of weeks when I first left Ellie."

"I'm sorry for your loss, Dave. Do you have any idea when the *Harry O* pilot will be aired?"

"Thanks, Mike! No, they are doing all of the technical parts so it will be a few weeks even before I will know. I'll call you and give you a heads-up when I know the date. How are things with you, Rose Marie and Baron?"

"No change. Everything is going smooth. Baron is still growing. I love my job, doing very well there; I hired some darn good people and they are making me look good to the boss."

"I'm glad to hear that. Give Rose Marie my best. How are you doing in your divorce?"

"Sorry to say, Dave, I really have been too busy to do anything about it. I haven't really even thought about it. My wife hasn't communicated with me so I've just been letting it remain as status quo."

"Well, my advice is you better start thinking about it. Now that you're making big bucks, I'd hate to see you lose a big chunk to a wife who's never really been a wife, after all this time."

"You're right, Dave. I'll do something ... real soon. How is Dani?"

"She is fine. I said I would marry her. Actually, I guess I proposed to her ... by way of telling some reporter we would be getting married."

"CONGRATULATIONS, DAVE! That is really good news! I mean, you've been a bachelor for what, almost three years. I guess you have finally decided SHE is the right one for you."

"Don't rush me, Mike! I said we were going to get married, but I didn't say when, and I haven't really been a bachelor for three years. You are forgetting a couple of years living with Rosemary and I have been with Dani since I left Rosemary, so I haven't really had the bachelor lifestyle," Dave said, then laughed.

"Well, I will be looking for my engraved invitation in the mail."

"Don't hold your breath, Mike. I have to get some sleep but I'll call you soon. You take care."

"Thanks, Dave ... talk later."

After that conversation, I felt totally confused. I could not help wondering IF Dani had been pressuring Dave to get married. I surmised it was a definite possibility and Dave had acquiesced but he was not completely, in his heart, ready to get married to anyone at this time. I could only wait and see.

2

I was surprised when Dave called me in my office on Friday morning, March 9, at 11:50.

"Good morning, Mike! I hope I'm not interrupting you; am I?"

"No, Dave, you are not ... what's up?"

"I just got word: ABC will air the pilot of *Harry O* on Sunday ... you will have to check the time there."

"Don't worry! I damn sure won't miss it! Have you seen the finished film? How do you feel about it ... do you feel good ... like it will be picked up by ABC?"

"I'm not sure yet. Yes, I saw the finished film but I have reservations. I don't feel I've really gotten the character down pat. I like him, but I'm not sure I portrayed him the way Rodman intends for him to be received by everyone else."

"Well, I will watch it very carefully and give you my honest opinion when we talk next. How are things with Dani? Any date set for your wedding?"

"Dani is fine. NO, there is no date set for any wedding. I told you, DON'T RUSH ME!"

"Oh ... Oh ... I feel I touched a raw nerve! SORRY! I won't make that mistake again ... I'll just wait for an invitation to come in my mail," I said, then laughed.

"I'm kidding, Mike ... don't take me seriously. I am not in any rush to get married. I'll let you know. I'll call you next week."

"All right, Dave! Thanks for the heads-up about *Harry O.* I'll watch it and see if I can find any flaws in your portrayal. Be sure to call me."

"I will, Mike. Take it easy."

I was excited and anxious for Sunday to come. Rose Marie would come over for dinner and watch the pilot with me.

Dave sounded good, even though he voiced some self-doubt about his portrayal of the character.

When Rose came over, I would ask her to watch the show very, very closely with me. Not only would we scrutinize Dave's performance but those of the supporting actors as well.

Friday evening I took Rose Marie for dinner and told her about the pilot of *Harry O*. She was as excited as me and we agreed we would do our best to pick apart everything about the show, from the plot, the dialogue, the scenery, the supporting cast and, especially, Dave's portrayal.

Sunday evening finally came. Rose Marie and I ordered a pizza and decided pizza and sodas would be our dinner. I had some ice cream on hand to make banana splits for dessert.

Harry O came on ABC at nine o'clock as a two hour special. There was no mention that it might be forthcoming as a series.

In the opening scene, Harry O is in bed, his alarm clock goes off and, as he fumbles for it, you see a hand holding it out for him. He awakes and Harlan Garrison, played by Martin Sheen, is holding a gun on him; Harlan Garrison is the man who shot him four years ago.

Marianna Hill plays a police woman who obviously wants more than a platonic relationship with Harry. Will Geer plays an elderly chemist-friend of Harry's who provides him with intelligence on the making of heroin. Sal Mineo is listed as a special guest star; he is the other robber who killed Harry's partner four years earlier.

As the plot unfolds, you see Harry O taking a city bus from a college to his home, which is somewhere on the beach.

An implausible scene shows a 19-year-old girl in the college office coming on to an obviously much older Harry. Harry notices this and his comment to the girl is actually funny.

As the story unfolds, Harry enters a bar and asks the lone female customer seated at the bar the name of the bartender. She tells him, "Stuart". Harry has a conversation with Stuart and ends up going home with the girl in her Mustang convertible.

The scene ends with Sal Mineo's character shooting and wounding a motorcycle policeman. Harry takes the officer's motorcycle and a wild chase ensues with Harry chasing the bad guy. After each spill off their motorcycles, a lengthy foot chase ensues. Harry finally captures him.

The two hour pilot was overall a good show, in mine and Rose Marie's opinions. Afterwards, Rose Marie and I spent an hour discussing the show.

My opinion:

First: I felt the lighting was way too dark and was such in almost every scene.

Second: I felt (at first) that, if I was in Harry's shoes and Garrison appeared as he did, I would take him into custody and lock him up. Of course, my opinion changed at the end of the show.

Third: the way Harry spoke to the police woman friend who wanted to vacuum his home, and the way he picked up the character in the bar was unlikely to ever happen, even for David Janssen.

Fourth: the way he spoke to Sergeant Granger was overall, plain rude.

Fifth: there was no explanation why he was using city buses to get around.

Sixth: there was really no character development of the supporting cast.

Seventh: For an ex-cop with a bullet lodged near his spine, the motorcycle and foot chase were just unbelievable.

Ultimately, I concluded that I may be off base on everything, except the lighting. I rationalized that this was the pilot, our introduction to *Harry O*, and in upcoming episodes we would get to know him.

Rose Marie's opinion:

She agreed with me on every point I made. Overall, we both liked it ... admittedly, we were both biased.

I drove Rose Marie home just before one o'clock.

I was anxious to hear from Dave again so I could offer our collective opinions. I knew he had no control over the lighting, the dialogue or the overall plot. However, he surely had control over the persona of *Harry O* and the characterization he portrayed. Then again, perhaps it was the director's orders whom Dave was following.

I did think it would evolve into a good series and would be a big hit for Dave and, once and for all, show his fans that Dr. Richard Kimble had been vindicated, then moved on with his life - that David Janssen was now *Harry Orwell*.

I contemplated calling Dave at his home Sunday night but hesitated. I always refrained from calling him because I knew how busy he was and didn't want to take the chance of interrupting him when he was involved either socially or in a business situation - so, as much as I wanted to talk to him, I refrained from making the call.

I did not have to wait long to hear from him. Dave called me Monday morning, March 12, at 2:15.

"Mike, it's me ... did you see it?"

"YES, we did! Rose Marie and I were entranced ... only ate our pizza during the commercials," I said with a laugh.

"WELL ... what's the verdict?"

"First, our collective opinion is you will have another hit; secondly, your fans will finally let Dr. Kimble get on with his life and welcome *Harry O* with open minds, arms and hearts. I think it will be a good series. I was glad it ended the way it did; you caught the guy who shot you and the one who killed your partner."

"Okay, I know you are painting a good picture ... but what did you two find fault with?"

"Okay ... I told you I would give you the whole truth and nothing but the truth. We both think the lighting was too dark in almost every scene. The way you talk to the women was *gruff*, almost to the point of being downright rude; it was almost like you gave the impression you were God's gift to women. There was not much character development for the other cast members, even Sal Mineo. The motorcycle and foot chase with Sal Mineo was plain unbelievable. Were you and Sal really riding the motorcycles? Also, there was no explanation why you don't have a car. However, that said, we both agree that it will be a good series and it will give you time to perfect his character."

"Thanks, Mike! No, neither one of us was really riding the cycles in the chase. I agree with you on the lighting; I will make that point with Thorpe. I'll also bring up your other observations with Rodman. IF we get the green light from ABC, I am sure there will be a lot of changes. Now, from your perspective, how should *Harry O* evolve ... what kind of character do you see him to be?"

"I would envision *Harry O* to be a good detective, personally a very nice guy, always looking for a one-night-stand and getting a decent car."

Dave laughed. "All right, Mike! I'm glad you and Rose Marie liked it ... overall ... and I'll keep your points in mind when we know whether or not it's going to be made. Thanks for letting me know; you have some good points. I'll call you later."

"Thanks, Dave ... now I'll go back to sleep."

"Yeah ... go back to sleep. Sorry I woke you."

"No problem ... call me when you can."

Regardless of the roles David Janssen assumed
throughout the years, he was largely recognized
for the series which made him famous
all over the world:
The Fugitive.

3

Over the years I had learned that, when Dave would say "I'll call you later" at the end of a call, it could mean anywhere from a few days to a few weeks. I did not hear from him again until Saturday morning, April 14.

"Good morning, Mike. It's me ... did I wake you?"

"No, Dave, I've been up for over an hour having coffee. How are you?"

"Good. I know it's been a while since we spoke; I have been pretty busy. My grandfather passed away ... a lot has been going on. How are things with you?"

"Good, Dave ... thanks. I'm sorry to hear about your grandfather. Was it your father's father or your mother's?"

"My mother's. He was 91; he had a good life."

"Where was he, in California? Did you go to his funeral?"

"No, he lived in Oregon, a small town. I sent my mother; I couldn't go. I don't like funerals ...or weddings."

"Well, I agree with you on disliking funerals ... and weddings. I've already decided I won't go to my own funeral ... and I'm on hold when it comes to weddings, but I will go to yours." I laughed.

"Well, you'll have to stay on hold for a long time if you're waiting on me to get married ... or die," Dave said, then laughed.

"Since it's been over a month since we talked, I thought you may have been angry with me for my opinions on *Harry O.* What is going on with that? Have you started production?"

"No ... no. Of course I wasn't angry with you! Apparently, the big shots at ABC, as well as the majority of viewers, were not impressed with *Harry O* either. It doesn't look like we'll be going forward with it."

"Damn ... as I told you, overall, we liked it ... really. We both feel it had a lot of promise. Maybe Rose Marie and I should send letters to ABC."

"I don't think that will have any effect, but it certainly can't hurt ... do it, if you want to."

"Believe me, we will! I bet we won't be the only fans of yours that will be doing it. So what are you going to do? Do you have anything else working?"

"Yeah, I'm scheduled to film another Movie of the Week for Spelling-Goldberg next month; it's called *Fast Freight*."

"What are you going to do, be a freight train engineer?"

"No ... I'm going to be a truck driver ... an 18-wheeler. Going to be going from LA to Houston with a top secret load. I like the script ... we're going to be hijacked by terrorists."

"Okay ... do you know how to drive a semi?"

"No ... but I'll learn." He laughed.

"Yeah, I bet you will ... with the magic of Hollywood," I said with a laugh. "Who else is in the cast?"

"Kennan Wynn is my co-star ... I don't know who else will be cast yet. I'll let you know."

"Okay ... at least, you're not going to be completely out of sight of all your fans ... and I know you were skeptical of doing another series, but it would have been nice to have at least an hour a week to look forward to. Will you be doing any other movies ... major films?"

"Abby is working on some things - too soon to talk about, but some are interesting. Don't worry, Mike! I always let you know when something is concrete enough to brag about," Dave said with a laugh.

"I know, Dave, but you know me. I'm on the east coast, you're on the west coast. For me, it would be good to know I can, at least, watch you on TV or go to a movie theatre and see you in a good movie, and I take the liberty of speaking for all your fans."

"Thanks, Mike! I know what you mean. Don't get me wrong! HAD *Harry O* gotten a green light, I would have jumped in running full speed ... something will come along, I'm sure."

"How is Dani? What does she think about the series not happening?"

"She is all right with it. I think she is happy I won't be spending weeks at a time in San Diego but, if it had moved forward, she would have accepted it."

"That's good to know ... that she will be happy with whatever makes you happy. I'm still looking for that invitation in my mail box," I said with a little laugh.

"Damn it, Mike! Don't push me! I'm nowhere near making that plunge ... I need time. Dani's divorce is nowhere near even making it into court yet."

"I'm sorry, Dave! Really, I was just kidding."

"I know ... I'll call you IF and when that time comes but, I say again, DON'T hold your breath!"

"I won't mention it again, Dave ... I promise."

"Okay, now that we have that straight, when will your divorce be final?"

"Touché ... you got me there, Dave. I haven't done anything about it. My wife has had no contact with me. I guess I have been kind of hoping she will file for a divorce there in Connecticut. Divorces are really expensive and hard to get here in New York; isn't that why Ellie went to Las Vegas to get hers?"

"I am sure things have changed in the divorce laws of New York since Ellie went to Vegas. I think you are just grasping at straws ... making excuses. You had better listen to one who has been through it! I guarantee you, IF I do get married again, it will be the last time. I will not go through another divorce. No matter what!"

"You are right, Dave ... I will look at all my options. Maybe I'll send my wife a letter and tell her IF she wants a divorce, she should file there in Connecticut, where we were married. I won't contest it. I'll pay for it. I could also look into filing in Indiana."

"Mike, as your friend, I am only trying to look out for you. You know what I went through, and I'm not just talking about the financial costs. Think hard and make a decision ... the sooner the better, for you."

"Okay ... okay, Dave! I will."

"All right, Mike ... enough of my lecturing. I'm going to grab a few hours sleep. You take care. Give Rose Marie and Baron my best."

"Thanks, Dave ... I will. You take care, too, and give Dani my best." I hung up the phone.

It was the beginning of a nice spring day in Manhattan and I decided to take Baron to Riverside Park for more than his usual hour of play time.

I was really disappointed in hearing that *Harry O* would not be made into a series. I reflected upon everything I had found fault with in the pilot.

The lighting was by far the biggest drawback, at least in my opinion. Then, Dave's attitude towards the three main female characters.

The motorcycle and foot chase at the end just seemed unbelievable; it covered some pretty rough terrain off the paved streets where he was bouncing all over the cycle. With a bullet lodged near his spine, wouldn't that be physically impossible? Would he have been capable of such strenuous physical activity without ending up paralyzed from the waist down?

Dave had told me it was a body double riding the cycle and doing the running but viewers were to believe it was DAVE, as Harry O - so my points were valid, at least in my mind.

As for the lighting - which was really, really bad - I kept telling myself that I was not well versed in the way that technical application was made by the Hollywood experts. Even so, to me, it was way too dark; it was just bad.

In addition to Harry's attitude towards the female co-stars, I found that the character Margot Kidder portrayed was not normal; she appeared to be curious about Harry but was cold in her expressions towards him. To me, it looked like she was just in it for the sexual expectations. I presumed it was just the writing since Margot Kidder is an excellent actress and I always enjoy seeing her on screen.

I comforted myself with the fact his agent had found a new project for him and, at least, he would be in something for his fans, including me, to see and, hopefully, enjoy.

4

Six weeks passed before I heard from Dave again. I was thinking he was angry with me for mentioning his getting married again. I felt positive Dani was putting pressure on him and he did not need to be getting that from me.

I was on the terrace watching a beautiful sunrise over the East River; it was the start of the Memorial Day weekend. I was enjoying my first cup of coffee when the phone rang; it was Saturday morning, May 26.

"Good morning, Mike. It's me. Is your divorce final yet?" Dave asked with his deep laugh.

"I know you're really trying your best to be funny, Dave. Maybe you should stick with drama," I said, then laughed.

"I'm just joking. How the hell are you? How are Rose Marie and Baron? How's the weather there?"

"In the order you asked: I am doing well, Rose Marie and Baron are both doing well. Summer has arrived here a little early. Now, how the hell are you? How is Dani? How is the smog in LA? Have you done that trucker movie yet or has it been cancelled, too?"

"Okay ... in the order you asked, Mister Wiseguy: I am good, Dani is fine, the smog is still the smog and we finished the movie ... and before you ask, no, I do not know when it will be aired."

"Thanks for bringing me up-to-date, Dave. So what else is new?"

"We closed my office ... don't really need it so you can throw that number away. I changed my PR guy; Victor sort of retired. Dani has been combing through my finances and she has shown me how to save a lot of money."

"Well, that's always good, but what about your secretary-valet, Victor? He's been with you a long time. Have you found a replacement? I thought you liked Liberman? What about Mr. Greshler? He's been very good for your career."

"I don't think Victor really approves of Dani. I like Frank as a friend but I don't really like the way Frank has been handling things lately. Of course, I am still with Abby; there is no one better at his game - at least, in my opinion. I have not been using my office much of late so it was really just wasting money."

"That all makes sense ... I guess. Dave, you know I would never intrude on your private affairs, but do you think it wise that you are giving Dani so much insight into your financial affairs? I'm just thinking of what Ellie cost you and that was through the court. In Dani's case, if she has all the details, she could just clean you out; she wouldn't even have to go to court. By the way, does Mr. Greshler have anything else lined up for you?"

"Yeah, there are a couple of things in the works. Don't worry about Dani taking me for a fool; she knows better. She does not have access to my accounts, anyway. Oh! I almost forgot to tell you. We met President Nixon a few weeks ago. He said he thought my portrayal of *O'Hara* was right on point. Personally, I don't like him; he's just a career politician, full of shit. He couldn't let go of Dani's hand."

"You were at the White House?"

"No, he was here. He attended a tribute to John Ford. I think he was at San Clemente, anyway. His whole damned entourage, secret service and all, just made a mess of Ford's tribute."

"I'm sorry to hear you don't like him; he seems to be making progress in ending the war in Viet Nam. I voted for him, twice."

"Kissinger is making progress with ending the war; Nixon hasn't anything to do with it."

"One thing he did, that I was happy to see, was stepping up the use of the B-52 bombers. I always said if we just sent a squadron of B-52s over North Viet Nam, the war would end within 24 hours."

"On that, I agree with you. I do think Kissinger will succeed in bringing it to an end. He is a master at negotiating very difficult situations," Dave said.

"I have to agree with you, Dave. I just don't like the idea so many of our guys are being killed and maimed for a country that has no appreciation. We will never change the politics of the world. So, changing the subject, what are you going to be doing next? When will we get to see you on screen?"

"I have a few weeks off and then I'll be going on location to do a guest appearance on the season premier of *Cannon*. Bill Conrad is the star; you never saw him but he was the narrator of *The Fugitive*."

"Yeah, I have been watching it since it started. I keep waiting for him to say, *The Fugitive*," I said with a laugh.

"The episode has a good storyline; I think you will like it."

"Quinn Martin is the producer so I am not surprised it's a hit series. I've seen photos of him with you. Has he ever acted before this? I can't see him winning any foot chases."

"It has Quinn Martin's 'Golden Touch' ... so I'll be having a sort of reunion with a lot of the people I worked with on *Fugitive*. That's the main reason I jumped at the role; I'll see a lot of old friends I worked with and haven't had much contact with over the past few years.

"Yes, Bill has acted in several projects. In this case, I'm sure the writers will have him using his brains more than his brawn," Dave said before laughing.

"Well, you have to admit, if he needs to, he sure has a lot of weight to throw around," I said with a laugh. "You getting together with some of your former crew ... I bet that must be something you are really looking forward to, Dave. I'm sure Mr. Martin will be glad to have you back with him. Maybe if he was the producer on *Harry O* it would have been better received by ABC. I bet the lighting would have been better, for sure."

"No, Mike, I don't think it would have made any difference at all. That's behind me, anyway. I am happy I will be working with Quinn and Bill and the rest of the guys; it will be fun."

"I bet ... you will have to tell me all about it as soon as you can. So how are you and Dani doing?"

"We're doing fine ... relaxing and going to lots of parties, some charity events, things like that."

"I am glad to hear that ... you sound pretty good ... happy."

"I am, Mike, for the first time in a long time. Listen, I have to go, but we'll stay in touch. You take care. Give my regards to Rose Marie, and a hug to Baron."

"All right, Dave! Thanks for the call and bringing me up to speed on everything."

Dave sounded in very good spirits and looked forward to working with a lot of his friends and colleagues from his *Fugitive* days. I was happy for him.

Weeks would pass without hearing from him. I continued perusing the newspapers and fan magazines looking for any articles relating to Dave and his work or Dave and Dani.

There would be an occasional photo of Dave and Dani together with short captions but nothing relating to the projects he had mentioned to me. I knew they would appear usually a couple of weeks before the project would be aired.

I would not hear from Dave again until Sunday morning, June 10.

"Good morning, Mike! How the hell are you? How is everything in the big city?"

"Fine, Dave ... everything is fine. The city never sleeps but it keeps getting better. How are you? How is Dani? How about the Quinn Martin film, *Cannon*?" I asked.

"We start production in a couple of weeks or so; I'll let you know. We'll be going on location in a few days ... somewhere near the Cal-Nevada line. Dani and I are doing well. How are Rose Marie and Baron? How about your divorce?"

"That's good news! I know you have no idea when it will air, but what about *Fast Freight*? Do you know when it will be broadcast? Yes, Rose Marie and Baron are both doing well. Dave, of all people, you should know divorces take a while ... no, to be honest, I haven't done anything yet ... but I will!"

"Yeah, you keep saying that. Oh, I have to go. I'll check back with you later," Dave said and hung up without telling me about a date for the airing of *Fast Freight*.

5

I did not have to wait long for my answer about the broadcast of *Fast Freight*. Dave called me at 11:40 the next morning at my office. It was Monday, June 11.

"Good morning, Mike ... sorry I had to rush yesterday. How is everything? Am I interrupting you?"

"Great, Dave ... and with you? No, you're not interrupting me."

"Good, real good. You asked about the *Fast Freight* movie. From what I'm told, there is some bickering going on between all the big shots and creative heads involved. There is no date set for it to be aired ... if it ever gets broadcast. I'm not involved in their hissy fit, so I don't really give a damn. They paid me so whether it ever makes it to the screen, who the hell cares?"

"I and a few million fans of David Janssen and Keenan Wynn's ... that's who will care," I said with a laugh. "Did you get to see the finished film?"

"Yeah, I saw it. I'd give it about a five ... that includes my performance. It really did not turn out to be as good as I thought when we were in production, but what the hell! You can't win 'em all."

"Hey, Dave! At least you were working and keeping yourself busy. How is everything going with Dani? Are you still keeping her happy?"

"Everything is good and she keeps me happy, too; it's a two-way street, you know. How are Rose Marie and Baron?"

"Both are fine ... Rose Marie and I are going to the Rainbow Room this coming Friday to celebrate her birthday. Baron is still growing! How are your mom and sisters? I haven't asked and you haven't mentioned them in a while. How about Kathy and Diane?"

"Give Rose Marie a birthday kiss for me. Mother, Jill and Teri are all doing well. I haven't talked to Kathy in a while. I saw Diane last week, had lunch with her. She is doing okay, still trying to get into the business. Thanks for asking."

"Will Dani be going on location to Cal-Nev with you? Does she care you are still seeing Ellie's daughters?"

"No, she'll be staying here; I'll only be up there for a few days. The rest of the shooting will be done around LA, mostly in the studio. I received the script yesterday and it is very well written, good storyline and great dialogue ... I am really looking forward to it. No, Dani knows I still love Diane and Kathy; they are still my step-daughters so she understands and has no problem with my seeing them."

"That's good. I will really be looking forward to seeing *Cannon* so you have to keep me up-to-date, especially when it will be aired. With Quinn Martin as the producer, it will definitely be a hit show; seems like everything he touches turns to gold."

"I have to agree with you, Mike; he is the best of the best. I have to go but I'll be in touch soon. You take care and be sure to give Rose Marie a big birthday kiss from me."

"Okay, Dave ... thanks for the call and be sure to keep me abreast of what's going on with *Cannon*, and *Fast Freight*, too."

"Don't hold your breath on *Fast Freight*, but I will let you know when I know, Mike. We'll talk soon."

It was rare that Dave would call me at my office but I was glad he did. I was curious about his latest movie, *Fast Freight*, so I was happy he called.

I don't think Dave was privy to the machinations going on between the studio executives and the creative heads; otherwise, he would have told me. Whatever was going on, Dave did not seem to care if the movie ever made it to public view. He had been paid and that was all that mattered to him.

Dave's next call to me came on Sunday afternoon, July 1, as I was about to leave my apartment.

"Good afternoon, Mike! It's me. How is everything on your end?"

"Good, Dave ... I was just going to pick Rose Marie up for lunch and a movie, which will most likely end in our having dinner at the Friar Tuck Inn. How are things with you? Any word on *Cannon*?"

"Everything is going well here. We just started production on *Cannon*. Before you ask, there is still no news about *Fast Freight*. I just had a few minutes and decided to give you a call at a time I knew you would be awake," he said, then laughed.

"That's nice ... it's always good to hear from you. Whether I am awake or not, doesn't matter. Are you on location?"

"No, we are still in LA, doing a lot of scenes in the studio. We will be going on location sometime in the next couple of weeks."

"How do you feel, seeing Mr. Martin, Mr. Conrad and all the other crew members you worked with six years ago?"

"Great, Mike! It has been just great! It's been like a high school class reunion. Working together again, it is like we never stopped. Mike, it's like we all know each others minds. Everything has been moving so fast, so smooth ... hardly any re-takes. The other cast members are so prepared ... it is great!"

"That is really good to hear! Maybe they could take your character and make it a recurring role, get you used to the series schedule again."

"I can tell you a definite NO ... not going to happen," he said emphatically.

"What role do you play? What's it about?"

"I play a character named Ian Kirk. It's a suspected murder-suicide but, again, as I've always told you, 'all is not what it appears to be'. You will just have to watch and see for yourself."

"All right, 'Mr. Mystery Man'! I should know by now not to ask you too many questions. I mean, it's not like I wouldn't watch it, but I guess you are right. You don't want to spoil it for me."

"No, Mike, I'm not worried about spoiling it for you. I know you will probably have Rose Marie with you and I don't want to spoil it for *HER*," Dave said with a sarcastic laugh.

"Okay ... okay, but you have to give me a heads-up for the air date."

"That I can do. So tell me, is there any progress in your divorce?" Dave asked, again with a sarcastic tone.

"Yeah, Dave ... there has been no progress at all. I will send you a telegram when I get the divorce ... you can come to New York and we'll have a party."

"Yeah, right ... just send me an invitation to your wedding. I know Rose Marie will make a gorgeous bride."

"Well, if you know the Catholic church doctrines ... maybe her father won't let her marry me. Divorce is frowned upon by the Church."

"Yeah, I know that ... but there are ways around it. You'll figure something out."

"I don't think she has told her parents that I am married. We don't discuss it and her parents seem to like me, so I don't think they know."

"Well, keep going ... you better listen to your big brother and get moving on your divorce. I have to go now, but we'll be in touch. Take care."

"Okay, thanks for calling, and my best to Dani."

I was glad he called. It was good to hear him sober and happy. I felt it was a combination of his being back to working with old friends and colleagues, his blooming relationship with Dani and the fact he seemed to have what he called 'steady' work.

6

I did not hear from Dave the rest of July, which I attributed to his busy filming schedule for *Cannon*.

I appreciated the fact that my older brother, Jack, had taught me patience. On many occasions when I did not hear from Dave for an extended period of time I had been tempted to call him directly at his office, but I always had the inert fear of interrupting him so refrained from calling him each time.

Saturday morning August 4, 1973, Dave called me at 10:15.

"Good morning, Mike. It's me. How are you?"

"Good morning to you, stranger! I'm doing fine. Now I'm glad to know you're still among the living ... haven't heard from you in weeks. I was ready to put out an 'All Points Bulletin'," I replied.

"Yeah, well sorry, but I have been very busy. You know, Mike - all the APBs Gerard put out on me ... they never helped him."

"Yeah, I know, but I was beginning to worry ... even started to wonder if you were pissed off at me."

"For what? I couldn't get pissed off at you. If I did, I'd damn sure let you know it upfront. Are you divorced yet?"

"Damn it, Dave! No, I'm not divorced yet, but thanks for reminding me. I really have to get on it and do something. So, what the heck has been keeping you so busy?"

"Yeah, and I will keep reminding you, for your own good." Dave laughed. "We wrapped up *Cannon*, at least my part, so I'll have a few weeks off to rejuvenate myself. We're going to the race track tomorrow so that will be fun."

"Have you seen the finished episode of *Cannon*? Did you have fun doing it, working with your old colleagues and friends?"

"No, they have all the editing and music additions to do and then I'll see it. Yes, it was a hell of a lot of fun ... a lot of work, but it doesn't feel like work when you're having fun. I wish I could have the same crew on everything I do; it would really be great."

"Is it the horse track you're going to tomorrow? Does Dani like horse-racing? Is it your horse that's running?"

"Yeah, Dani really enjoys it, too; we go with a few friends. No, it isn't my horse; I sold my share in her a long time ago. A friend of mine has a horse running so I'll bet a wad on her and hope she wins." Dave laughed again.

"So what will you be doing next ... anything exciting?"

"I've been asked to take part in the Democratic National Telethon towards the end of this month. It should be fun - a lot of laughs - and we'll be raising money for the national party."

"Damn, Dave! If you're raising money for the Democrats, I don't think we should be friends anymore," I said. then added a laugh.

"I vote for the man I feel is best qualified. I'm really only doing this to keep myself visible."

"Yeah, but hey, Dave! It may cost you a lot of fans who are Republicans; did you give that any thought?"

"I really don't think politics will have any real bearing with my fans. You'll still be a fan, won't you?"

"Yeah, of course! You know I will. Does Mr. Greshler have anything else lined up for you ... anything exciting?"

"Yes, he has me in a western called *Pioneer Woman* with Joanna Pettet and Bill Shatner. It sounds like it will be a good movie; it's a made for television movie."

"It sounds good; when will you be filming it?"

"Early next month. I'll let you know."

"Is it going to be filmed in Griffith Park and the studio?"

"No, we will be going on location, to Canada."

"Whoa! Canada? Is this supposed to be an American Western? They film a lot of westerns there in Griffith Park; that would be a hell of a lot cheaper than Canada, wouldn't it?"

"Yeah, I think it would be, but I don't make the call where they shoot it. I just go. It is supposed to be set in Wyoming but will be filmed in Canada, specifically around Alberta. You won't be able to tell the difference between there and Wyoming."

"Okay, Dave! I'll take your word for it. Have you ever worked with *Captain Kirk*? I know you've worked with Joanna Pettet."

"Yes, I've worked with him; he did one episode of *The Fugitive*. He's a little arrogant, but he knows his lines and he works hard. I'm sure we'll get along. He will be killed off early, anyway," Dave replied and laughed.

"Okay, all I ask is that you give me a warning shot when it will be aired and, of course, what network."

"A warning shot? Nice play on words, Mike. Of course, I will." Dave laughed. "So how are things with you and Rose Marie? How's Baron doing? How's your work coming along?"

"All is well with Rose Marie and I. Baron is doing well. My work is getting fast-paced - a lot of hours, but I love it."

"That's all good to hear. I have to go to a meeting so you take care and I'll be in touch ... sooner rather than later."

"All right, Dave! I really appreciate the call and, hopefully, you'll remember to call me sooner rather than later. Give my best to Dani and good luck at the track tomorrow," I said, then laughed.

"Yeah, I'll tell the horse and rider you said that. Talk later."

Dave sounded good and full of optimism. His agent was working his magic to keep Dave working and in so many diverse roles. I was happy to see that.

I knew Dave had a busy month ahead of him so I was surprised to receive a call just a week later, Saturday, August 11, as Baron and I came in from his park run.

"Hey, Mike! How the hell are you?"

"Good, Dave ... and you? This is a surprise; I didn't think I'd hear from you this soon. You sounded as though you had a busy schedule this month."

"Yeah, I do, but I have a few minutes this morning. I didn't want you to think I had forgotten you," he said with a laugh.

"I wouldn't think that ... at least, not in a week. It would take you at least a month to forget about me, or maybe at least two weeks, but surely not just one." I laughed.

"Hey, Mike ... don't worry! It ain't gonna happen. I just wanted to let you know I will be tied up for the rest of the month so don't get angry if you don't hear from me."

"Okay, Dave ... thanks for letting me know. I won't have to call my LAPD buddies to go looking for you," I said with a little laugh. "How are you and Dani doing?"

"Everything is going well, but I'm too busy ... and too tired ... to go to all her party invites."

"I can believe that. Any word on the air dates for *Fast Freight* or *Cannon*?" I asked.

"Not yet ... I don't even know if *Fast Freight* will ever make it. When I know something, I'll give you a call. *Cannon* may be coming up soon; it is the season premier so look for it in *TV Guide*. When I know the date, I'll call you. I have to run but I'll call you in a few weeks. Take care."

"Thanks, Dave ... I'll be here."

7

Sunday afternoon, September 30, Dave called me just before three o'clock.

"Hey, Mike! It's me ... how are you doing?"

"Good, Dave ... and you and Dani?"

"Good, everything is good. I just had a few minutes and thought I better check in with you before I have to start looking over my shoulder for your LAPD buddies."

"Yeah ... well, I'll tell you, they are looking for you. I am damn glad I like *Cannon*. I saw you in the season premier a couple of weeks ago. IF I was not a fan, I would have missed it; you didn't give me a warning shot." I laughed.

"Yeah, I'm sorry about that; I was in Alberta filming. I knew you wouldn't miss it. How did you like it?"

"It was really good. I like it. I saw the ratings here in the New York papers - solid, very good. So you're back home? Have you finished *Pioneer Woman*? What's next for you?"

"Yeah, we finished it and we're back home, which is nice. I have some good news from Abby; ABC wants to try *Harry O* - at making it worth a series."

"That is really great news, Dave! I am really happy for you. Do you have any details yet ... when you will be doing it? Did Dani go to Canada with you?"

"Not yet. We'll be shooting it here in the studio ... nothing set yet. Howard Rodman is doing the script now so maybe in a couple of months. I'll let you know. Yes, Dani, went up there with me; she made it easier for me. I was glad she came."

"Good, that's nice she could go. You have to PROMISE ME when you know the air date; that one I damn sure do not want to risk missing!"

"So how are Rose Marie and Baron? Have you taken any steps to getting a divorce?"

"Rose Marie and Baron are both well. Dave, I have really been too busy to even think about a divorce. Today is a good day for me to write Joanne a letter, see if she wants to file there in Connecticut. I won't contest; it will be much easier that way. I'll tell her I will pay whatever it costs for her to hire a lawyer there."

"Mike, that makes a lot of sense ... do it before she finds out you are making good money. I'm not pushing you; I'm just trying to look out for you."

"I know, Dave, and I really appreciate it. I'll send her a letter today. So, enough about me ... what about you? Did you enjoy working on *Pioneer Woman*? How are you two doing? When am I getting my wedding invitation?"

"All right, Mike ... yes, I enjoyed the work on the film. Joanna Pettet is a great lady and I always enjoy working with her. Yes, Dani is happy I'm home and we can go out and enjoy being together. I'm not even going to answer about wedding invitations," Dave said, then laughed. At least he did not seem angry I asked about the wedding invitation. I think he knew I was just kidding him, not pushing him.

"You know, I really hope Mr. Rodman writes a dynamite script especially tailored for you as *Harry O* and he either gives you a sleek Thunderbird or, if he insists on you riding the bus or borrowing strangers' cars, then he explain it. Living on the beach and drawing a pension from the police department, you can't be so broke you don't have a car; anyone who knows anything about California knows a car is a *must have*, not a want."

"I don't have any idea how he is writing it but, when I see the script, I'll find out ... maybe tell him I want a Rolls Royce like Gene Barry had in *Burke's Law*. Do you remember that show?"

"First of all, Dave, you already have a Rolls Royce. Secondly, you don't want to park a Rolls Royce on the beach; the salt water will rust it away in no time. Yes, I remember *Burke's Law*. I saw it a few times; it was pretty good, but a millionaire who was also Chief of Detectives and went to crime scenes in a chauffeured Rolls was a little hard to believe."

"Yeah ... well, it was a pretty good show. That's why I bought my first Rolls ... the one Ellie always drove and got as part of our divorce. By the way, Mike, Rolls Royces do NOT rust!" Dave said with a laugh.

"All right, Dave ... but you would look better in a T-Bird convertible. Just make sure to let me know all the particulars when you find out. I don't care what time it is; you know you can call me at three o'clock in the morning."

"Yes, I know, Mike ... but you wouldn't want me to wake you up at three o'clock in the morning, would you?" Dave asked with a hearty laugh.

"Yeah, right!" I said, returning his laugh. "So how are you and Dani doing? Has she finished with the apartment decorating?"

"She is doing very well. Yes, she has finished the apartment but she will change things every few months; that is one funny thing about her that I like."

"What do you mean, she rearranges the furniture?"

"Hell, no! She changes almost everything. Sometimes I come home tired; after having a few drinks, I walk in and think I'm in the wrong apartment ... but the key worked, so I just yell out her name. She appears and I know I'm in the right place."

"Tired after having a few drinks? Speaking of that ... how are you doing ... still cutting back?"

"Mike, you know me. I won't say I'm drinking more than I did a couple of years ago but then I won't say I'm drinking any less either. I'm doing okay in that department."

"It's none of my business and I've never asked, but does Dani drink?"

"No, she drinks very sparingly ... and she doesn't smoke. She hammers me about my smoking."

"Yeah, I know what you mean. Joanne never drank alcohol, nor smoked ... she hated my habits."

"Did you send the letter to your wife?"

"Yes, I certainly did. I wrote it the Sunday when we spoke and mailed it the next day ... have not received any reply, as yet."

"If you don't get a response soon, if I were you, I'd get a lawyer and file. I know divorce is a messy situation but you had better take care of it now before it gets too messy and costly for you!"

"I know, you are right. I'll do it! I just hope that doesn't put me in the same situation you are in ... Rose Marie starting to put pressure on me to get married."

"That you will have to face if, and when, it happens ... just play it the way you feel. There are 10 women for every man out there ... hell, in New York ... millions there. You can pick and choose."

"Yeah, Dave ... as I walk on the streets and see the beautiful women walking all around, I wonder if I would be better off being a confirmed bachelor ... take advantage of all the opportunities just for variety sake," I said with a laugh.

"Yeah, Mike ... you might want to give that a thought," he said, laughing.

"Hey, Dave! You went from a 10 year marriage to a three year relationship to now being with Dani, what - almost a year? You should take your own advice ... play the field a little."

"Yeah, well, Mike ...I don't see myself doing that. I need a woman to come home to every night ... one I can depend on, one that sort of takes care of me. You know what I mean?"

"Yeah, Dave, I do! On the other hand, for me, I am adjusting to living alone with Baron. I have everything I need right outside my doorstep and I don't feel any obligations to anyone - no one nagging me, telling me they want this or that or to go here and there. Right now, I like it; of course, that could change."

"Yeah ... well, you better get with the program and get a divorce or you'll end up paying and paying and paying."

"I will, Dave. I will follow your sage advice, big brother."

"I have to go now. I'll be in touch soon. Take it easy."

"Okay, Dave ... thanks for the call and your advice. You take care and keep me informed."

I knew Dave was not needling me about getting my divorce; he was truly concerned with my personal well-being.

I did have the feeling from an earlier conversation he was a little resentful about my questioning him about getting married to Dani so I decided never to broach the subject again. He had all the benefits of marriage without the financial risks of divorce. I knew he would make a decision about getting married in his own time.

"Quinn Martin is the best in the business."
- David Janssen

8

Saturday morning, November 3, 1973, was a beautiful day and practically all of New York City was enjoying the last days of Indian summer. Dave called at 9:45.

"Mike, it's me, Dave ... good morning. How are you?"

"I'm good, Dave, and you?"

"I'm okay ... have you done anything on your divorce yet? I have some good news and some bad news, both confidential."

I thought that was a strange way to start a conversation. Dave knew that anything he said to me, anything we discussed, I had never repeated to anyone.

"Not yet. I am going to check the laws in Connecticut; it's only an hour drive from Manhattan. I can go there and file myself. Now, what's your news?"

"Bad news first: my fucking ex-wife is taking me back into court. I was served Friday!"

"What? What for?"

"I stopped paying the bitch her fucking alimony ... that's why! I've been paying her over $3,000, almost $4,000, a week since the divorce; I stopped paying a few months ago. Now she has that shyster Mitchelson as her lawyer."

"Yeah, I've read about him; he represents a lot of celebrities in divorces, doesn't he?"

"Yeah, and he's a smart, slimy son-of-a-bitch. So, listen, get your ass in gear and get a divorce, as soon as possible!"

"Damn, Dave ... believe me, I will! How much does she claim you owe her?"

"Over thirty grand!"

"Wow ... did you stop paying her on purpose?"

"Hell, yes! She has been getting quarterly residuals from *The Fugitive*, the 10 percent I gave her as part of the settlement - and that's giving her a hell of a lot of money. I'm not willing to give her another dime. I work too damn hard for my money!"

"So what do you think will happen in court?"

"Don't know. My lawyer will try and show the judge I've suffered a loss in earnings ... try and get the alimony shut down. After all, we've been divorced for over three years. Hell, he can't give me any assurances ... I just have to wait and see."

"Well, I hope the judge is a fan of yours. Damn it, Dave! This is a shock! When will you know anything?"

"We have a hearing set for Friday, the 30th. We just have to show I'm destitute."

"Dave, that'll be kind of hard. Your lifestyle is kind of out and in the open ... in the public eye."

"Yeah, I know but, hopefully, the judge will understand I am - have been, in effect - supporting two women ... both with very expensive tastes."

"I can only imagine! Dave, I'll be praying for you! Now, what's the good news?"

"ABC wants another pilot for *Harry O*. Jerry Thorpe and Howard are sort of re-working it so they paid me a 'holding fee'."

"GREAT ... that is really great news, Dave! What's a 'holding fee'?"

"They pay me to keep me available so I won't take another series with another network, or any other project that will tie me up for any length of time."

"That is really, really great news! I liked the first *Harry O*. Do you have any idea what they will be changing?"

"No, Mike, not a clue. I won't know anything until they send me the script. To me, it looks like we have a second chance and that is good enough for me."

"Do you know when you will get a script - have any idea when you will start filming?"

"No, no idea ... you'll be the first to know when I do ... well, almost the first to know," Dave said, then laughed.

"All I can say, Dave, is I am now really excited at the prospect of seeing you again in *Harry O*. I'll also be in suspense until you let me know what happens with Ellie ... sure pray the judge will make the right decision."

"So do I, Mike ... so do I. Listen, I have to run now but I'll keep you well informed. Take it easy ... and start working on your divorce. We'll talk soon."

"Thanks, Dave. You take it real easy. Give my regards to Dani."

After the call I reflected upon all Dave had just shared with me. I was very happy for the prospects of a new *Harry O* but I was really disturbed at what Ellie was doing to him.

It seemed to me that she had turned from the woman who claimed to love him to the woman scorned and was not willing to let him go ... not willing to let him enjoy his life. In addition to the emotional stress she was causing him, she was determined to take as much of his money as possible to further embarrass him publicly.

I was not concerned the publicity surrounding Ellie's latest court action would have any adverse effect on Dave's career and his fans, nor the abilities of his agent to get him good work. I was concerned about the effect it would have on him mentally and the possibility it would drive him back into heavy drinking.

I was hoping the prospects of reviving *Harry O* into a viable series would spur his self-confidence and inspire him to devote all of his concentration to the project. That would surely have a profound effect on reducing his dependency on alcohol.

I could not help but wonder the effect Ellie's action was having, or would have, in the future in terms of Dave and Dani's relationship. I felt it would certainly cause Dave to give serious thought to getting married to Dani. The next unknown factor in that regard was whether Dani would stay with Dave or give up any dreams she had of marrying him and end up leaving him.

Dave's warnings to me, personally, to get off my rear end and take serious steps to obtain my divorce were now making me think of my own martial situation. It had become obvious to me over the last year and a half that there would be no reconciliation with my wife. Although I had not yet become a police officer, that did not seem to change my wife's feelings.

I was now earning a very good salary and had great benefits through my company. Dave had made his point many times; I had a lot to lose now. Although I did not believe my wife would leave me in financial ruin, the fact remained, she could.

I decided I would call the court clerk in Greenwich on Monday and inquire about the procedures I would need to take in filing for a divorce.

Dave called me again on Sunday, November 18.

"Good morning, Mike. It's Dave."

"Hi, Dave! How are you?"

"I'm good ... things are moving along ... waiting for our court hearing; it's on the 30th, nine o'clock in the morning ... just have to wait. I do have some good news to pass along to you."

"That's good ... I could use some good news."

"We started production on a second *Harry O*; we got a green light from ABC and it really looks good to me. I think we have a solid script, good guest stars and big names. I am really excited about it."

"That is very, very good news, Dave! I am really happy for you, and for all your fans, too!"

"Yes ... thanks, Mike. I think this one will be a winner and we'll have a series for next fall."

"When will it be finished, the pilot?"

"We will be done shooting by the end of the month - don't have an exact air date yet, but I'm led to believe it will be right after the first of the year."

"What would come next? When will you know if ABC wants it for a series?"

"That will depend on the ratings of this one. It is a two hour episode so it will have a good shot at pulling in good ratings. So, how are things with you?"

"I'm getting a divorce. I have an attorney in Indianapolis ... faster and cheaper than getting it in Connecticut. I'll only have to fly out there for one hearing. My wife will not contest it so that is good."

"I am really happy to hear that, Mike ... for your sake! I am sorry your marriage didn't work out but, at least, you haven't put a lot of time in it, and expenses. Is your wife expecting any alimony?"

"No, no alimony. She conveyed everything to me through her mother, who actually feels sorry for me. It's only costing me a thousand for the lawyer and a couple of hundred in costs."

"Man, you are really lucky ... you are getting off cheap!"

"Don't I know it! Now I just wonder if, and when, I should tell Rose Marie. I don't want to put myself in a situation where she will be pressuring me to propose to her."

"I know what you mean ... believe me, I know. I would advise you not to mention it until you feel comfortable with telling her. Listen, Mike! I'm sorry but I have to go. I'll call you back soon. You and Rose Marie have a Happy Thanksgiving – Baron, too. Take care."

"Thanks, Dave! I hope you and Dani have a nice Thanksgiving, too ... and CONGRATULATIONS!"

The call ended.

"This town is full of backbiting, gossip mongers ...
anyone here is lucky to claim any real friends ..."
- David Janssen, about Hollywood

9

I next heard from Dave on Tuesday morning, December 11, at 2:15.

"Hey, Mike! It's me, Dave. I hope I didn't wake you. I had some good news in court, wanted to share it with you."

"Good, Dave ... yeah, you woke me up, but that's okay. What is the good news?"

"We had a hearing and the judge ordered me to pay the back alimony to Ellie. Then he shocked the hell out of her by cutting her alimony from over $3,800 a month to just $2,200 a month, then he did something we did not expect. He set a cut-off date so I won't have to pay her a damn dime after December of 1978 – or, if she gets re-married before then, the alimony ends!"

"That is really great news, Dave! I am really happy for you! If you don't mind my asking, how much do you have to pay her in back alimony?"

"Just under $40,000 but, when you consider I've already paid her over $150,000 since the divorce was final - and that's not including all I paid her monthly while the divorce was going through the court or all she got from our settlement - it's not that much."

"Damn, Dave! I am sure glad I'm not in your shoes! Do you mean that before the judge's decision you would have had to pay her alimony for the rest of her life?"

"That's exactly what I'm telling you; unless she re-married, I would have been supporting her for the rest of her life!"

"Wow! That's wrong ... downright dirty! I'll tell you, from all the crap she laid out in the press while your divorce was going on, I don't think she would ever find a man who would be crazy enough to marry her! She did all that to you - just think what she would do to the next guy if they got a divorce."

"Yeah, you're right, Mike ... I'm just glad it's over!"

"Yeah, I bet you are. Is it really over or do you still face the risk she will take you back to court?"

"No, the judge made it perfectly clear. She has no other recourse as long as I make my monthly payments, the last one being December 1, 1978 ... or IF she marries some other sucker before then, I'll be completely free of her."

"Wow! Doing some quick math, that's over $130,000 you'll be paying her! Dave, do you need a loan?" I asked with a laugh.

"No, Mike, I don't need a loan. *Harry* will be paying the back alimony, but thanks for offering," Dave said, then laughed.

"I'm sure glad you have a friend like *Harry* and I can't wait to see you guys together again ... will you still be doing the show in San Diego? Did Dani go to court with you? What does she think of the judge's ruling? Did your lawyers ask the judge to cut the alimony off?"

"I don't know if we'll be filming in San Diego yet but I'll let you know when everything is confirmed. Yes, Dani went with me to court and she is ecstatic over the judge's order. She said, 'It really shows Ellie how she cut off her nose to spite her face.' Yeah, my lawyers asked the judge to reduce the alimony but, when he did that and then set a date for the alimony to end, that surprised me and my lawyers and shocked the hell out of Ellie and her dirt bag lawyer!"

"Was Ellie there ... in court? How did she react?"

"Yes, she was there, and she turned white when the judge set a cut-off date for her alimony. She didn't say a word to me but she turned on the tears; it did not have any affect on me. She has enough of my blood, sweat and tears."

"I really am glad it's over for you, Dave. Now you can have some peace of mind and get on with your life. If you don't mind me asking a personal question ... how are you doing, as far as your drinking goes?"

"I'm doing good, Mike ... being with Dani, we don't go out as much as I did before. Mostly we go to private dinner parties at our friends' homes or have people here in our home, so I'm not drinking nearly as much as I did when we went to restaurants. I feel a lot better, too."

"That is really good to hear. Do you have any idea when the new *Harry O* will be broadcast?"

"I don't know the exact date, but it will be after the first of the year, just a few weeks from now ... so watch for it in *TV Guide* and, when I know for sure, I'll give you a call. Okay Mike, I'll let you get back to sleep. Give Rose Marie and Baron my best regards."

"Thanks for the call ... all the good news. I'm happy for you. I'll tell Rose Marie you send your best."

"Don't forget Baron, too. We'll talk later," Dave said and we hung up.

I was glad he gave me the consideration of calling and telling me his good news. I knew how much the divorce and Ellie's allegations had hurt him emotionally, especially as she tried to drag him through the mud and damage his career. As it would turn out, the divorce didn't hurt his career at all.

I knew that his relationship with Rosemary had been good for him, at least for the first 18 months, but I could tell in the last few months of their relationship he was having serious reservations about her being the right girl for him. In her case, I think Dave felt that the age difference between them was a big obstacle.

Dave had been with Dani for about a year and they were now living together in a glamorous Penthouse apartment. They had known each other since they both were young actors at Universal Studios. Dave was only about three and a half years older than Dani.

Dave related to me that, although neither he nor Dani realized it at the time, each had a crush on the other at Universal but never acted on their feelings.

He married Ellie in August of 1958 and Dani married Buddy Greco in 1960. Ironically, they became neighbors in the Sierra Towers apartments. Dani and Buddy Greco hosted the Tenth Wedding Anniversary for Dave and Ellie and, unbeknownst to any one there, that was the evening Dave told Ellie their marriage was over.

I found it bizarre Dave and Dani ended up together after having known each other for all those years, each having feelings for the other, yet never having let the other know. Perhaps, had they acted on their feelings way back then, they would have saved each other years of heartache each suffered with their respective spouses. I know it would have saved Dave a lot of money.

What really mattered though – now, at least – was that Dave seemed very happy. I had to give Dani credit for that.

Dave had expressed his ambitions to become established as an actor with major films because the pay was better and the work was far less strenuous. He had not wanted to commit to another television series because the shooting schedule was hard and fast-paced. It took a heavy toll on any actor playing the leading role.

Yet, with the prospect of *Harry O* becoming a series, he seemed to embrace it and sounded excited. I was happy for him and I must admit excited that we, speaking for all of his fans, would once again have a good television series where we would see him on a weekly basis.

Dave had told me that the new *Harry O* pilot was much better than the original. Although the new one was produced by the same man and had the same writer, in his gut, he was far more pleased with the end result. He felt confident it would make the cut and he was willing to be fully committed to making it a success.

If, in fact, *Harry O* was bought by ABC, then I knew I could look forward to having some drinks with Dave as he would surely be coming to New York to promote the series on the various talk shows.

10

My phone was ringing as I entered my apartment just after midnight on Sunday, December 23.

"Mike? It's me, Dave. Don't tell me I woke you."

"No, Dave ... I just got in. How is everything with you?"

"Good ... everything is progressing nicely. I just wanted to give you a quick call and wish you a Merry Christmas. How is everything going there? How are Rose Marie and Baron?"

"All is great here ... I just got in from dinner and dancing with Rose Marie ... brought Baron a nice prime rib, so he will be happy in a few minutes. I hope you and Dani have a very nice Christmas, too." I could hear music and a lot of conversation in the background; maybe he was out at a restaurant or in a bar. It was difficult to hear him.

"They will be airing *Harry O* on ABC, February 3; that's a Sunday so make sure you get Rose Marie, some popcorn and soda and watch it, okay?"

"You bet I will! Thanks for letting me know. I'll mark my calendar. Do you know if they are going to make it a series yet?"

"No ... we won't really know anything until the Nielsen ratings are released. Get all of your friends to watch it and spearhead a letter writing campaign to ABC ... can you do that?"

"Hell, yes! I will definitely do that! You told me last month that you feel really good about this one ... what does the producer and writer think ... are they satisfied with it?"

"Oh, yeah! The consensus of the entire crew is 110 percent positive. Still, it will all come down to the ratings ... and a lot of positive letters to ABC will count as well."

"I never knew that. You mean like fan letters to you, or for you?"

"No, not for me - not just for me but the overall reception of the show; you know, the plot, the characters, the cast, the settings, everything. They try and gauge whether or not it is a show people would be apt to tune into every week. They use all that data to bring in sponsors and determine how much they can price each commercial."

"Oh, I get it ... that makes sense. What's all the noise ... are you in a bar ... restaurant? I can hardly hear you."

"We have some friends in for dinner ... little noisy, sorry about that. I just had a chance to call you before things really get swinging here. Listen, you have a great Christmas and, if I don't speak with you before, have a great and safe New Year's Eve. We'll talk soon. Don't forget to tell Rose Marie and everyone you know about *Harry O*. Oh, I have a court hearing on the 27th so the judge can see I paid the back alimony, so he won't put me in jail. I'll let you know how it turns out," Dave said and the phone went dead.

I was glad I came home in time to get his call. He was really excited and so was I. Immediately, I marked my new 1974 calendar.

I would wait and call Rose Marine in the morning and make certain that everyone in my office, everyone I knew - including my family in Indianapolis - would mark their calendars and also ask them to write positive letters to ABC. I made a mental note to get the address of ABC to send the letters.

Dave and Dani must be having one hell of a party, I thought to myself. I wondered if it was a Christmas party or a celebration of the date for the airing of *Harry O*. I was perplexed about his court hearing; I thought that was all over with. Dave did not seem the least bit worried, so I would not be.

I had decided to stay in New York for the holidays and was looking forward to the festivities. The city is transformed into a magical place for Christmas and New Year's; it seems everyone is in such a great mood. I love it!

I did not expect to hear from Dave for a few weeks but I was counting the days to February 3 in great anticipation of seeing the new *Harry O.*

David Janssen was the consummate professional.

11
~1974~

Dave called on Monday morning at 2:45, February 4, 1974. He was composed and from his voice, I could tell he was sober.

"Mike, it's me ... did you see it?"

"YES! As a matter of fact, Rose Marie and I are still talking about it ... we both LOVED IT! Dave, it seems to both of us that you had a complete change of personality. YOU ARE *Harry Orwell*! It was so well written, the cast were right on target for the characters they played ... the flow of the story was consistent ... really had us guessing. It was really outstanding ... WE are proud of you!"

"Gee, Mike ... thanks! I really appreciate that. I know you and Rose Marie are a little biased, but I am glad you enjoyed it. Dani and I watched it here at home. We had some friends over; everyone agrees with you guys. I really feel good about it. I think they will pick it up. Of course, then I'll have to get back into the grind but, you know, I am really looking forward to it. Rose Marie is still there? You guys are still awake?"

"Well, yes! The show ended at eleven. We had banana splits and we've been talking. Don't think what you're thinking, Dave; I'm taking her home in a few minutes ... if I don't, her father will kill me." I laughed. "I'm really glad to hear that you feel as good about the prospects as we do, Dave.

"Rose Marie and I are writing our letters tonight. I gave orders to everyone in my family, my office and all our friends to watch it and write letters. I'll be calling all my family tomorrow, I mean today ... and all our friends and my people in the office ... to make certain they all send nice letters. We're also sending letters to WABC Channel Seven here, in addition to the network big shots."

"Thanks a million, Mike! I really appreciate it! We're going to get the early editions of the papers here, see what the TV critics have to say ... that will be like a preview for us."

"When will you know the results of the Nielsen's?"

"Sometime tomorrow afternoon; I'll let you know when I find out."

"The big question though is when will you know if ABC is buying it?"

"I have no idea, but it will be probably be a couple of months, at least. Don't worry! I'll be sure to let you know."

"Assuming they buy it, and I know they will ... when will you know what day it will be on in the regular season line up?"

"We'll know that right away. We will have a lot of work to do to get it into shooting. There will be a lot to do with the writers, logistics, casting, costuming, all that stuff."

"Well, there are two New Yorkers here who will be watching it every single week. The world will just have to stop because we will be glued to the TV," I said, then laughed. "Will you be taking a little vacation, waiting on ABC's decision?"

"Thanks, Mike! No, no vacation. Abby has a couple of projects lined up for me so I'll be working. I'll let you know when things are locked in. Okay, I'd better let you go and get Rose Marie home. I appreciate your vote of confidence; that means a lot to me."

"We enjoyed it, Dave ... you play a damn good ex-cop!"

"Thanks, Mike! Give Rose Marie a hug for me ... talk later."

I was really happy to get this call. Dave sounded so positive and confident the show would be made into his fourth television series.

Rose Marie and I finished drafts of our letters both to ABC Network and the ABC station in New York. I then drove Rose Marie to her parents' home in Queens. I, finally, went to bed at around five o'clock after setting my alarm for eight.

I picked up the morning papers and drove to my office. I went straight to the television page of *The New York Times* and *The Daily News*. Both had lengthy articles extolling Dave's performance as *Harry O*. Both newspapers' critics felt ABC and David Janssen had a HIT on their hands. I would clip the articles and make sure I would read them to Dave when we spoke again.

David Janssen's roles were always serious, though he enjoyed comedy.

"I guess they don't think I'm funny. Do you think I'm funny?" he once asked Michael Phelps.

12

I did not hear from Dave again until Saturday afternoon of March 2.

"Mike, Dave ... I'm not interrupting you, am I?"

"No, not at all, Dave. I'm glad you called; I was just going out shopping. How the hell are you? How's Dani?"

"All is well here ... I'm finishing a movie of the week for CBS, been really busy."

"I understand ... now, first tell me about any good news you have about *Harry O.* Any word from ABC? Then, tell me about the movie you're doing for CBS."

"Okay, answer to your first question is we have no firm commitment on *Harry O* from ABC yet but, according to Abby, it looks very positive and we should have a firm answer in a few more weeks. The ratings, across the country and across the board, were higher than any of us expected. We're excited about it; I think we'll get the green light from the network - at least for a first season.

"Your second question: we're shooting a film called *Fer-De-Lance;* it is a wacky plot about a bunch of poisonous snakes on a submarine. I don't really care for it but, at least, it pays the bills." Dave laughed.

"Okay ... first, getting back to *Harry O*, all three of the New York papers had great reviews, but one thing I didn't really like ... they brought up a bunch of flat out bullshit about YOU. Bringing up things about you being a big-time gambler, a functioning alcoholic - that was the critic's words, not mine - and a rehash of your contentious divorce and how mean you were to Ellie. I didn't like it!

"In one paragraph, they said how great your acting was as *Harry Orwell* and what a great show it was, then they slam you, as far as your private life! Did Liberman let them get away with that?"

"No ... no, Mike! We - Frank and I - we wanted it that way. Hell, all of it has been all over the tabloids for the last three or four years anyway ... no point in trying to make me sound like a saint when we all know I ain't," he said and laughed again.

Apparently I was angry at the articles with no real need to be. "Okay,

Dave, I get it. You don't think it will hurt your chances of ABC buying the series then?"

"No, we don't think it will have any adverse effect at all. Now, let me give you a little more good news. I may be coming to New York City in a few weeks so keep some of your time free so we can have a few drinks together."

"That's GREAT news, Dave! Are you coming to promote *Harry O* or the movie you're doing now ... going on the Merv Griffin Show? How long will you be here?" Again, I caught myself peppering him with questions.

"None of that ... Abby has me doing another movie, a major film; it's called *Once Is Not Enough*, based on the Jacqueline Susann novel. It's an excellent script and my role is tailor-made for me. We will be doing a lot of exterior filming around Manhattan, and some restaurant and club scenes, then back to the studio here, and some other travel outside the country.

"I don't know yet when I'll actually be in New York or how long we'll be there, but I'll fill you in with all the details as soon as they are firm. I just wanted to make sure you could be on stand by so we could get together while I'm there."

"That is really great, Dave! I will make sure I have a clear calendar when you are here ... can't wait to see you! Are you bringing Dani?"

"We don't know yet. She may come along, do some shopping. I'll let you know what she decides. I have to go. I'm running late to take mother to a luncheon but I'll give you a call as soon as I have the details."

"Okay, Dave ... thanks for calling ... look forward to seeing you soon."

"Okay, Mike ... take care and my best to Rose Marie and Baron." Dave hung up the phone.

I was happy to hear Dave sound so good, sober and, actually, very positive with how his life had improved since his divorce. I would be looking forward to seeing him again, to be able to sit down and enjoy a few drinks, maybe even a lunch or dinner. I hoped Dani would accompany him; I would have the pleasure of meeting her.

I made a mental note to ask Dave what the chance would be of my bringing Rose Marie to watch some of the filming for the new movie. I knew Rose Marie would be thrilled and I could hope some movie big shot would 'discover' her. In my eyes, her physical beauty alone qualified her to be in the film business.

I also made a note to ask Dave who would be co-starring in the film with him. I had not read the book, but I sure heard of it. Jacqueline Susann was a best-selling author. Romance novels just did not hold any interest for me. I hoped Dave would call sooner rather than later and give me all the details.

I didn't have to wait long. Dave called me the next afternoon, Sunday, March 3, just after one o'clock. I was just finishing my weekly routine of devouring the Sunday edition of *The New York Times*. I always joked the *Sunday Times* was thicker than the Yellow Pages of the Indianapolis phone book.

"Mike, it's me, Dave ... are you busy?"

"No, Mike ... just finished reading the *Times*. How are you? How is Dani? Any news?"

"No ... I don't have any more than what I told you yesterday. Just wanted to check in and let you know the film deal is done. I've signed the contract and hopefully we can get this done before the network gives us their decision on *Harry O*.

"It is still up in the air whether Dani will come to New York with me. You know how women are and she'll make a decision five minutes before I'm supposed to be at the airport."

"I wanted to ask you, is there any way you could get passes for Rose Marie and I to watch some of the filming? I know she would love that."

"I really don't know yet, Mike. I have no idea where we will be shooting the scenes or if it will be a closed set, but I'll find out and, if I can get it done, I will."

"Thanks, Dave! I won't say anything to her until you let me know; I don't want to build up her hopes and then not be able to deliver."

"You're a smart man, Mike," Dave said, then laughed. "I signed the contract last Friday so I'm supposed to get the script on Monday. I'm also going to read the book ... get a feel for my character."

"So that's how all you big stars do it, huh?"

"I can only speak for myself ... and that's the way I do it," he said and laughed again.

"What is your character supposed to be?"

"I'm a nearly washed-up writer ... novels, screenplays, things like that. I'm an alcoholic. I smoke too much and I can't get it up anymore ... I'm a wreck!" he said laughing long and loud.

"Damn, Dave! You weren't kidding when you said the role was tailor-made for you. Do you think since you stopped running from Lieutenant Gerard, Hollywood is trying to change your stereo-type? We both agree you drink too much and you smoke too much, but ..."

"Hey, Mike, don't go there! I can still get it up. Dani wouldn't have stuck around this long if I couldn't." He laughed again.

"Oh ... believe me, Dave! I wasn't going there!" I laughed.

"Well, in this plot, I do get a much younger woman who falls head over heels in love with me!"

"See, Dave! It's true! 'Art imitates life' or is it the other way around? Rosemary was a lot younger than you ... and Ellie was a lot older than you," I said. Immediately, I regretted mentioning the two major women in his past.

"Yeah, Mike! You are right. Maybe Jackie Susann conjured this character up from reading about me." He laughed.

"Well, you have to keep me up-to-date; I will be going crazy with wonder."

"I will, Mike ... I have to go. I'll be in touch."

We ended the call and then I immediately kicked myself for not asking who else would be in the film. I'd find out next call.

"David Janssen was a lover, not a fighter."

- Michael Phelps

13

I was jolted out of a sound sleep by the persistent ringing of my phone. I stared at the blue hue of my digital clock radio; it was 4:15, Tuesday morning, March 26. I had to get up and get ready for work; I had gone to bed just after two in the morning.

"Hello, Dave," I managed gruffly.

"Hey, Mike ... you still awake? It's me."

"I am now. Of course, it's you, Dave ... who else could it be? Are you here ... in the city?"

"No, I'll know sometime Thursday or Friday when we'll be there. I wanted to let you know Dani may come with me, but she will only be there for a couple of days so we have to get together so you can meet.

"We finished *Fer-De-Lance*. I'll be doing a 'roast' of your favorite Quarterback, Joe Namath, for the Dean Martin show, so watch for it. I guarantee you will laugh your ass off. Abby has me doing a few other projects, fast ones that pay me way too much, but keeps me busy while we await the network's decision."

"That was going to be my first question ... you still don't know if they're going to make *Harry O* into a series? Why in the hell are they taking so much time to make what has to be an obvious decision? Can't they just look at the ratings and see it will make them a ton of money?"

"I know, Mike, but there is a lot more to it. They have their advertising people promoting it, running the new pilot to potential sponsors, that all takes time. Then they have to see where they feel it will bring in the highest ratings in the new fall line up ... a lot of technical and administrative details we have no part in. Patience is a virtue, Mike, and I learned to have patience ... a lot of patience. Don't worry! Abby and everyone at the studio feel we'll get the go sign soon enough."

"So will you be able to give me a call on Thursday or Friday and let me know when you'll be in New York? I've been meaning to ask you ... who else will be in the movie?"

"Yeah, I'll give you a call; it may be early so I'll call your office. Is that okay?"

"Of course, anytime. Are there any other major stars in it?"

"Some up-start named Kirk Douglas; he's the father of the girl, Deborah Raffin, who falls in love with me ... then there's Alexis Smith, George Hamilton, Brenda Vaccaro, Melina Mercuori and several others. Not everyone will be in New York; a lot of them will be appearing in the LA filming. I'll let you know all the details when we get together there."

"You've worked with most of them ... haven't you? I recognize the names. Of course, I know you've worked with Brenda Vaccaro. I like her. She's beautiful ... reminds me of Rose Marie."

"Yeah, I've either worked with most of them or, at least, know them from parties here. I'm excited about this one, a strong cast ... outstanding script writing. I read the book. I can tell you, Jacqueline Susann is an exceptional novelist ... YOU should read the book."

"I will. I'll get it today. So what else is going on? How is Dani?"

"Everything is going smooth ... with Dani and me. I'm on a diet for this film and she knows just what to feed me and keep me from screwing up. Okay, Mike, now that I have you wide awake, you can go back to sleep. Baron will be waking you at daybreak, anyway. We'll talk Thursday, maybe Friday, for sure."

"Okay, Dave ... thanks for waking me. I'll return the favor sometime. Don't forget to call me on Thursday or Friday when you know all the details."

We ended the call. I got out of bed, went to the kitchen, turned on my coffee pot and gave Baron his morning cookie.

I stopped at the Barnes & Noble bookstore and bought Jacqueline Susann's *Once Is Not Enough*. I would read it after dinner. It would be interesting to know Dave's character before seeing the film.

As promised, Dave called me Friday afternoon at my office just after five o'clock on March 29.

"Mike, it's me, Dave. I'm not interrupting you, am I?"

"No, you're not, Dave. What's the good word?"

"I'll be in the city on Sunday, April 7. I don't have my flight schedule but I plan on arriving early in the evening. If you're free, we could have dinner. Is that okay?"

"Yes, I'd really enjoy that. Is Dani coming with you? I could bring Rose Marie; she would love it."

"I still don't know if she's coming. I don't think so. She may come for a few days near the end of our shooting schedule there. You know how women are; they change their minds more often than we change our skivvies."

"Yeah, I know. It would really be nice to meet her and I know Rose Marie would love to meet her and, of course, see you again. Let me know your flight schedule and I'll pick you up at the airport."

"I'll let you know all the details, but you don't have to pick me up. The studio will have a limo there for me. If Dani doesn't come with me, maybe we can just have dinner and some drinks at the Carlyle; I'll be staying there. We'll play it by ear, okay?"

"Yes, of course ... but you're going to have to see Rose Marie while you're here; otherwise, you'll hurt her feelings."

"Don't worry, Mike! I wouldn't do that. We'll all get together for a dinner. I want to personally thank her for the letters you guys sent the network."

"Thanks, Dave! That will be nice and I know she will really appreciate your gratitude. Do you have any more information on your schedule here? Will you be able to get us in to watch some of the filming?"

"I won't know our schedule until we all meet there and I'll see then if I can get you two passes to watch the shooting. Don't worry! I'll try my best."

"That's good enough for me, thanks. It will be great having drinks with you again; the only thing I miss about LA is meeting you at *The Formosa*."

"Yeah, Mike ... I still haven't found another drinking buddy." Dave laughed.

"Yeah, but from what you've told me, you don't go there that often after work; you rush home to Dani." I said with a laugh.

"Yeah, that is pretty much what I do. I go home and Dani and I may have something light to eat and some wine, or a few drinks together ... and relax together. She is a real pleasure to come home to."

"That is good to hear, Dave. You deserve someone nice to come home to ... and I'm happy you, finally, found the right one."

"All right, Mike! I'll call you over the weekend and let you know my arrival time. I'll get settled into the hotel, have a shower and then we can meet there, okay?"

"Perfect, Dave! I'll wait for your call. Have a good flight and I'll see you soon." The call ended.

I must admit I was excited knowing I would be sharing drinks with Dave again in person. I was anxious to know all about the new film and full of hope that it would be the catalyst for his move into major films.

With an all-star cast in the leading roles, it would be the perfect vehicle for Dave to connect with fans who enjoyed going to theatres as opposed to being captivated by their televisions.

Dave was a mega-star on television and was easily recognized on the big screen with *The Green Berets, The Shoes of the Fisherman, To Hell and Back, Where It's At, Generation* and many others.

Still, he had yet to realize stardom on the Silver Screen. Maybe this film would give him that, which he richly deserved.

14

I received Dave's call Friday afternoon at 4:20.

"Mike, it's me, Dave ... real quick ... I don't have a set date, other than sometime near the end of April. The studio is still putting all the logistics together but that is when we expect to be in the city. I'm pressed for time so I'll have to call you when I know everything is confirmed, okay?"

"Yeah, Dave ... I'm a patient man ... I'm just learning that."

"You have a good teacher ... we'll talk soon." Dave laughed then ended the call.

I told myself I would just have to be patient and accept I would be in suspense until Dave either told me the details over the phone or in person over drinks at the Carlyle. I had a feeling it would be over drinks.

Sunday morning, April 7, Dave called at 7:55.

"Hey, Mike! It's me. I'll be landing at JFK at about 5:10. Can you meet me at the Carlyle around eight? We can get some dinner."

"Yes ... I can do that ... look forward to it. Is Dani coming with you?"

"No, she has things to do here, but she will be coming for a few days before we finish shooting. We will have a pretty tight shooting schedule, but I'm pretty sure we can fit some time in for a few drinks."

"That's all good, but I'm really looking forward to meeting Dani," I said with a little laugh.

"Yeah, I bet you are, Mike. You will like her, I guarantee you! Okay, I have to get ready to go to the airport. I'll see you tonight."

"Thanks, Dave ... see you then."

Sunday evening, Dave called around 7:30 to let me know he was in his suite at the Carlyle and to confirm our dinner was set for eight o'clock. He sounded exhausted. I suggested we could have dinner another night; he would not hear of it.

"Hey, Mike! I don't know about you but I'm hungry and, when I'm hungry, I eat - so be here at eight. Don't be late," he said and laughed.

"I'll be there."

I arrived at the Carlyle at 7:45 and went straight to Bemelmans bar. I scanned the interior and did not see Dave so decided I would wait near the door. Dave tapped me on my shoulder at 7:55.

"Mike, it's really good to see you! You're on time, too," he said with a broad smile as we shook hands.

We entered the bar and were immediately escorted to a nice banquet towards the rear of the room.

Dave was dressed in charcoal grey slacks, a navy blue blazer, light blue dress shirt, no tie. He looked fresh but, from his slightly bloodshot eyes, I could tell he must have had a few drinks on the plane and he must be tired.

We sat down and were immediately handed menus. The waiter took our drink order.

"It is really good to see you, Dave. How was your flight?" I asked. I could not help but notice several people staring at Dave, yet trying not to be noticed. I knew Dave was used to that.

"It was good - long but smooth. It's good to be back in the city. How have you been doing?"

"Good, everything is going great. I hope you will have time to come by my apartment and say hello to Baron. You won't recognize him; he's all grown up."

"I'm sure I can find the time. How is Rose Marie?"

"She's fine. I told her you were coming and she hopes we can get together for dinner. Maybe when Dani comes, you can find time for us all to have dinner, my treat."

"We can do that. I am not certain how long we'll be here, all depends on the shooting schedule. If everything goes well, we will be here about three weeks."

"That's good. Now tell me all about the movie. I bought the book ... I haven't finished reading it yet, but it has some pretty steamy parts ... and your character is a real scumbag, the way you treat the poor little rich girl."

"Yeah, I agree with you ... as long as you know I'm just playing the role. I'm not really a scumbag ... at least, I don't think I am. You know I would never treat a lady like Jacqueline wrote it," he said and laughed.

"Of course not ... but I think you are perfectly cast for this role," I said with a smile. "So tell me, when will Dani be coming?"

"I won't know that until she calls me; you will be the first to know."

Our drinks arrived and the waiter took our dinner order. We both selected the lamb chops. Dave made sure the waiter knew to bring another round of drinks after he put the dinner order in.

"In the photos of you and Dani I've seen in the media lately, you really look happy ... for the first time in years. I'm glad to see that."

"We are happy together; I didn't know you could tell from what are, mostly, staged photos, but everything is perfect for us. Now, don't you even mention the 'M' word!" Dave laughed.

"I was not even thinking that, Dave! 'Why spoil a good thing?' some wise old guy once told me," I said with a laugh. "I'm sure she is just as happy with your relationship the way it is, as you are."

"Yeah, I think she is. I can tell you I'm a hell of a lot happier with Dani than I was with any other woman I've been attached to - you know, living with," Dave said with what I presumed to be a direct comparison to both Ellie and Rosemary.

Our second round of drinks arrived and the waiter provided clean ashtrays.

"Which cast members will be here for the filming of the movie?" I asked.

"Kirk Douglas, Brenda Vaccaro, Alexis Smith, Melina Mercouri and Deborah Raffin will all be here for the shooting of some scenes, mostly interior shooting ... which will be closed sets. There will be some street scene shots so I'll let you know when and where."

"Thanks, Dave! That would be really exciting if I could take Rose Marie to watch the filming. We've never seen a film shooting on the streets of New York. I've seen them filming television shows but the cops always have everything blocked off. We will look forward to seeing this."

"Some of it may be done during your normal working hours ... but I'll let you know, anyway."

"Dave, believe me! We can both take time off to watch you make a movie on the streets of New York!" I exclaimed and smiled.

Our dinner arrived along with another round of drinks. I was glad I had chosen to come by cab and leave my car in the garage.

We enjoyed our dinner at a leisurely pace and Dave kept a steady flow of drinks coming from the very attentive waiter.

I was well aware Dave could handle his alcohol intake better than anyone I had ever known, but I wondered if there were underlying problems driving him to drink more than what had become usual for him. Perhaps he was already missing Dani. Could it also be the long flight and three hour time difference? I could only wonder.

It was almost ten o'clock when our dinner finished and we both enjoyed coffee and a cigarette.

"Dave, this was great ... great food, good scotch, great seeing you again. You look very tired so we should call it a night. You need to get some sleep."

"You're right, Mike. I have to call Dani and say good night. I'll give you a call later in the week when I have a clear picture of our schedule here. Thanks for coming. We'll see each other soon," Dave said as we made our way to the lobby.

We shook hands and Dave got into an elevator. I walked outside and the doorman waved down a cab for me.

15

I arrived home just before the eleven o'clock news on ABC Channel 7. I watched the first 15 minutes and then took Baron for his evening run in Riverside Park as I reflected upon my dinner with Dave.

We had not seen each other since he was in New York for a guest appearance on *The Merv Griffin Show* which was taped in late February of 1973. I was glad to see him.

Although he appeared tired, with a few drinks under his belt, he did look content. He seemed happy with his work schedule and the possibility of *Harry O* being bought by ABC for his fourth television series.

I could not help but consider how fast he appeared to be aging. His new hairstyle, with his hair almost covering his ears, was in style but I noticed how the grey was becoming quite pronounced. He was only 43-years-old but I attributed his, what I considered pre-mature greying, to the stress in his life; Ellie and her never-ending court battles, his work schedule and perhaps some to do with his heavy drinking and smoking. I felt Dani had a very positive effect on Dave, at least in giving him the happiness that had eluded him for so many years.

Dave called me at my office on Monday afternoon at 4:45.

"Mike, it's me ... will you be available for drinks later?"

"Sure, Dave. I plan on leaving here in about an hour, go home and take care of Baron ... a quick shower and I'll be available. What is a good time for you?"

"We will be wrapping up here in about an hour; I'll go back to the hotel and take a shower so, if you can, we'll meet at Bemelmans say around eight o'clock, okay?"

"Perfect! I'll see you then."

I left the office and went to my apartment to take Baron for his run in Riverside Park. After preparing his dinner and giving him fresh water, I took my shower. I watched the local and national news on NBC and made myself a scotch and water to relax before going to meet Dave at the Carlyle.

Dave was already seated when I arrived at Bemelmans and I was escorted to his banquet in the back of the bar. I had the thought that no matter where we were, he always chose a table in the rear of the establishment; was that for privacy or for the long walk back so the other patrons would see that David Janssen was there?

"Hey, Mike! Good to see you. How was your day?"

"Good to see you, too. A hectic day at the office but I got through it. How was your day?"

"We spent the day with Guy Green, our director, going over the scripts for the scenes we'll be shooting here and being fitted by the wardrobe people. I would say it was a productive day."

"How is Dani? Missing you already?"

"No, she's not missing me. She's doing fine ... parties and shopping. How is Rose Marie?"

"I'm sure Dani is missing you and I'm sure she has told you that," I said with a smile. "Rose Marie is fine, sends her best regards to you. So when will the actual filming start? Do you know where the scenes will be filmed?"

"We start tomorrow morning, six o'clock for hair, make-up and wardrobe and shooting will start around ten o'clock. We'll be doing some scenes in a rented penthouse apartment, the El Morocco, and in a studio in Long Island City. They are all closed sets. When I find out if there will be any street shooting, that you and Rose Marie can get close to, I'll let you know."

"That will be appreciated. I know Rose Marie is very excited to see how it's done, especially a scene you will be in. Who will be appearing in the scenes here?"

"Deborah Raffin ... my love interest; she's much younger than me. Actually, I'm supposed to be older than her father, played by Kirk Douglas. Brenda Vaccaro will be in some of the scenes with Deborah and me, but only Deborah will be in scenes with me as we *fall in love*. Kirk and Deborah will be in scenes together in his lavish apartment."

"That's interesting. As I mentioned, I love Brenda Vaccaro ... did I mention that before?" I laughed.

"Yeah, you certainly did, Mike ... more than once. I'll see what I can do for you to meet her, or would just her autograph do?"

"No ... a face-to-face meeting ... and I wouldn't want Rose Marie to be around or to even know about it," I said, smiling.

"Come on, now! You don't think she would be jealous ... do you?"

"Uh ... yeah, I think she would be more than a little jealous. She's 100 percent Italian. She probably has a big brutish relative who would break my legs if she even thought I was cheating on her."

Dave laughed. "I don't think she would go that far. She may have you dumped in the East River with a cinder block tied around your waist ... but you'd get out of that."

"Yeah, right! I just don't want to take that chance. I'm just kidding; I don't think she'd be jealous at all unless Miss Vaccaro hit on me ... nah ... I'm sure I'm not her type." I laughed.

We were finishing our third round of drinks. Dave appeared very tired and as if he had not caught up on the time change or his sleep. Dave caught our waiter's attention then motioned for another round.

"I'm going to call it a night after our next drink ... are you hungry?" he asked.

"No ... not at all ... have you already eaten?"

"I had a roast beef sandwich and coleslaw in my room when I came in from work ... not hungry at all. We can order you something."

"No, Dave, I'm fine. Thank you! You look like you need a good night's sleep. I guess your real work will start tomorrow. Do you guys do any rehearsing before you actually do the filming?"

"Yeah, I need the sleep. We do a fast rehearsal of lines, the director will run through the expressions, body language that our lines depict ... the way he wants them ... and then the actual filming begins. I'll give you a call in the next few days."

Our last round of drinks arrived and Dave asked for the check. We finished our drinks and I walked Dave to the elevators. We shook hands and I left to get a cab.

I felt good seeing Dave again, twice in two days. He was excited about the film and working with so many talented and accomplished actors. I had started reading the book. After reading the descriptions of 'Mike Wayne' and his spoiled-rotten daughter, 'January Wayne', I jumped forward to the part where 'Tom Colt' enters 'January Wayne's' life. Brenda Vaccaro, who plays book editor, 'Linda Riggs', introduces 'January' (her best friend) to 'Tom Colt', the writer.

I am not one who reads romance novels or anywhere near that genre but, since this book made it to the big screen and Dave is one of the major stars, I had to read it.

Dave's character is that of a successful, award winning playwright and novelist who is suffering from 'Writer's Block', has not been published for a while and has turned to booze to help break his block. He is much older than 'January' ... hell, he's older than her father 'Mike Wayne'.

It is insinuated that his maturity is what drew 'January' to him ... to fall in love with him. When her father finds out she is having an affair with a much older man ... a 'loser', he goes into a rage.

This movie was sure to be a box office success. The book had made it to the New York Times Best Seller List, as had her book *Valley of the Dolls*.

Valley of the Dolls was also made into a film in 1967 and was a huge success. Dave's good friends, Paul Burke and Martin Milner, had leading roles in the movie. Actress Sharon Tate was one of the stars, who had been tragically murdered in 1969 by some of the followers of Charles Manson. Miss Tate was pregnant at the time of her death; she was happily married to Director Roman Polanski.

16

Dave seemed happy to be starting the film and, although I could see he was physically exhausted, I was sure that with a good night's sleep he would be his usual energetic self and go at the filming with his determination for perfection.

It would be Sunday afternoon, May 12, before I heard from Dave again.

"Hey, Mike! It's me, Dave. Sorry I haven't had a chance to call you. We've been very busy and on a tight schedule. How is everything with you?"

"All's well here. How is the filming going? Has Dani arrived?"

"We are about to wrap up this coming week, then back to LA for some studio work, then they will move onto Switzerland and Spain. The director is keeping us on a tight schedule and moving everything along smoothly. By the time we finish shooting, I am too damned tired to do anything but shower and sleep, so I'm sorry we haven't gotten together. Sorry I haven't called sooner."

"That's not a problem, Dave. I understand how you have to work. Are you happy with it so far? Are you telling me you'll be filming in Switzerland and Spain for this movie, too?"

"Yeah, certain scenes require it, but I won't be going; I'm not in those scenes. As for the film, so far ... I'm pleased with it. Everyone has been prepared, right on the mark. I think it's a good film. Dani wasn't able to make it here and I'll be going home next week. Can you make it for dinner tonight? It will probably be the last time we can get together before I leave."

"Of course! It is nice of you to offer. Where and at what time ... you sure you are not too tired?"

"No ... not too tired ... and we have to eat. You pick the place. What's your favorite restaurant?"

"Okay ... how about the Friar Tuck? It's one of my favorites; it's on Third Avenue, corner of Fifty-Fifth Street ... mostly American cuisine ... great prime rib, steaks, chops."

"Perfect! How about 7:30? I'll take a nap and see you there."

"Great! I'll be happy to pick you up ... no need to take a cab."

"Not necessary, Mike. I have a car service available. I'll meet you there," Dave said before hanging up.

It was a nice surprise to hear from him. I knew he must have a very busy schedule and that he always memorized his lines at night for filming the next day.

I had seen a couple of blurbs in the newspapers about the frantic filming schedule in New York City and the cast were all on the *Hollywood 'A' List*. I had not yet returned to reading the book and was unaware that parts of the story took place in Switzerland and Spain. I returned to reading the book.

I had called and made a reservation at the Friar Tuck and requested my usual table in the downstairs dining room.

The Friar Tuck appeared as a small, old English castle. The interior was all stone walls with stone steps leading to the downstairs dining room. It had oil burning sconces along the walls and a long oak bar upstairs. Behind the bar were autographed photos of many celebrities. Dave's photo was not there ... yet. The food was delicious and the service impeccable; I was certain Dave would enjoy it.

I asked Dave if he had a publicity photo of himself and he said he thought so. I told him to bring one. I knew he always carried a manila envelope with a few to hand out to fans that got up the nerve to approach him.

Dave was on time. He exited the Cadillac and I noted he was casually dressed. He had an envelope in his hand which I presumed contained his photo. He looked rested and refreshed.

We shook hands by the car and entered the restaurant. I was glad I had not chosen to wear a suit and tie.

We were greeted inside the door and escorted downstairs to my table. I discreetly palmed $20 to Anthony, the Maître D".

I could tell Dave liked the theme of the restaurant. Dale, a waiter who knew me from frequent visits was at out table instantly, bringing menus and taking our drink order.

I had noted both the Maître D' and Dale instantly recognized Dave. Dale had often pointed out celebrities, even 'Mafia' members, to me. I was never impressed.

"Well, you are looking good, Dave. New York agrees with you. Too bad you can't do all your filming here," I said with a smile.

"I feel great, Mike ... caught up on my sleep, the work is good, great people working on this project and everything is going smooth. How is Rose Marie? I wish I had told you to bring her tonight."

"She is doing well ... I think she may be a little disappointed in not being able to see you working on this, even the street scenes, but she understands. I did not tell her we would be meeting tonight."

"I'm sorry, really. You have to convey my apologies to her, let her know I'll try and make it up to her."

"I will, Dave, but don't worry! She does understand; she won't hold it against you, I promise. So, when you wrap up here, are you going home first, and then to Europe?"

"Yes, home first. We'll be doing some work in the studio and outside locations and then they go to Switzerland first for two weeks, then down to Spain for another two weeks, back at the studio and finish everything there."

"So the whole project will take about three months before they do all the technical stuff ... editing and all that?"

"Closer to four months of actual shooting and then I can relax; my part will be done. I'll be free for a few weeks and I am sure Dani will have plenty of things for us to do together."

Another round of drinks arrived and Dale took our dinner order. We both selected the Caesar salad. Dave chose a New

York Strip steak with baked potato and asparagus spears. I chose the prime rib because I would always have some left over, with the bone for Baron.

"After dinner, if you feel up to it, we can go see Baron; my apartment is only a block away. I have some scotch and soda there."

"Yeah, Mike, I'd like that. Do you think he'll remember me?"

"Of course, are you kidding me? You're his Uncle Dave; he sees you on television all the time," I said, then laughed.

"Yeah ... does he like television?"

"Sure does! He climbs onto the couch and watches it with me all the time. When I tell him, 'Look! There's your Uncle Dave,' his ears perk up and his eyes are glued to the screen," I said with a laugh. Dave laughed as well. "Yes, I'd like to see him again ... all grown up. I bet eating steaks and prime rib all the time, he must be big."

Our bread arrived with another round of drinks. Dale removed the ashtrays.

"He's a lot bigger than when you first saw him; he was only about six months old then," I said. "It'll only take a few minutes. We can have a drink."

"That's good with me."

"Dave, have you heard anything about *Harry O?* I haven't seen anything in the papers."

"Not yet ... we should be getting word soon, though. They will call Abby and he will call me the minute he hears from the network. Personally, I feel good about it; I think we'll get it."

"Promise me you'll let me know immediately ... I damn sure do not want to miss seeing it!"

"I will, Mike, so don't worry about it."

We finished our dinner and I asked Dale for the check. As was Dave's habit, he immediately reached for the check. We had a brief tug-of-war and I won. I insisted on paying the check. After all, I had only done so once and that was because he had had quite a few drinks and did not notice I paid, or just expected the bill to be added to his monthly charges.

17

On the way out of the restaurant, I introduced Dave to Anthony, the Maître D.

Anthony shook Dave's hand vigorously and advised me, "David Janssen needs no introduction! I'm a fan," he said with a smile.

"You are right, Anthony, but I noticed Mr. Janssen's photo is not behind your bar so I asked him to bring one for you."

"That is very kind ... I will ensure it is put in a place of honor," Anthony said. "Will you sign it?" he asked, looking at Dave.

"Of course ... my pleasure," Dave said, removing the photo from the envelope. He signed, *To Anthony & Friar Tuck. All the best. David Janssen.*

I thanked Dave for signing the photo for Anthony and he thanked me for the gesture in having his photo placed in the restaurant behind the bar with all the other luminaries.

Dave's car was waiting right outside on Third Avenue. Dave told him we were walking the block and he could pick him up in front of my apartment building at 209 East-Fifty-Sixth Street in about half an hour.

As I opened the door of my apartment, Baron was waiting. The smell of the prime rib and Dave's left over steak had him salivating. He sat at attention, his tail wagging. He was accustomed to seeing Rose Marie enter with me but I had no doubt he remembered Dave as Dave bent down to pet him.

"Hey, Baron, big boy ... remember me?" Dave asked with a

broad and sincere, if not loving, smile.

Baron stood up and began licking Dave's hand and wagging his tail but his eyes were on me as I moved into the kitchen and placed the take-out container on the counter.

Dave continued petting him as they moved into the living room. I cut a few pieces of prime rib with the huge bone into his dish and set it on the floor; he rushed to it.

"Scotch and soda, Dave?" I asked.

"Yes, Mike ... one for the road. I'm not driving."

"Coming right up! How was your dinner?"

"It was excellent! Now I know why you rave about the place so much. Do you eat there often?"

"Yes, at least three or four times a week. Rose Marie likes it, too. Being a bachelor ... at least, almost - the only thing I can cook is coffee, so I eat out almost every night."

"Doesn't Rose Marie cook for you?"

"Not really ... I think she has cooked dinner here one time and that was for a couple of our friends, and she had help."

"How did it turn out?"

"She and our friend made sirloin steaks, baked potato and fresh broccoli; it was actually pretty good. I don't think she likes to cook, unless it is one of her mother's Italian recipes."

"That's Dani's specialty - Italian food - and she is a great cook. She's always watching my weight so everything she does is healthy."

"I wish she had made it here. Maybe she could have inspired Rose Marie about cooking ... and I love Italian food."

"Yes, I wish she had made it here, too. By the way, she was busy there; her divorce became final last month ... so now she's a free woman."

"That's good ... isn't it? I mean, at least now she will no longer feel she is living in sin with you."

"Yeah ... I guess. However, I will be wondering what bearing it will have on our relationship. I'm still not ready to get married again and I won't be pushed into it ... by anyone."

"Oh, boy! I see what you mean but, from what you've already told me, I think Dani will see that or you can just tell her and she will be satisfied with your present arrangement."

"I hope you are right, Mike ... I hope you are right."

I served Dave his second drink and we sat down and watched Baron as he stripped the bone of its meat and began gnawing on the bone. Dave seemed entranced watching him.

"He loves that bone, doesn't he? How often do you get those for him?"

"At least three times a week. They are good for his teeth - makes them stronger and keeps them clean."

"I can see he has big k-nines ... has he ever bitten anyone? Have you trained him, like your dog in the service?"

"No, he's not bitten anyone yet ... and, yes, I've trained him, but he's pretty social with people as well as other dogs. I think most people are in fear just by his size and the fact they think of a German Shepherd as a police dog."

"I can understand that. I envy you, Mike; he must be a lot of fun, especially when you take him to the park."

"Oh, he is! He's great to come home to ... never asks for anything, never asks where I've been, who I've been with, doesn't ask for diamonds ... he's really a great companion."

"How does he get along with Rose Marie?"

"They love each other. He's okay with anyone I bring home, as long as I introduce them first. I'll tell you, Dave: if he doesn't trust someone, he lets out a low, deep growl - very discreet – and, if Baron doesn't trust someone, I won't either!"

"I don't blame you ... I can see why you trust his judgment. Has that ever happened?"

"Yes, once. I take him to the office sometimes and I was interviewing a guy for a job. He snarled his lips and let out a low growl; I don't think the guy noticed but I trust Baron so I ended the interview."

"Well, Mike ... I better get going. It's been great seeing you and I thank you for dinner. I may not have a chance to call you before I leave the city, but I'll be in touch soon."

"Thanks, Dave! It really has been good seeing you. I wish Dani had made it. I'm really looking forward to meeting her but it was good seeing you ... in person. I hope you have a good flight home and every place you will be going. Please keep me informed, especially about *Harry O.*"

"I will, Mike ... again, thanks for this evening ... and allowing me the visit with Baron."

"You're his Uncle Dave. If you had not come to see him, he would have growled at you the next time he saw you." We both laughed.

I rode down in the elevator with him and we shook hands. He got into his car and left. It was just before eleven so he would get enough sleep for the night. I returned to my apartment in time for the Eleven O'clock News on ABC.

I enjoyed the evening and was especially happy to see Dave so refreshed, 90 percent sober and very optimistic about the film he was shooting and the prospects for ABC to buy *Harry O.*

I reflected on his remarks relating to Dani's divorce being final and how it might affect their relationship. Judging by all he had told me, he seemed to have settled into a comfortable home life with Dani, the same as it would be IF they were actually husband and wife ... seemingly the same as he was with Rosemary.

Even so, the thought of actually making their relationship legal and binding by the laws of marriage seemed to scare the hell out of him. I could see the hurt he endured through his divorce from Ellie and her continuing demands. Dragging him back into court - wanting more and more of his hard earned money - was something he feared beyond fear itself. I believed his fear to be real and would hate to see him go through that again.

I convinced myself to put it out of my mind. After all, I could not change the course and Dave was man enough to chart the course of his own life without any input from me.

I felt certain he would get married again but, when he made that decision, it would be to a woman he chose and at a time he chose. Still, from all the recent photos I had seen of them out and about in Hollywood, it appeared they were both very happy ... as though they were meant for each other.

Dave had not given me any indication that there had been a

single instance where he had cause to be upset with Dani or that there was anything other than constant happiness within their relationship. It was obvious to me, from articles I had read, the Hollywood media considered Dave and Dani to be a couple ... a happy couple.

Dave told me he would be extremely busy with the film shooting in Los Angeles. Therefore I did not expect to hear from him for an extended period of time.

"David Janssen was courteous no matter what he was facing in his own life, on any given day. If he took the time to ask a person about his or her day, he took the time to listen to their answer."

- Norma Budden, author

18

Friday evening at 5:45, May 31, Dave called from Los Angeles.

"Mike, it's me! *Harry O* is a GO! I just talked with Abby; they bought, at least, the first season!"

"CONGRATULATIONS! Man, I am really happy to hear that! Do you know when they will air the premier episode?"

"No date set yet; we assume it will be in the first week kicking off the new fall season. I'll be sure to let you know, but watch for it in *TV Guide* in case I don't reach you ... I don't want you to miss it."

"Don't worry, I won't! So have you finished with *Once Is Not Enough*, at least your part in it?"

"No, about another week and I will be, then I'm going to Ankara, Turkey for a few days."

"Turkey? Are you doing a film there? Have you ever been there? Is Dani going with you?"

"They invited me ... promotion for the syndication of *The Fugitive* ... guess I'm pretty popular there. No, I've never been there but I understand they are really nice people and, no, Dani isn't going."

"My brother, Gene, was stationed at Incirlik Air Force Base during the Korean Conflict. He liked it ... guess he thought it was better than being in Korea."

"Yeah, back then, I guess any place was better than being in any part of Korea." Dave laughed.

"Wow ... here it is seven years since you finished *The Fugitive* and it is just now getting to Turkey!"

"I think this is the re-run syndication. I don't really know but I'll also be promoting other projects I've done."

"That is really interesting. I knew you were an international star, but Turkey? I never would have thought it! At least, send me a postcard, will you?"

"Yes, Mike, I'll do that. I just wanted to let you know about *Harry O* and that I'll be incommunicado for a while, so don't think I'm ignoring you. Give Rose Marie and Baron my regards; we'll talk as soon as I get back."

"Okay, Dave ... thanks for calling and giving me the good news. Take it easy. Have a good time in Turkey and be careful."

"You know me, Mike. I'm always careful," Dave said, then laughed before ending the call.

I really appreciated when he thought enough to give me a quick call just to let me know the latest events surrounding his life so I would not be overly concerned when he was too busy or unable to call.

I was certain that, with our friendship having developed over the past nine years, Dave knew without my saying that I valued his friendship as well as truly appreciating his talent on television and the big screen.

I knew he had several actors and actresses in Hollywood whom he considered good friends: Martin Milner, Clint Eastwood, James Farentino, his wife, Michele Lee, Paul and Peggy Burke, James and Lois Garner, Johnny and Joanna Carson and Angie Dickinson to name a few.

I knew he enjoyed socializing with them; it made the obligatory 'Hollywood Party Circuit' he was required to be involved with more palatable for him. He respected them for their work and valued them as friends he could relax with and enjoy being around.

Of his non-Hollywood friends, I knew his driver Bud White (replaced by Elliot Shapiro when he started filming *Harry O*) and Victor Gentille, his valued and trusted Secretary/Valet, were people whom he considered and trusted as valued friends.

I considered myself, as an outsider, honored to be one he trusted and considered to be a true friend. I would learn as time passed that Dave really liked Elliot Shapiro, his sense of humor, his confidence and his ability to keep Dave's *secrets*.

When Dave and I were together in a restaurant, I had noted on more than one occasion that he appeared to feel embarrassed at the staring looks of non celebrities. It was almost as though he didn't feel their approval of him was warranted. I think he felt he was *no one special*.

It could also be, as I think back, that he knew he WAS someone special but did not like being stared at.

One thing was certain to me: Dave was a very complex man. IF he wanted you to know something about himself, he would tell you. He did not like being questioned about his getting married again, that I knew for sure. He also did not appreciate anyone telling him not to drink too much.

I had resolved over the past nine years to accept our friendship, to accept that no one could change Dave, even if the intent would be for his own good. Still, I could not help but think about Dani's divorce being made final. How would that affect their relationship and would Dave make the right decision for himself?

As June passed with no contact from Dave, I continued scanning the newspapers and fan magazines. There were occasional articles about Dave and the big announcement that ABC would be bringing *Harry O* to its fall line up. That pleased me and I would plan a 'watch party' at my apartment with Rose Marie and a few close friends.

I was surprised when Dave called on Monday, July 1, 1974.

"Mike, Dave ... how are you, stranger?"

"I'm good, Dave ... more important ... how in the hell are you? It's been a long time since we spoke. Where are you?"

"I'm back in the States. Actually, we're in Palm Springs for the Fourth of July weekend. Just wanted to let you know that, when we start production on *Harry O* later this month, we'll actually be shooting in San Diego."

"Dave, that is music to my ears! We LOVE the show! I have no doubt it will be another *Fugitive* type success for you! Wait a minute! You will be actually shooting it in San Diego;

have you ever been there? Do you like it? WHY San Diego; why can't they just shoot it in LA, like you did the pilots?"

"Damn, Mike! You're just full of questions, aren't you?" He laughed. "ABC decided it would be more realistic to film there. I've been there but I'm not really that familiar with the city, but I'm looking forward to it, for sure."

"Will you and Dani be moving there?"

"No ... no ... I will lease a place there and come home on weekends ... or whenever we wrap an episode. It is a quick flight between here and there so it won't be too bad. Dani will hold down the fort here."

"Wow! I am really happy for you, Dave. Actually, I'm excited just knowing you will be on TV every week and doing a show we love! I think you will see a huge jump in your fans, considering the differences between *Dr. Kimble* and *Harry O*; you are going from being the hunted to being the hunter."

"Yeah ... quite a leap, isn't it? You really think I can pull it off?" Dave asked with a little laugh.

"Hell, YES! You already have! Personally, I really liked both of the pilots ... I didn't see anything really wrong in the first one, except the lighting and the way you treated the women. I did see the changes in the second one and it was much better, but the first one was not as bad as the network seemed to think."

"No, Mike! They were right. The first pilot lacked a lot. At least, the network saw enough potential to give us another shot at it. *Gertrude* is the new ... the first episode. I don't know if that will be the one the network chooses to air first, but it is the first we'll be shooting. You'll see a lot of differences - a lot of improvements, even in the way I treat the ladies." He laughed heartily.

"I believe you, Dave ... I can't wait to see it. I know we will love it. What is it about?"

"I'm NOT going to tell you, Mike. I don't want you to blab it to Rose Marie and spoil it for both of you," he said, laughing.

"All right, Dave ... but, in case you don't know this, *TV Guide* will give us a synopsis so I'll play detective and figure it out," I responded with a laugh.

"Yeah, but you will still watch it, right?"

"Of course! I'm planning a 'watch party' here in my apartment."

"That's good to hear so take a consensus and let me know."

"I will be sure to do that. I think I'll even make all our guests write letters to ABC before they leave ... positive letters ... even if they don't like you," I said jokingly.

"Okay, Mike ... I have to run but I'll be calling you in a few days. You and Rose Marie have a good Fourth of July."

"Thanks, Dave ... the same for you and Dani," I replied before hanging up.

David Janssen was blessed with true friends in
spite of the (sometimes) cutthroat nature of the business
he had been involved with for most of his life.

Among those friends were Paul Burke, Jimmy
Farentino, James Garner, Johnny Carson
and Clint Eastwood – not to mention
his non-Hollywood friend,
Michael Phelps.

19

I next heard from Dave on Sunday, July 21; he called at 8:15.

"Hey, Mike! It's me. Just wanted to let you know I'm in San Diego. We begin filming the first season this coming week."

"Hi, Dave ... that is really great news! Is Dani with you?"

"No ... she will be staying home. I'm in a hotel for the time being. Victor is looking for a place I can lease while we are filming here, something on the beach."

"Hell, Dave, Harry O has a beach house! Why don't you just move in with him?" I asked, laughing.

"He won't let me and I would not do it anyway. When we finish work, I need my space and privacy," he said with a big laugh.

"Right. That I can understand. Will he, at least, let you use his boat sometimes? What about a car? I hate buses. So do you have any idea when it will air?"

"No ... I won't know that for several weeks. You know, as I've told you, all the technical stuff takes time. I will be sure to give you a call and let you know. I don't think Harry's boat will ever see water. You have to wait and see about Harry having a car. How are things going with you?"

"Hectic in the office, but that is the norm. Otherwise, all is going along smoothly. Rose Marie and I are considering her moving in with me; she is working on it with her parents. My Indiana lawyer is working on an uncontested divorce and Baron is still growing; he wishes you'd come back. He loved your left-over steak."

"That's good to hear. So you are finally taking your big brother's advice and getting a divorce? Tell Baron I'll send him a whole steak from California. Be careful! If Rose Marie moves in with you, it won't be long and you'll start hearing the 'M' word," he said with a hearty laugh.

"Don't scare me like that, Dave! Actually, I had not thought of that! Maybe I'll be lucky and her parents won't allow it."

"She is over 18, isn't she?"

"Yeah, but she's Italian, living at home and her parents - especially her father - have very strict, Catholic values. I don't think they will allow it; they are afraid of her even moving to Manhattan."

"She's Italian - then she has a strong will - and, Mike, one thing I know about is women! I'm just trying to warn you."

"Yeah, and I appreciate that, Dave ... but hell! Look at you! You spent three years with Rosemary. You've been with Dani almost two years. You seem to have it worked out to where you have the benefits without the legal binds."

"Yeah, but I know deep in my mind it isn't going to last. I'm just riding the cool wave; when it crashes, I'll move on."

"Well, thanks Dave! You've given me something to think about ... something I have to worry about. It may be a few months before my divorce is final so who knows what will happen? Maybe I'll just follow your plan ... ride the cool wave."

"Just remember we had this talk ... be careful! You've been warned, young man," he said with a laugh.

"Okay, Dave ... I consider myself warned! Now, let's get back to *Harry O*. Do you like him? Do you think you will work well together?"

"Yeah, Mike ... I really like him. He's a pretty cool guy, laid back ... analytical mind ... doesn't get shook up easily. I think he will be a hit. WE will definitely work well together, that I promise."

"Well that is good enough for me. Since I know you won't give me any of the juicy details about any of his cases, I'll still have to wait and read the synopsis in *TV Guide*."

"I don't want to spoil it for you, Mike; it would ruin any

enjoyment you get out of watching. You know it's funny: when we are working, shooting the scenes, that is all I concentrate on. I sometimes watch the dailies but that is only to find flaws in my own performances. Then, when it is finished, I don't think about it until it airs ... and then I WATCH IT! I look for every mistake, no matter how minute, and make certain not to make the same mistake again ... at least, I try."

"Dave ... being honest here ... in every episode I've ever watched you in, on every show on TV, or even in the movies you've made, I cannot remember any scene where I could consciously see a mistake in your performances," I said with sincerity.

"Thanks Mike, that is good to hear, but believe me! I make mistakes. Hopefully, and like you, most people don't see them. I mean, I don't think my mistakes are so blatant; they wouldn't get past the director or the film editors if they were - but I can see them and I don't like it when I know I could have done better. The fans of the show ... especially *my* fans ... deserve better."

"I know, Dave. I figured that out since knowing you as a person. Personally, I think sometimes you may be too hard on yourself, too critical ... and I think most of your fans, and your real friends, think you push yourself too hard."

"You have a point ... and I know that, but I won't change. Perfection is what I demand ... of myself as well as the people working with me. Listen, Mike! I have to get organized here in the hotel and get to bed early; we have an early call in the morning. I'll give you a call soon. Take it easy."

"Okay, you too, Dave ... and thanks for the call."

I was happy to get Dave's call and to know he was finally getting started on *Harry O*. Based on my friends' and my own opinions, as well as the critical reviews of the second pilot, *Smile Jenny, You're Dead*, I had no doubt whatsoever that Dave would have a huge hit on his hands and would be working with *Harry Orwell* for several years to come.

I called Rose Marie first, then my family in Indianapolis, followed by all of my friends and colleagues in New York to let them know they MUST watch *Harry O* coming to ABC in the fall. I asked each one to write positive letters to ABC after watching the show and was assured all would comply with my request. Of course, I would follow up with another call when I knew the air date.

I did not know, nor could I understand, how the television networks calculated the viewers to set the ratings, but I did know enough that the show needed all the viewers it could get to receive a high rating.

I figured it would be six or seven weeks before the premier of *Harry O* and I marked it on my calendar to keep track, as well as a reminder to keep a close eye for any announcement in *TV Guide*.

I scanned the New York newspapers each day as well as my weekly *TV Guide* looking for announcements about the premier of *Harry O*; there was no mention of it in any of the media.

Dave surprised me with a call on Monday morning, August 19, at 4:45. I had just poured my second cup of coffee.

"Mike ... it's me, Dave ... did I wake you?"

"No, Dave, not at all. What is going on with Harry?"

"That's why I'm calling you, as promised. We've finished three episodes, starting the fourth this week. The premier will be on Thursday, September 12, at 10 o'clock ... prime time! Make sure you don't miss it!"

"No way we will miss it, Dave! We've waited too long to see it. Rose Marie and I will be holding a watch party with about 12 of our good friends. We're going to have Bar-B-Que ribs, baked beans, beer, scotch, you name it ... oh, and popcorn for when the show starts."

"You do go all out, don't you, Mike? Will Rose Marie be barbecuing?"

"No ... no way! We're getting them from a restaurant. I want our guests to be healthy and happy ... just kidding. I'll call everyone and make sure they know."

"Good ... I appreciate that. You should be seeing some publicity promoting it soon. I just wanted to give you a heads-up."

"Thanks, Dave. You've already completed three episodes?

How are you adjusting to the rigors? Is it like when you were filming *The Fugitive*? Have you been home, seen Dani at all, since you started?"

"Yeah, we've finished three; I think they are pretty damn good. Yeah, I'm getting used to the grind ... and that is what it is ... it's brutal. I've been home a couple of times; all is well there. How are things on your end? How is Rose Marie? How's Baron?"

"Everything here is going great. Rose Marie and Baron are doing well. How is Dani?"

"Dani is fine. Has Rose Marie moved in with you?"

"No ... she is getting too much flack from her parents, so you had me worried for nothing. Actually, I am glad. I am getting used to living alone, with just Baron. I put in 12 to 14 hours a day at the office, sometimes taking clients for happy hour or even dinner; I don't know how Rose Marie would deal with that."

"Well, I think you are better off, really. Baron doesn't give you any BS when you come in ... you don't have anyone nagging you to go here-go there ... no one to really answer to. You're a lucky guy, Mike."

"You are right, Dave ... and I see it clearly now. Don't get me wrong! I would have loved for Rose Marie to move in with me but I am too busy working on my career and I can't afford any distractions, so I have to be able to put in all the hours necessary.

"New York is not a cheap city to live in. IF, and when, I really feel she is the right woman for me, I want to be financially secure - to be able to give her anything she wants."

"You are thinking the right way, Mike ... but don't push yourself. Don't marry your work and neglect your personal happiness."

"I know ... I'm keeping a clear and open mind but my work is demanding and it is important - especially now, at my age."

"You're right ... you keep focused. I have to get some sleep so we'll talk soon. If I don't have a chance to call before, remember September 12[th;] it's on a Thursday."

"Don't worry, Dave ... not a chance we'll miss it! Thanks for calling."

20

At eight o'clock on Thursday evening, September 12, 1974, Rose Marie and I plus 10 guests made ourselves comfortable in my living room. Rose Marie, Jan, Phyllis and Liz attended to setting up the delicious Bar-B-Que ribs and baked beans. Phil and I played the bartender role and everyone enjoyed a good dinner and relaxing drinks.

The conversation was all about David Janssen; our friendship, *Richard Diamond, The Fugitive, The Green Berets* and, of course, tonight's premier of *Harry O*.

Of all our guests, only Liz Connors knew a real celebrity; Liz's mother was good friends with Jackie Gleason. As a comedian, I felt Jackie Gleason was among the best. I loved *The Honeymooners*.

At 9:50, the girls had all cleaned up the dishes and Phil and I made everyone fresh drinks as Rose Marie made big bowls of popcorn. Precisely at 10 o'clock, the ABC Television Network began the introductory scenes with jazz music by composer, Billy Goldenberg.

The screen flashed as Dave is seen walking down towards a car with a bullet hole in the window. *David Janssen* flashes, followed by 'as *Harry O*'. Tonight's episode title, *Gertrude*, flashed on the screen.

The volume was turned up much louder than I would normally have it. Even so, you could hear a pin drop on my plush carpet as the first scenes rolled.

The plot involved a somewhat scatterbrained blonde girl

(played by Julie Sommars) who comes to Harry with a man's shoe. It belonged to her brother, Harold, who had disappeared; he was Absent Without Leave (AWOL) and his sister, Gertrude, was adamant her brother would never desert his beloved Navy. The character of Harold was played by Les Lannom, an excellent actor Dave would work with on several future projects.

Harry O takes the case but not Gertrude's money since she had sold her furniture and nearly every worldly possession she owned to hire him to find her brother.

Harry O is met with resistance when he seeks information from the Navy at the San Diego Naval Base, as well as the San Diego Police Department. Even his old friend, Detective Lieutenant Manny Quinlan (played by Henry Darrow) balks at getting involved.

The story revolved around Gertrude's brother Harold, a couple of his shipmates and a plan to smuggle stolen diamonds. There are no high speed chases, no fist fights and no murders. It was still a good plot, well written and it showed Dave's comedic talents with some well chosen lines.

In all, everyone at our party seemed to thoroughly enjoy the show and each felt it had great series potential. Several of our friends prodded me to divulge any *secrets* I knew about Dave and really wanted to know what kind of guy he was off screen. I told them simply, "He is a great guy and a good friend."

Our guests left around 11:30 and each promised to send letters praising the show to ABC headquarters in New York.

I was awakened at 2:20 in the morning, Friday, September 13, by a call from Dave.

"Mike? Sorry to wake you and I know I did ... but did you see the show?"

"Yes, Dave, we did ... and it is okay that you woke me. All our guests really enjoyed it. It was really well put together. I liked your opening lines about the circus - showed you do have a sense of humor. With most of your work, your fans don't know that you can make jokes. Now I know why you take the bus ... and I'm glad to see you were nice to Julie Sommars, even when you had to borrow her car.

"I did get a big laugh seeing you drive a Volkswagen, knowing your Rolls Royce was probably in your parking space. Everyone here liked it and promised to send letters to ABC. Have you talked to Dani ... did she see it ... like it?"

"I'm glad you and your friends liked it. Thanks! Yes, I spoke with Dani. She had a party at home with a few of our close friends; everyone liked it ... but, of course, they are all biased. Dani is going to get the early papers for the reviews and call me. So you think we have a good shot at it in the long run?"

"I definitely do ... you have moved into the character already. Everyone knows why you are now a private detective - about the bullet in your back, your car in the shop ... laid back attitude, detective's mind ... you have mastered the character and I know your fans are going to love it ... and YOU!"

"Thanks a lot, Mike! Now I feel good. Hey, I'm sorry I woke you, but I couldn't wait to get your opinion and those of your friends."

"That's fine, Dave ... I couldn't wait to tell you so your call is good. Is the schedule as bad as it was on *The Fugitive*?"

"It is pretty rough but, for a television series, turning out an episode a week, that's how it has to be ... no way to make it any easier."

"I liked the scene where Harold knocked you down on the mattress. I know you still have your bum knee, even with all the surgeries you've had ... does it still bother you?"

"Yeah ... every now and then, but it had nothing to do with that scene. The way it looked to you on television, well Mike, that's what I do ... it's called acting!" He gave a big laugh. "All right! I'll let you get back to sleep. I know you have to work in the morning."

"Okay, thanks for calling, Dave ... and good luck with the reviews and more important, the ratings." I hung up and went back to sleep.

I picked up the papers from my corner newsstand as I went to my office. After getting a fresh cup of coffee, I turned to the television page of *The New York Times*, followed by *The Daily News*. I was very pleased to see the TV critics were very kind to the series' premier and the show's potential. Both lauded Dave for his performance, even saying he "brought life to *Harry O* that made him a likable character."

Yes, I was convinced in my heart and mind that Dave had, finally, cemented a deal for a new series that held great promise for him.

I expected he would be *Harry O* for at least the next four years, unless he became as physically and mentally tired as he did beginning the fourth season of *The Fugitive*.

I was very pleased when he called me at almost 2:30 in the morning to hear how happy he was with the consensus of me and my guests and Dani and their friends. I gathered from his tone of voice that he got what he was hoping for, affirmation of his having turned in a great performance ... that he proved he was in fact *Harry Orwell*.

I also noted Dave was completely sober when he called and that was a very good sign to me that he was putting his full concentration into the character and had full control over his alcohol consumption.

21

Rose Marie and I set a standing date to watch *Harry O* at my apartment every Thursday night. We agreed to play it by ear whether to invite friends, or just watch it ourselves.

On Thursday, September 19, I took Rose Marie to the Friar Tuck Inn for an early dinner. We were back at my apartment by 9:45. She made a big bowl of popcorn and I prepared Baron a good dinner with some steak tidbits mixed in. He was happy when I gave him a special dinner.

Rose Marie and I cuddled up on the sofa and had the television tuned to ABC. At 10 o'clock, *Harry O* commenced with this week's episode titled, *The Admiral's Lady*.

The guest stars in this episode were Leif Erickson, who played retired 'Navy Admiral, Tannehill'; John McMartin played 'Jordan Briggs'; Ellen Weston played 'Mrs. Lucas' and Sharon Acker played the part of 'Andrea Tannehill', the Admiral's much younger wife.

Harry O was hired by the Admiral to find his wife; he refuses to believe she was killed when their boat was lost at sea. Soon, the body of her best friend - who had been with her on the boat - washes ashore; it was determined her friend had been murdered.

Harry O gets on the wrong side of the Admiral when he suggests his wife was having an affair, so the Admiral fires him. The Admiral did not know that *Harry O* was a very stubborn and determined man.

Throughout the episode I made notes on a legal pad. I knew I would have a lot of questions when I spoke with Dave again.

After the first 15 minutes of the Eleven O'clock News on ABC, I drove Rose Marie home then returned to my apartment and took Baron for a midnight run in the park.

The week passed and on Thursday, September 26, my copy of *TV Guide* had told me tonight's episode would be *Guardian at the Gate,* which Dave had told me was the first episode they had filmed in San Diego.

Rose Marie and I decided to again host a 'watch party' with our close group of friends. We decided on Rose Marie and the girls fixing hamburgers, homemade fries, sodas and beer, as well as my bar for those who preferred.

The guest stars were Barry Sullivan - a star in his own right through films of the 40s, 50s and even some television shows - and Linda Evans, a close friend of Dani's, so I assumed Dave's as well. Others with prominent roles were Anne Archer, Katharine Woodville and Richard Kelton.

The storyline involved Barry Sullivan as 'Paul Armin Sawyer' - a famous architect and conservationist with a mean demeanor. He has alienated everyone in the community costing a developer a lot of money by getting the county commissioners to halt a multi-million dollar development. He's also alienated a local politician. Linda Evans plays 'Marian Sawyer', his devoted daughter.

In the opening, Sawyer's German Shepherd is poisoned and rushed to the veterinarian's office. Marian is sure whoever poisoned the dog made an attack against her dad. She hires *Harry O* to find the person responsible for poisoning the dog.

Since the dog had markings similar to Baron, I made sure he was watching it with us; I knew Dave would be angry if I didn't.

At the end of the show, we all expressed our opinions and everyone gave it a very high rating. After giving Baron a hamburger, he agreed. I knew Dave would like that vote of confidence. Again, I took notes, filling a page and a half on my legal pad.

"Well, did any of you notice the looks Harry gave Marian when she was driving him from the vet's office? To me, it looked like he had lust in his eyes - and I don't think it was acting," Liz said.

"No ... no ... he didn't know her well. They were neighbors; he was just sizing her up," I said, almost in a defensive tone.

"But he does know her! Linda Evans is one of Dani Greco's best friends. I read that!" Liz countered.

"Yes, and I'm sure she and Dave are just friends, too. He probably helped her get the part," I said.

"I still think he had the look of lust in his eyes," she said with a smile.

"Okay ... I'll ask him," I said, then laughed.

"Well, I've read that he is a real womanizer and he chases anything in a skirt," Jan said, adding her two cents.

"No, Liz ... Jan," Rose Marie said, interrupting the conversation. "I met him with Mike here in the city. He took us to dinner; he's not that way at all."

"I can tell you for a fact, he is not ... nowhere near it. If he becomes involved with a woman and has feelings for her, he won't cheat on her; he doesn't jump into bed with every woman he sees or works with," I said.

I felt uncomfortable in having to defend him. Hell, these girls did not know him; they actually believed all the crap in the tabloids. Now I knew what Dave had warned me about.

Our guests left just before midnight, then I drove Rose Marie home.

On the drive to Rose Marie's parents' home, we discussed Liz and Jan's comments. I was relieved when she had taken Dave's side, but she told me she was cautious because, when she met Dave, he was in love with Rosemary Forsyth.

"Well, Rose Marie, I did not like Liz and Jan drawing the conclusions they did about Dave's private life but as long as I, or I should say we, know the truth and they like the show, I guess that's all that really counts."

"Yes, I agree. Maybe we shouldn't invite them over for the show again," she responded.

"No, that wouldn't be nice ... and they would think we were being hypocritical."

"Yes, you are right, but let's not invite people every week. It's nice for us to watch and enjoy it ... just the two of us."

I had hoped to hear from Dave but we had seen two episodes of *Harry O* since I last spoke with him. I knew he must be extremely busy so I wasn't concerned. I was burning to ask him my questions but resigned myself to having patience. I'd get my answers when Dave had the chance to call me.

Another week passed with no call from Dave. I joked with myself that, at least, I knew I would see him Thursday evening for sure.

When Thursday came, I picked Rose Marie up from her office at East Forty-Ninth and Madison Avenue at 5:15. We went to my apartment and took Baron to the park for a run. After having a couple of drinks to relax while watching the evening news, we went to dinner at the Park Lane Hotel. We were back in my apartment by 9:40 and I prepared Baron's dinner.

I had picked up a couple of the tabloid papers and one Hollywood fan magazine where it was reported that "based on reliable sources" it was rumored that Dave and Dani were heading to the "altar" now that her divorce from Buddy Greco had been made final.

That was a shock to me, as Dave had made no mention of his giving any serious consideration to re-marrying. Rose Marie was also shocked. Neither of us had met Dani, although I had told Rose Marie that Dave spoke very lovingly of her and that she had many talents in the home that made him happy.

Having met Rosemary Forsyth, Rose Marie honestly felt that Rosemary was madly in love with Dave, that they made a perfect couple; she was sad when they broke up.

I quickly changed the subject out of fear Rose Marie may compare me to Dave. She did not even ask how my divorce was progressing.

Tonight's story was titled *Mortal Sin*. A friend, or perhaps his 'Priest' (played by Laurence Luckinbill) wakes Harry up early one morning. He tells Harry that a man had confessed to him of having committed a murder and was going to kill again. The Priest asks Harry to find the man before he kills again.

Of course, Lieutenant Quinlan (Henry Darrow) races to the scene in the final act and saves Harry's life.

This episode was the result of extraordinary writing and excellent acting by everyone in their respective roles.

Rose Marie and I both found this episode to be one of the best we had seen so far. I kept my routine of taking notes for questions I would ask Dave.

I told Rose Marie I was starting to have some reservations about asking Dave all my questions, some of which I would have to admit may have been stupid. Dave and I really did not discuss his work in any great detail and I did not want to risk aggravating him.

"Mike, this is his new series. He wants to know your opinion and I don't think he will mind, least of all be offended by, your questions," she said.

"I hope so ... okay, I'll ask him when we speak again."

"Don't forget to ask him if he's getting married to Dani."

The episode over, Rose Marie and I made our critiques. I thought it was very good but I, again, found fault with the lighting in several scenes. Rose Marie agreed with me on every point, or did she? I was wondering about Rose Marie. Was she just trying to please me by agreeing with my opinions of the show, just because Dave and I were friends?

I drove Rose Marie home, taking Baron along for the ride. I decided we would stop at the park on our return if I could find a parking space so Baron could have a midnight run.

David Janssen always wanted a dog but never had the opportunity to own one. Even as an adult, he didn't get one; he thought it would be unfair to the dog since he was rarely home and would have little time to spend with it.

22

Another week passed without hearing from Dave. Again, Rose Marie and I decided that we would watch *Harry O* together - just the two of us and Baron. It was her idea, to which I readily agreed.

I picked Rose Marie up from her office and we settled on having our Thursday evening dinner at the Friar Tuck Inn. We were in my apartment in time for me to fix Baron his dinner, with a good portion of New York Strip steak.

We settled onto the sofa with Brandy Alexanders and waited for the boring commercial messages. I knew, however, that it was the commercials that paid Dave and the crew their salaries.

Tonight's episode was *Coinage of the Realm* with guest stars Kenneth Mars, Joan Darling and Dawn Lyn. Of course, there is Henry Darrow as Lieutenant Manny Quinlan.

A woman comes to Harry asking him to find her ex-husband - who had been a suspect in an old hit-and-run homicide case which Harry had been the lead investigator on when he was a cop; he had not solved the case. The woman's daughter needs a life-saving kidney transplant and her father may be a match.

Harry is not the only one seeking the missing father; the suspense builds. The little girl is precious and quite a good actress. She collects coins and, through that, she and Harry become friends.

This was a well written story and the acting was above par. I was not too impressed with the actor playing the girl's father nor the one who portrayed Harry's snitch; they were the only faults in the casting, in my opinion.

Rose Marie and I watched the first 15 minutes of the news and then I took her home; again, Baron was happy to go along.

I was surprised when Dave called me a couple of minutes before three o'clock in the morning.

"Mike, it's me. I know I woke you. Hope you don't mind ... just wanted to ask if you've been watching the show."

"Hey, Dave! It's okay. I'm glad you, finally, found the time to call. Of course, we have been watching the show! We've even had a few people over to make it a party."

"We've been really busy; the crew tried to kill me a couple of weeks ago so we lost a day of shooting. It has been pretty hectic lately. Well ... I'm waiting ... what's your verdict?"

"What in the hell do you mean ... the crew tried to kill you? It doesn't sound like it would be part of the script. Hell, they would all be out of a job without YOU!"

"A light fell on my head ... caused a slight concussion and required a few stitches. It was an accident, but it got us all out of filming on a Saturday," he said with his deep laugh.

"You are okay now though, right? As for the show, YOU should already know; it is going to be a big HIT ... a real ratings-buster. Is that the way you say it? I've even been taking notes, questions I have for you. Truthfully, all our friends really like it ... all my family likes it."

"I'm fine. You know I have a hard head; it didn't hurt at all. I really do appreciate your opinion of the show. Thanks, Mike! T

hat is really good to hear. What are your questions?"

"I don't have my notes here by my bed. We'll get to them later ... there's too many to go over now, but I'll ask a couple that have really been bugging me.

"One: as a retired police detective sergeant with over 15 years on the force, you (as Harry) must be getting a good pension, right? You seem to have very little living expenses ... right? So why in the hell don't you get a reliable car? Two: at Harry O's age, you must have other clothes yet all we see you in is the sports jacket, khaki pants or, when at home on the beach, all you wear is what looks more like boxer shorts than swim trunks and that fisherman's jacket. Get a better wardrobe."

"Okay, Mike, first question ... it isn't that I can't afford a decent car; it's part of the mystique of Harry - the car always being in the shop and a city bus to get around. Second: the persona of Harry is that he lives a simple life, he's very frugal ... no need for a big wardrobe.

"Besides, that's how the studio saves money; the guest stars demand BIG bucks. Those are swim trunks and I wear something under them ... oh, and they wash them several times a day. The swim trunks make me look sexy. Don't you think I'm sexy, Mike? They save money on the car and my wardrobe, do you get it? Actually, Mike, I have several pairs of identical swim trunks." Dave laughed loudly for a good minute.

"Yeah ... okay, I get it. I'll ask Rose Marie and the girls if they think you're sexy," I said, then laughed. "One other thing from tonight's episode ... at the shoot-out between the bad guys and the cop, we see bystanders walking right up behind the uniformed cop. I can tell you that would never happen and, by the time we see all that, you'd be hearing a lot of wailing sirens in the background."

"Hey, Mike! The director has claim to 'dramatic license' ... it's his show, after all. I'll remember that about the sirens, though." He laughed.

"Okay, one last question for now ... you're an ex-cop, now a licensed private detective. You are involved in cases with some pretty bad perps. Why in the hell don't you have a gun, like a .38 caliber Smith and Wesson Detective Special?"

"I have a bullet in my back, Mike. I don't like guns; I know how dangerous they can be - and the studio won't give me one." He laughed.

"All right, Dave! I'll just resign myself to watching the show and not be so critical ... still, I have to tell you, Rose Marie and I both agree it is our favorite show on television. We won't miss a single episode, I promise," I said, then laughed.

"Good ... thanks, Mike! I have to get some sleep; we have an early call. You get back to sleep and we'll talk soon."

"Okay, Dave ... don't make it so long between calls. I worry."

"All right, Mike. I'll be in touch soon." Dave ended the call.

I had not asked about the rumors of him and Dani getting married. I had not asked how he is adjusting to spending so much time in San Diego, away from Dani. I was tired and he sounded tired as well. I would have a lot more questions for him the next time he called.

I called Rose Marie at her office the next morning to let her know I had spoken with Dave. She asked me if I had told him about Liz and Jan's comments and if I asked about the marriage rumors. I told her it was three o'clock in the morning when he called and I had not mentioned the comments or what we had seen in the tabloids about his wedding plans.

I told her I would ask him the next time we talked but I may not ask about the 'M' word. I would let him tell me if, and when, he wanted. She understood.

23

On Thursday, October 17, *TV Guide* told us the title of tonight's episode was *Eyewitness*. The synopsis stated the only witness to a murder was a blind teenager.

On this evening, Rose Marie and I decided to invite our group of friends. I had arranged for the Friar Tuck to prepare 10 New York Strip steaks, 10 baked potatoes and 10 sides of Broccoli, with plenty of garlic bread.

Rose Marie and I set the dining room table and our friends all arrived around 8:30. I prepared a batch of Brandy Alexanders and a Grasshopper for Liz. After the Brandy Alexanders, the guys all opted for beer; I stayed with the Brandy.

Dinner was delivered at nine o'clock and we all immediately enjoyed a great meal. Rose Marie and the girls cleared the table and put the dishes in the dishwasher. We were all relaxed with fresh drinks when *Harry O* began to roll.

The episode was written by Herman Groves and was, by consensus of our friends, the best as far as script and acting. I was the only one who still voiced disapproval of the lighting. Several of our friends told me to have my eyes checked; I would definitely voice my objections to the lighting in my next talk with Dave.

Everyone was very pleased, not only with the show, but with the catered dinner. I had Rose Marie home just before midnight and drove Baron to the park; I think Baron knew it was Thursday and it would be his night for a midnight run. He sure had me trained.

Dave called me on Saturday morning, October 19, at 10:45.

"Good morning, Mike ... it's me. How are you doing?"

"Great, Dave ... thanks, and how are you? Are you working today?"

"No, I'm in LA. Did you see the show Thursday?"

"Of course! We had eight of our close friends in. I had steak dinners catered by Friar Tuck and we all had a nice dinner, plenty of booze, great conversation ... then silence when YOU came on the screen."

"What did you ... your friends, think of it?"

"I can tell you honestly Dave, without exception - everyone loved it! We all thought the script was outstanding and the acting, award-winning - especially the blind kid. I still had only one complaint ... the damned lighting!!!"

"I am happy to hear that, Mike ... but, as far as the lighting goes, that's out of my purview. The director and the lighting man has full control over that; to be honest, I look past it."

"All right, Dave! I'll try to accept it and just look past it, too. Seriously, though, in my opinion, each episode seems to be getting better and better. Do you know anything about the ratings yet?"

"Yeah, the ratings are climbing which means more viewers are tuning in each week; that's good for us."

"I'm glad to hear that ... means you'll be solving cases for a long time to come. Are you getting any fan mail yet? Are any of your *Fugitive* fans writing to you, telling you what they think about *Harry O* as compared to *Richard Kimble*?"

"Yes, we have been getting lots of fan mail ... keeps climbing each week. I haven't really seen them yet ... but I'll make the time to read and answer some pretty soon. I don't know if anything has been said about comparing Kimble to Harry, but you've raised an interesting point. I will look into that when I get to the studio here; that's where all the mail comes."

"Well, what can you tell me about this coming week's show?"

"Nothing; you have to watch it. All I will tell you is we worked hard on it and it's finished and we go onto the next one. I will have to watch it, too ... just to see if they got the lighting right in every scene," he said, laughing.

"Okay, smart ass. My *TV Guide* will tell me what it's about then I can decide if I want to watch it," I said, then laughed.

"You BETTER watch it! You and Rose Marie are my East coast critics ... my sounding board. You'll like it. I think it was very well done. So how are things with you and Rose Marie? How is Baron?"

"Everyone and everything here is good. Are you just home for the weekend or on a break? How is Dani?" I asked.

"Yeah, I'll be going back to San Diego tomorrow evening. Dani is fine; we have a party we have to go to this evening and she demanded I be present. I'll give you a call next week - try and call you after the show, see how you liked it.

"Are you having a party Thursday? I can only imagine how much the Friar Tuck catering must have cost. You have to stop that; save your money. I don't think I could get it past the accounting department for the show to pick up the tab," he said with a laugh.

"I bet Dani is happy you are home even if it is for just a few hours. Dave, I don't do that often, the catering ... but I enjoyed doing it, seeing everyone enjoying a good meal, the drinks and then your show. I wouldn't think of sending you the bill, but if you want to try to get the studio to reimburse me, I don't mind," I said before laughing, then added, "So tell me, Dave ... what do you do all week in San Diego after work ... with Dani in Los Angeles?"

"Mike, by the time we finish the day's shooting, I honestly just take a shower and go to bed. Rare occasions I may go to a local bar with some of the cast and crew and have a couple of drinks but, usually, everyone is too damned tired to do anything but get some sleep and get ready for the next day."

"I can understand that. I know from what you have told me, it is hard work, but when the whole thing is done, and you see it on television, it looks so easy; it looks like you could shoot an entire episode in an hour, even taking breaks during the commercials."

Dave laughed. "Yeah, Mike ... that would be nice if it were the case; it will never happen, though."

"I still have a lot of questions about the episodes we have already seen; maybe when you have some time to talk, I'll hit you with them."

"We can do that ... unless you want to just write them down and mail them to me."

"No, I like instant answers ... no rush; we can do it at a later time."

"Rose Marie wanted me to ask you one thing, Dave. We read in a couple of the tabloids, not the New York papers, and in one of the fan magazines, that you and Dani are pretty close to tying the knot. I told Rose Marie I would ask you, but I still haven't received any invitation in the mail, so I didn't believe the articles."

"Mike ... it is all bullshit! I know what's going on. Dani is spreading this crap to her friends and getting them to leak it to the tabloids. I know what she is doing; she's covertly trying to pressure me. I don't like it and I won't be pressured; she knows that. It is plain bullshit," he said firmly.

"So she hasn't come out and said anything to you? You haven't had any arguments over it, have you?"

"No, she knows better than to say anything to me. We haven't had any fights about it. I just ignore the subject and, if any reporters catch me out and ask about it, I will flat out tell them it is BULLSHIT! If that happens, then Dani will get the message loud and clear ... hell, we may even have a fight about it. She is a pretty strong woman and she sure as hell has a temper ... let me tell you!"

"Okay, I will let Rose Marie know that. As a matter of fact, I'll tell her that IF, and WHEN, you decide to ask Dani to marry you, I figure that my divorce will be over and I'll ask her to marry me," I said with a laugh.

"Yeah ... good luck with that, Mike. Okay, I have to run. Give my regards to Rose Marie and a steak for Baron from me. I'll give you a call sometime during the week."

"Thanks, Dave! I'll look forward to it. You take it easy." The call ended.

24

We decided we would watch *Harry O* alone on Thursday, October 24. Rose Marie even suggested we just order a pizza and have a relaxed and easy night. I was happy with that.

The story titled *Shadows at Noon* involved a sinister plot between a sister (played by Marla Adams) and her brother-in-law (played by Guy Stockwell) having her younger sister (played by Diana Ewing) committed to a mental sanitarium in order to take control of the younger sister's deceased father's business empire.

Harry O walks up to his front door with a bag of groceries, only to find the door locked. He finds that funny since he doesn't lock his door ... ever! Hell, he doesn't even have a key!

He knocks on the door and the young lady who escaped the sanitarium opens it. She does not know it is Harry's house. The back and forth dialogue between he and the girl is really funny. The writer slipped in some humor in Dave's lines and his deliverance showcases, albeit briefly, that Dave loves to joke.

I noted actor Michael Strong was also a guest star; I remembered watching him on the set in Los Angeles when I was Dave's guest while they were filming *In a Plain Paper Wrapper*. I felt Mr. Strong put in a good performance.

Rose Marie and I both enjoyed the show, especially the ending - which shocked both of us. It had a twist we could not have foreseen, totally different than either of us expected.

During the course of the evening, I told Rose Marie what Dave had said about the marriage rumors. She was shocked because, like a lot of fans of celebrities, she believed what she read, even in the tabloids.

Based on what Dave had told me, I detected a little anger in his voice - and his suspicion that it was Dani herself having the rumors planted did upset him. I decided I would not touch that subject with Dave again. If he wanted me to know anything, he would tell me. I would not believe anything I read about Dave and Dani; after all, most of it was all crap as Dave had told me many times.

I could not help but think problems may be coming to the surface in their relationship. I hoped I was wrong and that Dave would have a very happy life with Dani. Only time could tell.

Rose Marie and I really enjoyed *Shadows At Noon* and agreed, at least in our opinions, *Harry O* was improving as the episodes played out. To us, it was like watching Harry O's personality develop as we learned through his voice-over - listening to his thoughts - just what a nice guy he really was. I felt it somewhat uncanny just how much Harry Orwell was like the real David Janssen.

Dave did not call during the following week as he had said he would. I knew how busy he was and how tired he must be after a day of filming so I was not concerned.

On Halloween night, Thursday, October 31, we again invited our same group of good friends to a watch party. Tonight's fare would be pizzas, sodas and candy. Our friends started arriving between nine and 9:30. That gave us time for eating and socializing before the start of the program.

As it neared ten o'clock, I read the synopsis from TV Guide. "Tonight, the episode is titled *Ballinger's Choice*. The guest stars are Paul Burke as Philip Ballinger; Tim McIntire, Lisa Gerrit'sen, Tom Atkins, Mel Stewart and special guest star, Juliet Mills. A friend of Harry's - wealthy publisher, Philip Ballinger - mysteriously disappears. His wife calls Harry for help in finding him. What Harry finds is a murder which leads to his discovering a lurid affair his friend had been involved in, and then a second murder. Soon, Harry's friend becomes the target of the killer."

I had met Paul and his wife, Peggy Burke, through Dave when I lived in Los Angeles. I knew that he and his wife, Peggy, were two people Dave and Ellie considered to be close friends. Paul Burke had been the star of his own television series, *Naked*

City, on CBS Television from 1960 to 1963. Dave had guest-starred in two episodes of *Naked City* a couple of years apart.

Ballinger's Choice filled the television screen and held us all in suspense all the way through the commercials, through the scary boat chase and the subtle conclusion with Harry receiving a check and the gratitude of Ballinger over drinks at a bar.

I was very pleased to see the interaction between Dave and Paul. To me, it was evident that anyone seeing this episode would readily recognize that the friendship between Harry and Ballinger was real; it was not just part of the script.

Our party concluded just before the end of the Eleven O'Clock News. Baron and I drove Rose Marie to her parents' home then went to Riverside Park for a quick run.

Although I had expected and hoped to hear from Dave sometime during the week, again there was no call. I had already decided that Rose Marie and I would watch the coming episode of *Harry O* together, without guests.

As it turned out, Rose Marie had gone home from work early; she was not feeling well. After speaking with her and being assured it was just a slight stomach bug, I was relieved it was nothing serious and resolved to watch the show with just Baron.

November 7 was Thursday and, at ten o'clock in the evening, on ABC Television Network aired *Harry O* with that night's episode titled, *Second Sight*. The guest stars were Stefanie Powers, Mitzi Hoag and Martin Brooks.

A psychiatrist is missing and Harry's name appears in his appointment book. As Harry launches his investigation parallel to Lieutenant Manny Quinlan's, people start getting murdered. Each of the murders has, at least, one commonality: they were predicted ... by a psychic, Fay Connors.

As the ending credits rolled on the screen, Baron and I agreed it was an excellent episode, very well acted by every cast member. I decided I would not complain about some of the lighting in certain scenes when I spoke with Dave.

I took Baron to the park for his run and returned home and went to bed.

I was looking forward to a relaxing weekend. I spoke with Rose Marie and she was still not feeling back to normal; she was being nursed by her mother. She asked about last night's show and I gave her the quick synopsis.

Having no plans with Rose Marie for the weekend would only mean extra time spent with Baron in the park, time to do some shopping and spend a little time at Barnes & Noble.

I left my office just after four o'clock, as is customary for everyone in our office on Fridays. I went home, leashed Baron and we were in Riverside Park before five o'clock.

I was trying to decide what to do about dinner. I settled on just grabbing something light from the corner deli. I spent a leisurely night at home watching television and was in bed by 11:30. I would rely on Baron to be my alarm clock, at whatever time he wanted to go out.

Instead of Baron, the sound of the phone ringing awakened me just before five o'clock in the morning on Saturday, November 9.

"Good morning, Dave ... how are you?"

"Hey! Good morning, Mike! How did you know it's me?"

"Because it is Saturday ... it's five o'clock in the morning, which means it's two o'clock in the morning in San Diego ... which means you are the only one who is awake and would think to give me a call ... just to wake me up."

"Well ... that all makes sense. I see you are learning some of Harry's logic ... very good, Mike. How are you? How is Rose Marie and Baron? Have you guys been watching the show?"

"Yeah ... Dave ... uh last week we had our usual group of friends in; this week, Rose Marie had a stomach virus so Baron and I watched it alone. General consensus is both episodes were excellent. Even if I had a slight disagreement with your lighting genius, they were really good, Dave. Even Baron liked them. So tell me, how the hell are you? Where are you? How is Dani? Is everything going well with you?"

"I'm in San Diego ... stayed here this weekend. Dani has a party in LA tonight and I don't want to be there. We wrapped up another episode last night. Most of the crew have all gone home.

This will give me a chance to look around San Diego. You know, it is quite a nice little city. I think I like it."

"Well, that's nice to hear. I mean, you did serve and protect the city for what, 15 plus years. So when will you be going back to LA?"

"Probably in a couple of weeks, maybe three. We will be shooting a two-part episode starting next week; it may take a few extra days to get it finished so I'll be staying here until it's wrapped."

"Okay, well let me know how you like the city. I hear it's a pretty good town, mostly a military town, Navy and Marines. So is everything all right with you?"

"Yeah ... I just need some downtime ... no party-time, if you know what I mean."

"Yeah, I know what you mean. I haven't seen anything in the newspapers or tabloids lately. How is everything with you and Dani?"

"Delicate, for the moment ... and you know why. I'm just playing it one day at a time. I' m ignoring the topic completely. I figure, if she really loves me, she will be satisfied with having me the way I am ... happy with the way we are together ... if not, then it was not love in her heart to begin with."

"I have to agree with the way you are looking at it; you are absolutely right! Is she pissed you are not there for the party tonight?"

"Oh, yeah, but I am doing it for that reason. She has to know that she cannot and I will not allow her, or anyone, to control me."

"Okay, Dave, I'm on your side. How is the show doing ... ratings wise?"

"We seem to be gaining each week and that is very good news. I think the scripts are a little wavy for now but they get better. Oh, hey I have to run! I'll be in touch next week," Dave said and the phone went dead. I reflected and wondered why, or where, he had to run so suddenly and thought maybe the bar was closing.

I could tell that my suspicions of a few weeks ago had some

merit. I just hoped Dave was handling the situation with Dani in his own best interest, putting himself before others for a change. I still had not asked him the many questions about each episode I had watched and written down.

25

I enjoyed a very relaxing weekend at home with Baron. I called and spoke with Rose Marie several times and was relieved to know she was feeling much better and would go to work on Monday. We agreed to have dinner Monday evening.

I reflected on our early Saturday morning conversation and felt a pain in my gut thinking that, again, Dave was having problems with the woman he loved ... or, at least, it appeared to everyone that he did love Dani.

I was not in a position to form any opinion of Dani or her feelings for Dave. I hoped I would meet her in the near future and then feel comfortable in any assessment I could form regarding their relationship. I had serious doubts that her liking to host and attend parties was the only problem rising to the top of Dave's mind; I felt there had to be something else.

I had been right in my assessment of Ellie and the way she treated Dave. I had been right in feeling that Rosemary was determined to get Dave to marry her as soon as his divorce was final. However, Dave had known Dani when they were both student actors at Universal. He was only about four years older than she. They had been good, close friends for years; she and her husband, Buddy, had been good friends with Dave and Ellie and she supported Dave during the trials and tribulations he endured during his divorce proceedings. Dave had told me that, in his mind, he was not the easiest man to live with. He needed to have solitude and space.

He enjoyed time with his friends but only when he felt he

could be himself and relax. He had told me Dani was the type of woman who loved a crowded room. She enjoyed cooking and hosting parties as well as being a guest.

Dani had, for all intents and purposes, given up her career as an actress, even though she was very talented and held great promise of being at the top of the craft. Dave realized and appreciated her decision, knowing she had made her decision when married to Buddy Greco; it had nothing to do with Dave or his career. Dave was very impressed with her intelligence and astute abilities in judging people.

In recalling his words in this morning's conversation, I held hope I was wrong. Perhaps during the extra time he would spend in San Diego alone, he would examine his relationship and determine the pros and cons of his inner feelings.

Dave called me on Sunday evening, November 17, just before nine o'clock.

"Mike, it's me, Dave. How are you?"

"I'm good, Dave ... and you? How's Dani?"

"All is good. I'll be going home next weekend. How is Rose Marie; has she recovered from her illness? How's Baron? Did you see the show last week?"

"All is well. Rose Marie has bounced back and Baron is doing fine. Yes, I saw it and really enjoyed it. All I can say is, in my opinion, *Harry O* just keeps getting better. How was your week? How your weekend last week ... did you enjoy your downtime?"

"Yeah, I really enjoyed my downtime ... played the tourist role and enjoyed the city. Of course, just about everywhere I went, I was approached by fans ... both from *Fugitive* and *Harry O*, even a couple from that stinker, *O'Hara* ... but everyone was nice and I didn't mind the interactions. Actually, I kind of enjoyed it. The native San Diegans appreciate we are doing the show here. I really had some time to relax and it was wonderful. So how was your weekend?"

"I went to Greenwich Village - walked around, went to Barnes and Noble for a couple of hours, took Baron to his park and mostly just relaxed. Fortunately, no one on the street even recognized me ... didn't have anyone come up to me and ask for my autograph," I said, then laughed.

"Well that's just dandy ... lucky you! I love Barnes and Noble; hell, I love libraries! I just wanted to check in and see how you're doing. We have an early call in the morning so I'm going to make it an early night. Take it easy and we'll talk soon, okay?"

"Good, Dave ... I will, and you take it easy, too. Don't work too hard! Talk later."

I felt better just hearing how relaxed, sober and positive his voice sounded. I was convinced in my mind, though he did not go into the matter, that Dave had spent his downtime to think and determine how his relationship with Dani would proceed. In this conversation, he sounded refreshed and happy.

There had been a few photos of Dave and Dani enjoying an evening on the town in a few publications and always with captions declaring how happy they were and accolades for *Harry O*, making it clear Dave had another 'hit' television series. I concluded his publicist was doing a good job for him.

I received my next call from Dave on Tuesday, November 26, just before six as I was leaving my office for the day.

"Mike? It's me, Dave. I'm calling to wish you, Rose Marie and Baron a nice Thanksgiving. What are your plans?"

"Hi, Dave ... thanks! I'm flying my mother, my aunt and favorite niece in from Indianapolis. I'll be taking them and Rose Marie to dinner at the Plaza Hotel, then to see *Over Here*; it's a musical at the Schubert Theatre."

"That is really nice of you, Mike. Has your mother ever been to New York?"

"No, neither she nor my Aunt Madge, nor my niece, Sherry, has ever been on a plane, or even out of Indiana, other than Kentucky. It will be a lot of fun showing them around the city, all the history of it ... and, of course, a Broadway musical will really impress them. I think they will really enjoy it. They'll be going back on Sunday morning."

"I'm happy for you, Mike. That is really nice you can do that for your mother, aunt and niece. So, you are introducing Rose Marie to your mother. Is that a sign of some imminent milestone in your life?" Dave asked, then laughed.

"No ... no ... no! Once my divorce is final, I plan on remaining a 'happily divorced man' for quite some time. I'll be following the sage advice of a good friend who has been through the agony," I said with a laugh.

"Well, it will be nice for Rose Marie and your mother to meet. At least, it will be interesting. Dinner at the Plaza, huh? That is a very nice place; I am sure they will all enjoy it."

"Yes, I'm renting a limousine, really going all out. I want my mother and aunt and, of course, my niece, to see that I am moderately successful and that the city is not full of Mafia, gangsters and drug dealers running around. So, what are your plans? Are you home yet? What will you and Dani be doing?"

"That is good you can do that, Mike. I'm home. The network has decided to move *Harry O* to the LA studios; they decided it is too expensive filming on location so we'll be filming it all here. We will shoot one more episode in San Diego then pack up and move back here.

"As for Thanksgiving, Dani and I have been invited to dinner with some friends. I've been invited to dinner by my mother. Dani wants to do a big dinner at home with a few friends. I'm sure Dani will decide for me by Thanksgiving morning."

"WHOA ... wait a minute! You won't be filming in San Diego anymore? What about the scenery, the local sites, signage ... all that stuff? What about the San Diego Police Department, Lieutenant Quinlan? Are we to believe you just move to Los Angeles and become a private detective there?"

"All of that is being worked out ... there are a lot of changes being made that I'm not even privy to, at least not yet. The network thinks it will be a good move so I'll just play along and we'll see what happens. I'll let you know. Don't worry! I have to go but I'll be in touch. Enjoy your Thanksgiving with your family ... give them my best regards."

"Okay, Dave ... thanks a lot for the call and the heads-up about the move for *Harry O*. Please keep me informed. I hope you and Dani have a great Thanksgiving ... whatever you end up doing." The call ended.

26

I enjoyed a nice Thanksgiving with my mother, aunt, niece and Rose Marie. My family seemed very impressed with my success and in awe of New York City. They could not even comprehend how eight million people were crammed into the five boroughs.

They were amazed at the view of the city as they were coming in for a landing. They were dazzled by the Broadway play, *Over Here*, the storyline of life here during World War II. They were equally impressed with the opulence of the restaurant at the Plaza and the fabulous Thanksgiving Day dinner.

On Sunday, December 22, I received a call from Dave at 4:15 in the morning.

"Merry Christmas, Mike! It's me, Dave."

"Good morning," I managed in a gruff voice. "Is it Christmas already?"

"Not quite, but close enough. How are you? How did your plans work out with your family on Thanksgiving Day? How are Rose Marie and Baron?"

"Boy, you are just full of questions. I am fine, as is Rose Marie and Baron. The Thanksgiving weekend with my mother, aunt, niece and Rose Marie was outstanding. Everyone had a great time, a great dinner and they loved the play. Now, how in the hell are you? Did you and Dani enjoy a nice Thanksgiving? What did you do? What is the status of *Harry O*?"

"I am fine ... we went to some friends for Thanksgiving dinner. We wrapped everything up in San Diego; there are three episodes that will be airing soon. We have already finished two episodes here and will start on another after Christmas."

"That is good to hear; we have been watching every week and, yes, we agree it is the best show on television. How did you make the transition from San Diego to Los Angeles; what will we, the fans, see?"

"I take a case for a relative of a friend in San Diego; she lives in Los Angeles and has helped her boyfriend steal some negotiable bonds from her boss's office safe ... so I rent a small apartment on the beach in Santa Monica, meet a lovely airline stewardess, and then I get rudely awakened by 'Lieutenant Trench' of the LAPD, played by Anthony Zerbe. It's a well written script and we leave you hanging as to whether I make the move to LA permanent."

"What about Lieutenant Quinlan? Is he going to remain a regular in the series?"

"No, he'll be killed in the line of duty ... poor guy," Dave said, then laughed.

"All right, Dave! Damn it ... don't leave me in suspense! Is *Harry O* moving to LA or not?"

"You'll have to watch it to get your answer! I'll tell you this ... I get a new wardrobe," Dave said with a big laugh.

"You are rotten, Dave! I will write ABC and ask them what the hell they are doing to Harry! I bet they'll tell me. What do you mean you get new clothes? Are they from Sy DeVore?"

"No, they won't ... they'll send you a form letter asking you to watch the show. No, the clothes aren't from Sy's, but they fit," he said and laughed again.

"Okay ... well, can you at least tell me if Dave Janssen is happy to be back in Los Angeles or not?"

"Yeah, Mike, I am. I don't mind being away for a few weeks or even months working, but it is always good to come home."

"I bet The Formosa staff are all happy to see you back; I bet you go there every day now."

"No, I don't get to The Formosa as often as I would like; first of all, we are shooting *Harry O* at the Burbank Studios and that's quite a distance from The Formosa. Secondly, my drinking buddy deserted me and moved back east," he said with a laugh.

"Yeah, Dave, I wouldn't believe that at all; you would have no problem finding someone to drink with you. So how are things with Dani? I bet she is happy to have you home every night."

"Yeah, she seems happy, but she's dropping hints about the 'M' word again and I am just not anywhere near being ready to make that commitment again. She's taking it upon herself to make a lot of changes in MY life ... some seem to be good and make sense; some I don't think are the right changes for me. Right now, I'm just letting things ride; if there is something I don't like, I'll make the change myself."

"What do you mean, Dave? What kind of changes? Does she, at least, ask you or does she just do something behind your back and then tell you?"

"I think I told you ... last spring she decided I no longer needed my office, so we closed it. I don't really miss it; I had kept it mainly for a place to find some solitude away from Ellie's tirades.

"She decided I didn't need my publicist so she let him go. She decided I didn't need Victor so she let him go ... she decided I didn't need a business manager so she let Fred go. That is okay because she is handling my financial affairs; she pays the bills. Hell, the only one she dare not get rid of is Abby. He is the only real friend I have left.

"You know, I was paying out a hell of a lot of money for Frank, Victor, Fred, the office rent and really stuff I hardly used, so I went along with her ideas. The studio handles my publicity so that's good. Dani seems to do everything else so she is saving me a lot of money ... and she is a whiz when it comes to managing money. It is just that I feel I am losing control over my own life ... and I don't like that kind of feeling."

"Have you talked with her about the changes ... about how you feel? I'm sure she, at least, believes she is doing what is in your best interest. I'm sure she would undo any changes she made that you are not comfortable with."

"Yeah, I know ... you're right. I haven't discussed any of it with her. I just say 'fine' and let it go at that. Yeah, I think I'll find the right time and the right words to let her know what I think."

"That's a good plan. You have to have communication between each other or, eventually, your relationship will crumble - and you damn sure don't want that."

"I know ... we'll see. I'm sure things will work out ...they always do. Okay, listen, I have to go, but I wanted to wish you, Rose Marie, Baron and your family a Merry Christmas and all the best for 1975. I'll be in touch later, Mike. Take care."

"Thanks, Dave, and thanks for the call. Keep me informed about *Harry* and I wish you, Dani and your family Happy Holidays, too. You take care, too, and be careful." We ended the call.

In reflecting upon Dave's revelations about Dani making changes in his life, and again making hints about their getting married, I deduced he was feeling deep concerns over their relationship.

Dave had been separated for two years at the time his divorce from Ellie became final on August 27, 1970 – a little more than four years ago. Of those six years, he had spent about three years with Rosemary, between dating and living together, and had been in a monogamous relationship with Dani for over two years.

I had thought in my own mind - the fact he and Dani had been friends for, at least, 15 years and that she was only about four years younger than he - they were a perfect match for each other. This call from Dave gave me reason to think he was not completely happy with the way this relationship was going.

I knew Dave was the type of man who was happy to be with just one woman and he would go out of his way to give her anything and everything she wanted. His only desire was the relationship had to be stress-free and they both be happy.

I did not know if she was exerting unwanted control over his business matters - his career as well as maybe choosing his friends. If she was, she was driving their relationship on a road to certain disaster.

27
~1975~

The world welcomed 1975 with celebrations to top all celebrations. New York's Times Square always attracted a mass of people - at least one million by NYPD's estimates.

Dave and Dani had plans to attend several parties and end up just before the stroke of midnight at their condo with a group of their most intimate friends.

My plans were to deliver Rose Marie to her home, take Baron for a New Year's run in the park and be in my bed long before the clock struck midnight in Hollywood; I succeeded.

I was surprised when Dave called me on Friday morning, January 10, just after five o'clock.

"Up and at 'em, Mike. It's me, Dave. I didn't wake you, did I?" he asked with slightly slurred speech.

"Good morning, Dave! No, you didn't wake me ... would it matter if you had?"

"Well ... uh, yeah it would ... because then I'd have to apologize and then I'd have to hang up and wait a few minutes and then call you back when I knew you were awake," he said, then laughed.

"Oh, I see ... well, I've been awake for over an hour ... sounds to me like you are just about ready to go to bed. How are things with you?"

"Just moving along. How was your New Year's Eve? What did you do ... spend it with Rose Marie?"

"Yes, we had dinner at the Rainbow Room, then champagne, and watched the fireworks and all from there.

"I learned from the last couple of years that celebrating in Times Square is a real hassle ... too crowded and way too noisy. It's fun a couple of times but it was much better seeing everything from the Rainbow Room; we had a real 'bird's eye view' and Rose Marie loved it. We had a good dinner and danced until about one in the morning. What did you and Dani end up doing?"

"I'm glad to know you had a good time. We went out to several parties at some of our friends' homes, and then we were home around 11:30 and had some good friends in for a little party of our own. It was a grand evening, a lot of fun. We were in bed by three."

"That's nice. I'm happy to hear it. Are you on a break or back to shooting *Harry O*?"

"We're back to work. I was just calling to tell you to buy this week's *TV Guide*; Harry is on the cover. Make sure you tune in to *The Tonight Show*; I'll be on with Johnny on Wednesday."

"Thanks, Dave! I have a subscription to *TV Guide* so it should be in my mail today or tomorrow. I usually just watch Johnny's monologue but, since you will be there, I'll watch it. How are things with Dani?"

"Things are rocky right now ... but I am just going with the flow. I have to concentrate on the show so I don't let anything at home bother me. I don't have time to get into details but I'll let you know when I have more time to talk. I'm heading home to bed ... I'll touch base with you later. Have a good weekend," he said and hung up the phone.

Dave sounded as though he had been drinking but still in control of his faculties. He sounded upbeat and happy until I mentioned Dani. I hoped he was not having problems again. My instinct told me, based on the time of his call, that he was not home with Dani and his slightly slurred speech told me he was near his limit of alcohol. That did worry me.

The January 11 issue of *TV Guide* was in my mailbox when I arrived home Friday afternoon. Dave appeared on the cover, wearing his *Harry O* khaki slacks, blue button-down dress shirt and carrying his sports coat walking towards the camera on the beach. It was a good photo.

The cover story Al Stump wrote about Dave was pretty good from a public relations point. The story seemed to concentrate on Dave being some kind of a 'klutz'. Yes, I knew there had been incidents where he would consider himself a klutz, but we both knew it was far from the truth. Dave was not a klutz in any sense of the word.

The story also made prominent mention of his 'Silver Bullet' mobile home. It insinuated Dave had purchased the mobile dressing room - however he had not; it was a gift from Quinn Martin and Q-M Productions in 1965 during the filming of *The Fugitive* series.

The story also stated Dave had quit drinking long ago. Dave, I and anyone who knew him had to have a laugh over that statement. Nothing could be further from the truth.

It is true Dave preferred to do as many of his own stunts as the producer and insurance carriers would permit. In doing so, he would always do careful rehearsals and do them in slow motion.

The article related his debilitating knee injury while pole-vaulting in high school; it made no mention that he had endured four surgeries during hiatus periods of *The Fugitive*. The surgeries resulted in considerable relief from the constant pain yet the relief didn't last or provide a permanent rehabilitation of his knee. He sometimes struggled to play tennis, a game he thoroughly enjoyed.

I was pleased with the article and assured the studio publicity people were doing a good job for Dave and *Harry O*. Although I knew Dave had enjoyed a good relationship and considered his former publicist, Frank Lieberman, a good friend perhaps Dani's dismissing him was not so bad. Dani was, no doubt, saving Dave a lot of money.

Rose Marie and I had not missed an episode of *Harry O* except one she missed when she was ill. We would often host four of our close friends. I held high hopes the series would be renewed by ABC but Dave said he had no clue if it would be.

He enjoyed the character, especially the voice-overs where the viewer was hearing Harry's thoughts as he described the scenes, not to mention the humor he was allowed to inject. He considered Howard Rodman as one of the best writers in television. He loved working with Richard Lang, a good friend who directed the original pilot of *Harry O* which did not receive the ratings ABC expected. Dave said it was no fault of the director. Mr. Long would go on to produce a total of 18 episodes of *Harry O*.

I made certain to watch *The Tonight Show* with Johnny Carson the following Wednesday, January 15. I knew Dave and Johnny Carson were good friends and Dave enjoyed appearing on the show to promote whatever project he was doing at the time. With Johnny, Dave was always relaxed and could really show his fans his true self, and his sense of humor.

The remainder of January passed into February without another call from Dave. At 5:45 on Saturday morning, February 15, I was awakened by my phone.

"Mike, it's me, Dave ... I know it's Saturday morning ... but Baron still needs to go to his park. Did I wake you?"

"Yes ... yeah, you did Dave but, if you hadn't, Baron would have. He's right here telling me to get out of bed. How are you?"

I could tell Dave was almost what I would call 'falling down drunk'.

"I'm okay ... a little tired ... but still okay. How is everything on your end?"

"Good, Dave. It's good to hear from you ... been a while. What's going on out there? Any word yet about *Harry O* being renewed? How is Dani?"

"Yeah, I'm sorry to be out of touch. I've really been kept busy. We wrapped up the last episode a few days ago ... no word on if it's going to be picked up for another season. I have at least three or four months off and Abby has a couple of pictures offered me ... I may take one. It will be filmed in Switzerland ... I haven't decided yet. Dani and I aren't speaking at the moment ... which is good - gives me time to rejuvenate myself," he said and let out a little laugh I took as being insincere.

"What's going on with you guys, Dave? Don't tell me she is becoming like Ellie."

"No ... not that bad ... at least, not yet, but she is heading that way. She's trying to limit everything I like doing. She's even trying to tell me how to dress ... picking out clothes for me that I don't even like ... a lot of bullshit. I need some time away."

"Well, Dave, you can count your blessings. At least, you're not married; you can just walk away."

"Yeah ... that is under serious consideration ... but, then again, I think I love her ..."

"The only thing I can say about that is for you to consider everything ... the pros and cons ... think of how your life was when you went through your divorce. Just take it easy and do what is best for YOU!"

"I know, Mike ... I will."

"Dave, this series is a damn good television show and you need a clear mind to be able to do your best. Don't get into another situation where it takes away from your ability to do your best and make all your fans happy."

"You know, Mike, funny you should say that. I know in the last season of *The Fugitive*, with all the bullshit at home, I was making a lot of stupid mistakes and they slipped passed the directors. I'm not going to let that happen here. When I get out of make-up and wardrobe, I AM *Harry Orwell* ... David Janssen doesn't exist."

"Well, if it makes you feel any better, both of us - Rose Marie and I - watch the show carefully ... and you have both of us convinced you ARE Harry Orwell!"

"Thanks, Mike ... that does makes me feel better. I have to go. I'll call you soon. Take it easy; give my best to Rose Marie and Baron."

"Okay, Dave ... you take it easy. Stay sober," I said and hung up the phone.

"No, you would not want to
walk in my shoes."

- David Janssen, to Michael Phelps

28

I spent over an hour reflecting upon Dave's conversation, the tones of his voice - the fact that he sounded pretty close to being inebriated. I really felt bad and my thoughts were racing.

Here was a super-mega-star of television and film in the prime of his career. He was successful, happy with his work and had millions of adoring fans around the world. He didn't have the worries which afflicted the ordinary man – lack of disposable income, for example. Considering he had attained a status far beyond what most men would even dream of reaching, in my mind, he should be HAPPY.

However, that was not the case. Though he was thankful for his blessings, David Janssen was a tortured soul. He was a very unhappy man in the deep recesses of his soul. He was unhappy with the state of his personal life. He wanted so badly to be loved, wanted and needed for the man he was yet, it appeared, the only time he felt true happiness was in his work - when playing a character, a role which came from the mind of a writer.

Monday, February 24, 1975, Dave called me in my office just after ten o'clock in the morning.

"Good morning, Mike! It's me, Dave. Sorry to bother you at work. I'm flying to Philadelphia to be on the *Mike Douglas Show*; it's a short drive from Manhattan - wanted to see if you could run down and we could have dinner before I head back to LA."

"Wow! I would love to but I don't know if I can get away. When are you coming? What time?"

"I'll be there on the 27th and I'll be taking the last non-stop flight in the evening. If you can't make it, no problem. I understand."

"I have a meeting scheduled with our CEO, but let me see what I can do. It's only about an hour and a half drive; I think I'll be able to do it. Is Dani coming with you?"

"Hell, no! She's staying here. It will be a fast trip but it's for *Harry* so I have to do it. Douglas is a good friend so it will be fun. If you could drive down in the morning, you could watch the show."

"I'll see what I can do ... can you call me back?"

"Yes ... how much time do you need?"

"Give me about an hour. Is that okay?"

"Perfect! Talk to you then," he said and ended the call.

I called my boss, Arnold Ginsberg, and explained my situation. He had no problem with my taking Thursday off. I was thankful and looking forward to seeing Dave again even if it meant driving 100 miles to the City of Brotherly Love.

Dave called me back at 11:35. "Mike, it's me. What's the good word?"

"The good word is I will be there. What time does the show start ... where do I go?"

"The NBC station, KYW-3; it's at Fifth and Market Streets. Can you be there by 11:30? I'll leave your name at the door. The show actually starts at 12:30 but it takes time to get the audience in their seats. I'll see you right after the show ends. I'll have you brought back and introduce you to Mike. Then we can go have a drink and something to eat."

"That sounds great ... looking forward to it! What time will your flight back leave?"

"I haven't gotten the reservations yet; they'll let me know. I'll see you Thursday. Take it easy." Without a further word, Dave hung up.

I was always eager to see Dave when he came to the east coast so driving an hour and a half to Philadelphia was no inconvenience for me. I let the people in my office know I would not be in on Thursday.

I arrived in Philadelphia just after eleven o'clock. I found a parking garage and walked across the street to the NBC building. I entered the KYW-3 lobby and was directed to Studio A, where there was another lobby and reception area.

I gave the receptionist my name and she summoned an usher to take me into the studio. I was surprised at how small the seating area was as opposed to the massiveness of the stage.

The seats were empty and I was taken to a seat front row center. I asked if I could sit in an aisle seat so I could still see where Mr. Douglas and his guests would be sitting; my request was granted.

At 12:05, the doors opened and ticket holders entered, filling every seat. There were three purple fabric covered chairs on center stage.

Promptly at 12:30, Ms. Cybill Shepherd entered the stage.

"Hello, I'm Cybill Shepherd. Welcome to the *Mike Douglas Show*; I'll be co-hosting all this week with MIKE. With us on the show today will be the star of *Harry O*, David Janssen; World Heavyweight Champion, Muhammad Ali; Heavyweight Contender, Chuck Wepner; the jazz group, *Two Generations of Brubeck*, and the star of *The Walton's*, Richard Thomas with his lovely wife, Alma."

Light boxes on either side of the stage started blinking *Applause* and we, the audience, complied. Mr. Douglas walked onto the stage and welcomed the audience.

There were more blinking *Applause* lights, with thunderous applause from the audience.

A loud round of applause. The camera remained on Mr. Douglas and Miss Shepherd as they made small talk out of hearing range of the audience. The show cut to commercial messages.

"My fans are the reason I have what I have."

- David Janssen

29

The actress, Cybill Shepherd, was spending the week as Mr. Douglas' co-host and promoting her new film, *At Long Last Love*. She is a beautiful blonde with an effervescent personality. I was captivated watching and listening to her speak. The first segment was about the filming of *At Long Last Love*, starring Ms. Shepherd and Burt Reynolds, which was written, produced and directed by Ms. Shepherd's fiancé, Peter Bogdanovich.

Two and a half minutes later, the small band played the intro and Mr. Douglas announced: "This gentleman is starring in his fourth television series, has made over 40 films and made numerous theatrical appearances and has established himself as one of Hollywood's most popular leading men. He is currently starring in *Harry O*. Please welcome ... David Janssen!"

The blinking *Applause* lights came on. The band played. The audience broke into applause and I think I was the most exuberant in clapping my hands.

David Janssen entered from stage left, waving to the audience, walking briskly over to where Mr. Douglas and Miss Shepherd were standing. He shook hands with Douglas and leaned over and kissed Miss Shepherd on her cheek.

The applause died down just a bit as Dave took his seat between them. Dave was dressed in a black suit, white shirt, black silk tie and black shoes. He looked refreshed considering he had spent just under five hours on a plane.

Mr. Douglas welcomed him. Dave jokingly asked where he was. Mr. Douglas replied, "Philadelphia." Dave asked if that was in Pennsylvania, to which Douglas assured him it was. Mr. Douglas then commented that Dave had been doing a lot of traveling, to which Dave responded he had.

Dave asked Mr. Douglas about his health, as he had experienced a recent health scare and Douglas responded it was fine. Dave noted Douglas had lost some weight and they joked about Dave's weight and then Douglas asked him about his having been kidnapped in Istanbul, Turkey. Dave responded and related it was a true story and went into detail how he was 'kidnapped' and held on a magnificent yacht for two days, not realizing he was actually kidnapped.

It turned out the kidnappers were Turkish journalists wanting to ensure they had an exclusive interview with David Janssen, who was loved by the Turkish people.

A clip of an *Harry O* episode was shown, lasting about two minutes, with Henry Darrow who played San Diego Police Lieutenant, Manny Quinlan, Dave, Anthony Zerbe and special guest star, Sal Mineo, playing a bad guy.

It was from the episode, *Elegy for a Cop*, wherein Quinlan's character is shot and killed in Los Angeles. *Harry O* takes it upon himself to find his killer and relocates to Los Angeles from San Diego. The episode introduces Anthony Zerbe as 'LAPD Lieutenant Trench, who will be Dave's co-star for the remainder of the series.

Dave's segment lasted just about 10 minutes. Mr. Douglas announced his next guest would be the World Heavyweight Boxing Champion, Muhammad Ali then went to commercial. Dave spoke with Mr. Douglas and Miss Shepherd for another two minutes. The show resumed with Muhammad Ali.

I was impressed with Mr. Ali. He was so soft spoken and humble.

The show continued with Chuck Wepner, scheduled to fight Muhammad Ali in March. Apparently, Muhammad Ali and Wepner really do not like each other and there was quite a bit of verbal sparring. Muhammad left the stage. There was another commercial.

When the show returned, the band called *Two Generations of Brubeck* were introduced and played a song for the audience. Next, 'John Boy' (Richard Thomas) and his wife, Alma, were introduced. They had a conversation about being famous and trying to live a normal life.

The show ended just before 1:30. As the audience was filing out, the usher approached and escorted me back stage where Dave greeted me and introduced me to Mr. Douglas and Miss Shepherd as his 'good friend'.

I told Ms. Shepherd I was looking forward to seeing her film, *At Long Last Love*. I shook hands with Mr. Douglas and told him I was honored to meet him and my mother was a devoted fan. Prior to leaving, I asked Mr. Douglas for an autographed photo for my mother; he graciously provided one, writing my mother's name on it.

I really wanted to meet Muhammad Ali but he was nowhere to be seen.

Dave excused himself to have his make-up removed and told me he would be back in a few minutes and we could escape. He returned with a small carry-on bag, shook hands with some people around the hallway, looked at me and motioned for the exit. We walked out of the building and went to the Omni Independence Hotel for lunch.

We were ushered to a nice table and provided menus. The waiter took our drink order. The restaurant was quite crowded and, of course, Dave attracted a lot of stares, especially from the female patrons.

"You didn't tell me you were kidnapped in Turkey! Now, what's the rest of the story; did it really happen?"

"Yeah, it really happened. I did not know what was going on; it certainly wasn't what I expected. I wasn't worried, though. I mean, let's face it: how many kidnappers would take their hostage to a luxurious yacht, serve champagne and caviar and have a nice 'Q' and 'A' conversation?"

"So it had nothing to do with really kidnapping you for ransom? You weren't in any real danger, right?"

"No, I wasn't in any danger ... although, after I was delivered off the yacht, the government agents were a little scary - but no, no real danger. It's a good thing I wasn't; I don't know if Dani would have paid a ransom," he said, then laughed.

"I never saw anything about that in the newspapers or magazines. Why didn't you tell me about it when it happened?"

"I guess I just let it go, didn't think it was that important. I don't know - maybe the Studio or the State Department kept it out of the media. It wasn't a big deal, after it was over and I was out of Turkey. I'll tell you, though, Mike ... the Turkish people are really nice people, very genuine and good. I was surprised to see I have so many fans there ... or I should say *Dr. Kimble* has a lot of fans there," he said with a smile.

Dave ordered another round of drinks and we placed our food order. We both lit another cigarette.

"Was that blow-up between Wepner and Muhammad Ali serious ... was it for real?"

"I don't think so! I'm sure it was staged ... looked good though, huh?"

"Yeah, it sure looked real to me, and the audience. I hope Ali kicks his white ass! You look pretty fresh for having come in on the red eye flight," I said. "Your quick wit came through really well; your fans don't get much chance to see your comedic side ... although you show some in *Harry O.*"

"I slept like a baby once the plane took off from LA. I had a lot of coffee this morning and a Bloody Mary just before the show went on the air. Mike is a good friend and when he asks, or they book me on his show, my ratings get a big boost. I enjoy being on his show. You know, this is a talk show - a chance to promote the series and there really isn't a script so I can relax and be myself. I try to be funny sometimes ... do you think I'm funny?"

"Dave, there are times I think you're funny ... even without you trying," I said, then laughed. "What time is your flight back to Los Angeles?" I asked.

"I was lucky; I have a reservation on a flight that leaves Philly at six o'clock and arrives at LAX at 7:30, LA time."

"Will Dani meet you at the airport?" I looked at my watch; it was 3:15.

"No, my driver, Elliott, will pick me up. Dani can't handle the traffic around the airport," he said and laughed.

Our food was served. Dave put his cigarette out and ordered another round of scotch.

"How are things with you and Dani going?"

"Well, she had planted the rumor all around town that we were getting married on Valentine's Day ... DIDN'T HAPPEN!" he exclaimed and laughed again.

"Yeah, I saw that in the New York papers ... kept looking in the mail for my invitation. Saint Valentine's Day came and passed so I figured either you did not get married or you were pissed off at me and didn't send me an invitation."

"Mike, I would never get pissed off at you, no matter what. As for getting married ... I told her I am just not ready and that's that!" he said with a serious expression on his face.

We finished our lunch and Dave ordered coffee for both of us.

"So is Dani calmed down about getting married or is she still pushing you?"

"She keeps silent for a few weeks, then she drops little, subtle hints. I stay silent and she knows I'm not willing to even discuss it."

"Well ... do you think you will ever be ready again? Do you think Dani is the right woman for you ... the ONE you could see yourself spending the rest of your life with?"

"Hell, I don't really know! I'm sure I will get married again. I just can't say when ... or even to whom. Dani has a lot of baggage, but then, so do I; it is just not the time for me to say I want to get married."

"What if time passes and Dani gives you an ultimatum ... either marry her or she'll leave you?"

"Then she will leave! I'll be damned if I'm going to allow myself to be forced into marriage by anyone. Enough of that ... did you enjoy the show?"

"Yeah, Dave, I did. Your 'kidnapped' story was really interesting. My mom will love Mike Douglas' autographed photo; that was really nice of him."

"How is everything else going for you?"

"Good ... work is great and Rose Marie and I are doing well. Life is good."

"Well, I had better be getting to the airport. Thanks for coming down; it was good seeing you. I'll stay in touch."

Dave ordered the check and paid the check with a credit card and left a cash tip. We walked out of the hotel and back to the NBC building where a car was waiting for Dave.

"I'll be happy to take you to the airport."

"No, Mike, not necessary. It would be out of your way and the traffic here is insane. Not a problem; they have a car for me. I'll give you a call in a few days. Take it easy driving back."

"Okay, Dave. Thanks for inviting me; I really enjoyed it and thanks for lunch and the drinks."

"Are you okay to drive ... not too drunk are you?" he asked with a laugh.

"Damn, Dave! I only had three drinks." I laughed.

We shook hands and Dave climbed in the Cadillac sedan and was off. I retrieved my car from the garage and headed for the bridge to the New Jersey Turnpike.

30

Dave called me at 3:45 in the morning on Friday, March 14.

"Good morning, Mike. It's me, Dave. Time to get up and smell the coffee ... I know Baron wants to go out. How the hell are you?"

"Good morning to you, too ... yes, I'm getting up. How the heck are you doing?"

"Great ... just great. Did you see the show, *Street Games,* last night?"

"Yes, of course. Rose Marie and I had some friends over - pizza and sodas. Everyone liked it; excellent plot, solid acting all around. I even thought the lighting was right on. I was surprised and glad to see you have a dog ... a Great Dane, no less ... but, tell me, Dave, after meeting Baron, don't you have enough clout to get a German Shepherd actor?"

"I'm glad you all liked it. Grover - that's his name; he's not my dog. My dog wouldn't eat my sandwich! He'll have a recurring role if we get another season. The studio placed some pretty big ads in the trade papers touting it. They're trying to buy me an Emmy ... do you think I'll get an Emmy?"

"He's not your dog? Well, at least, he seems to like you ... at least, he liked your sandwich. Hell, YES! You should get an Emmy; you should have gotten 20 by now!"

"Yeah, I agree with you, Mike. Spread the word around. Maybe I'll get lucky this time." Dave laughed.

"I think you've got a hell of a good chance. *Harry's* ratings keep climbing ... you always give a great performance, you've had very good storylines and great supporting actors ... you're going to win this time."

"It would be nice, but I have some pretty stiff competition. We'll just have to wait and see. The ratings are not as good as we want them to be but, you're right. They keep going up so that is a blessing."

"Have you heard anything about next season yet? I know you will have another season ... all the write-ups here in the New York papers are great, especially about your portrayal of *Harry O.*"

"No, we haven't heard anything yet, but there is still time. None of the networks have announced their new fall line ups yet; we'll get the word just before they make it public. I'll let you know as soon as I do. How is everything going with Rose Marie? Is your divorce progressing? How's Baron?"

"All is well here. Rose Marie and I are doing well. Baron is great and still a big, spoiled puppy ... at least, he thinks he's still a puppy. I haven't heard anything about my divorce yet but it will happen when it happens. I know she wants it and, to be honest, I'm glad now. Rose Marie has helped me get over her so it wasn't true love on either part, I guess. How is everything with you and Dani? Has she calmed down any about getting married?"

"Good to hear all is well with you. Give Rose Marie and Baron my best regards. No, Dani is still dropping her little remarks about how much better it would be for us to be married and all I can think about is that is the way it happened with Ellie. I was with Ellie for 10 months before we got married and, the last six months, that's all I ever heard from her ... badgering me about getting married so she would not appear to be a slut!"

"Well, yeah, but you've known Dani for years; there's a big difference there and, hell ... Ellie had been married and divorced at least twice and she was having an affair with Sinatra when she met you. I'm surprised she was faithful to you all those years."

"Look, Ellie was with me when Abby took over and got me *The Fugitive.* It made me ... the fame, the money rolling in. Ellie knew what she had. She couldn't spend the money fast enough. Yeah, Mike, I know she loved me but, when jealousy seeps in and she starts treating me as one of her 'possessions', that kills the love. I don't want to go through that ... ever again." Dave's voice was very firm and I could feel his stress.

"Then why don't you just break it off, move out - live the bachelor lifestyle like you had when you played *Richard Diamond?* You seemed to have it all back then - money, fame, any woman you wanted."

"No, Mike ... I wasn't making that much money with *Diamond* until Abby took over and, by then, I was with Ellie.

"I'm not really the playboy they made me out to be; that was all publicity crap. I want a home ... I want a wife - well, a woman - the ONE woman who can make me happy, the one I can make happy ... one I can come home to and relax ... be with, alone. Someday, I would love to have a couple of kids, even if we would have to adopt."

"So, what you're telling me is you want the nice little ranch style house in the suburb with the white picket fence, two cars in the garage, a loving housewife who stays home and a couple of kids ... just like the all-American family, huh ... is that what you're telling me Dave?"

"Well, yeah ... except I want to live close to the studio ... not suburbia ... and, with my public persona, I need a big six foot high fence around for privacy ... but, yeah! That would be a dream - a wife that stays home, has dinner on the table when I come home from work. A couple of kids, a son and a daughter ... that would be perfect."

"Well, what's Dani position on all this? Have you talked with her about it? What about kids ... is she okay with having kids? A dog, too; house and kids, you have to have a dog."

"Dani likes kids as long as they are not hers and she doesn't have to deal with them. We have the condo and everything is done for us there: no lawn to mow, no pool to clean. Dani is a great cook and she cooks at home quite often but, she is in the party circuit. She loves parties ... she loves crowds. Me? I'd rather be home listening to music while I read a book, or even watch television.

"I don't mind having a few friends in for dinner, poker -

even a party once in a while - but not five nights out of seven. Mike IF, and that's a mighty big IF, I ever have the house, the fence, the kids ... yes, I would have to have a dog ... just like Baron," Dave said and his voice dropped, as if he was feeling a little depressed.

I could tell he was not as happy as he appeared in the media photos taken when he was out on the town with Dani. I really felt bad for him and changed the subject.

"What are you going to be doing when you go on hiatus?"

"I'm gonna be working. What the hell do you think I'd be doing? I need money; I'm paying alimony to the bitch, I'm supporting another woman ... I have to work," he said and let out a good laugh.

"Do you have anything lined up? Are there any movies we can look forward to ... any TV movies of the week?"

"Abby has sent me a pile of scripts. I'll be going through them in the next couple of weeks ... nothing has been set as yet. I'll be sure to let you know. Okay, Mike, I'll let you go now. Have your coffee and take Baron for his run. You have a good weekend and we'll talk sometime next week."

"All right, Dave! Thanks for calling and you take it easy, too. Have a good weekend." The call ended.

It was about 1:15 in the morning in Los Angeles and, from the background noise, I think Dave was in a bar. However, he sounded as if he was completely sober and in a fairly positive frame of mind. I was happy for that.

31

The next call from Dave came on Friday morning, April 18, 1975.

"Mike, it's me, Dave ... up and at 'em. Baron wants to run. How the hell are you?"

"Good, Dave. I'm good. Yes, I am already up ... having my first coffee before taking Baron out. He knows the rules. How is everything on your end?"

"We received the word yesterday. *Harry* will go another season so we are all kind of excited about that. We'll be taking hiatus so I've accepted a film which will shoot mostly in Switzerland. I have the lead role so I'm excited. It's a well written plot, has a strong supporting cast - good crew ... a lot of people I've worked with before."

"That is really great to hear! CONGRATULATIONS! What is the name of the movie?"

"The working title is *The Swiss Conspiracy.* It's about some wealthy Americans who have hidden lots of their money in Swiss banks to evade the IRS. They're on a blackmailer's hit list and, when they come to move their accounts, they start getting killed.

"I'm an investigator hired by the bank to protect the survivors and find the conspirators of the crimes."

"It sounds like it has Oscar written into it. Who else will be starring with you?"

"Elke Sommer, Ray Milland, Senta Berger, John Saxon and John Ireland are the main players. Jack Arnold is the director; he's pretty good, a rising star as a feature film director. I don't know if it will rise to the Oscar level; I'll think about that after I see the finished product," he said and laughed.

"They are all pretty good, although I've never heard of Senta Berger; the others are well known. When will you go over to Switzerland? Do you know how long you will be there? Is Dani going with you?"

"Berger is a German actress but she's done a few films here as well. We'll be going over at the end of this month, be there about six weeks ... hasn't been decided if Dani will go. Actually, I think we need some time apart and this is a perfect reason to allow that. I'm pretty sure she'll insist on going, though."

"Is everything okay between you and Dani?"

"Somewhat volatile ... one day everything is peachy-keen; the next it is like we're on the brink of a full scale war. I don't know, Mike; it's like, am I better off with her or without her? Know what I mean?"

"Yes, I definitely know what you mean but, Dave, you can't live in a relationship that is a constant battle. With the stress your work puts you under, you are certainly entitled to come home to peace and love."

"Yeah ... you would think so, huh! When I get home from work, I am physically drained. I still have to read the script for the next day's shoot. She has plans to go to this party or that party; it's every damn night! I don't mind once or twice a week ... on a weekend ... but not every damn night of the week!"

"Damn ... sound's like a re-run of what you went through with Ellie."

"Tell me ... I know. I just have to deal with it. I love her ... in a way ... and she is a great cook. She just has to learn I'm not the party guy I used to be."

"Yeah ... 20 years of partying, one has to slow down a little - or think about slowing down, at least."

"Yeah ... I have to admit it has caught up with me," Dave said, then laughed.

"One thing in your favor: you're not married. You can just walk away. Like you said, though, you have to decide if you are better off with her or without her. If you're not 100 percent happy, don't marry her. That's my advice."

"I know, Mike. Thanks for the good advice but I repeat ... I am nowhere near getting married. I'm still licking my wounds." He laughed again.

"Speaking of your wounds ... do you see Ellie at all, maybe in one of the restaurants, or do you see her daughters at all?"

"No, I was told Ellie has moved to London. I still see Diane, occasionally; she is doing well. Kathy is working; I haven't seen her in a while.

"I hope Ellie meets a nice, wealthy Brit, finds happiness, gets married and my alimony stops." Dave laughed again, but it was a halfhearted laugh.

"Well, Dave, I hope Ellie does just that. I thank God I am not in your position; if my wife wanted alimony, I'd have to take on two more jobs," I said with a laugh.

"Yeah, it is a hell of a drain. Okay, Mike, I have to go so keep watching *Harry* and I'll be in touch. I may not have a chance to call you while I'm overseas but I'll be in touch as soon as I can. You take it easy; give Rose Marie and Baron my regards."

"Okay, Dave ... have a good trip and work hard. Let me know when you're back and what you think of the new movie."

"I will, Mike ... talk to you later." We ended the call.

Dave sounded sober, upbeat and happy, with exception of his status with Dani. Not having met Dani, as yet, I had to rely on what Dave would say to me and, of course, my allegiance was to Dave even if any disagreements between them were 100 percent Dave's fault. I held hope that he would not rush into a marriage that would end up hurting him, emotionally and financially.

Dave had said it was not yet decided if Dani would accompany him to Switzerland. Not decided by whom? It was not clarified. Personally, I hoped she would not go with him. It would give Dave time alone to concentrate on his work and to be able to relax and enjoy himself.

I would continue to watch *Harry O* and continue watching anything else Dave appeared in on television. I would peruse the New York newspapers and the major Hollywood fan magazines for any news of Dave, both professionally and personally; Rose

Marie would do the same.

I knew not to expect any communication with Dave for at least the next six weeks so it would be good to, at least, read of any news about him.

32

Sunday morning, June 29, 1975, Dave called just before six o'clock.

"Good morning, Mike. It's me, Dave ... I hope I didn't wake you. How are you?"

"Good morning, Dave! No, I'm already awake; it's been a long time since I heard from you! I was just getting ready to take Baron out ... sure glad I didn't miss your call! I take it you're back from Switzerland? How did the filming go? Have you finished it? Are you happy with it?" I replied with a barrage of questions.

"Yes, I've been back a couple of weeks. I haven't seen the finished film yet; they are still working on it. As it is, I'm pleased with it; I think it will do well at the box office. We finished shooting the first *Harry O* episode yesterday, so I'm back to the grind ... but I am really looking forward to it. I don't have any time to relax, but that's okay. It will keep me and my mind busy."

"When will the new season start being aired? I have to get everyone psyched-up ... plan my watch parties."

"I don't have an exact date, but you'll see the ads in *TV Guide* and the newspapers. When I know the exact day and time, I'll give you a call. It has been a while since we spoke so how is everything with you? Are you still with Rose Marie? How's your work? How is Baron doing?"

"Everything is going well. Of course, I'm still with Rose Marie! All is well at work and Baron is a full-grown monster. I'm thinking of getting a female to keep him company. How are things with you and Dani? Did she go to Switzerland with you?"

"Dani is doing well. Actually, she is like a princess; she's treating me like a king! Yeah, she went with me; we had a good time in between work. We'll see how things progress now that I'm back to work on *Harry*. I'll tell you, though, I am really glad to be home. We had some good times over there but it really is good to be home ... see friends again and relax just a little."

"Is Dani keeping you in the party circuit?"

"No! We have an understanding now ... when I'm working, I'll only go to one party and it has to be on the weekend. She can go to as many parties as she wants - every night of the week if she wants to - but not me."

"You seem to have your home life under control; that is good to hear. Is Dani okay with that ... does she mind going out to parties and leaving you at home?"

"Hell, no! She doesn't mind at all. Actually, I think she likes it. She can have all her girlfriends believing that I'm a spoiled-sport ... no, I don't really think that. She tells everyone I'm working and couldn't attend with her."

"Well that's decent of her. So tell me, Dave ... are you happy with the way things are with Dani? Do you love her enough that you would marry her?"

"Well, Mike, to be honest ... yes, I do love her. She has everything I want in a woman and, to be honest, I'm not the easiest man to live with. I would have to admit, truthfully, I'm probably very hard to live with. I'm very moody, especially if I'm not working and, when I'm working, that comes first - above all. Then there's my drinking. I enjoy drinking; it calms my nerves, even bolsters my self-confidence. What do you think? When you're having a few drinks, what do you feel?"

"Well, I've never really given it a thought but, now that you mention it, I have to agree with you. It does calm my nerves and I do feel a little more self-confident, but I have to be honest. Observing you ... I like to think I know when to stop, before I lose control of my mental faculties."

"Well, I am glad to know I've taught you something," Dave said, then laughed. "You always seem to have control of yourself; I know you are a damned good driver even after a few drinks."

"Okay, Dave ... don't get me wrong! I'm not chastising you for drinking; I'd be the last one to do that. As for Dani, you say you do love her, but are you in love with her? I mean, you've been together three years, give or take. Do you see yourself married and spending the rest of your life with her?"

"I take 'The Fifth'," Dave said, then laughed hard.

"Well, just don't forget to send my invitation to your wedding," I said, then laughed.

"You may be waiting a long time, but I'll remember to send you one. Seriously Mike, IF and WHEN I do get married, it will be for the last time in my life. I guarantee you that."

"I believe you ... all the more reason for you to be absolutely, positively IN LOVE and to be absolutely, positively sure that SHE is IN LOVE with you! I damn sure would not want to miss your wedding!" I laughed.

"Okay, Mike, I have to get some sleep. You take it easy. Give my regards to Rose Marie and Baron. We'll talk soon."

"All right, Dave! Thanks for the call and the good news ... glad you and *Harry* are back to work. You take care, too ... talk soon." The call ended.

I felt Dave was excited about the movie he just finished and being back to work with *Harry.* He also had a reprieve in that, for the time being, Dani was not pressing him about getting married. I believed he had slowed down and was controlling his drinking. He seemed to have realized he could not continue to 'burn the candle from both ends'. It appeared to me he was happy with his relationship with Dani, as long as she allowed him his 'space' and did not insist on his being a 'party boy' as he had been in his past.

He seemed adamant about not being ready to get married again and, when he did, he would be certain the marriage would last, 'until death do us part'.

By all published reports, Dave was earning a very good living. Still receiving residuals from *The Fugitive*, his pay for *The Swiss Conspiracy* and other films and TV Movies of the Week, as well as his salary and ownership percentage of *Harry O*, he was quite comfortable financially.

I knew Dave was a generous tipper at restaurants and bars,

that he was also generous in helping total strangers in emergency cases, such as single mothers hit with catastrophes. I had no doubt Dave was supporting Dani in lavish style and not giving it any thought. Whatever Dani could want, Dave would provide.

I knew from talks with Dave that Dani came into their living together relationship with her own money and it was a substantial amount. I also knew since moving in with Dave, she had not spent a dime of her own money. Dani was not a 'gold-digger' in any sense of the word; Dave was just old-fashioned and his principles called for the man to always pay the tab which, in this case, meant everything.

Dave called me Wednesday evening, July 23, at 10:45.

"Mike, it's me, Dave ... just a quick call to let you know I'll be on Johnny Carson's show this Friday. Don't miss it!"

"Okay, Dave ... thanks for letting me know. I won't miss it, I promise. How is everything else with you?"

"Good, everything is good. I have to go ... just wanted to let you know about Johnny's show. Don't miss it! I'll call you later."

"Sure, Dave ... thanks for the heads-up. Talk later."

The phone went dead.

33

The Tonight Show with Johnny Carson on Friday night, July 25, 1975, was a great show. Dave was his main guest star and it was obvious to anyone watching that Dave and Johnny Carson were good friends with a lot of mutual respect.

Dave spoke of some work he did on radio as a voice-over. He then promoted the upcoming release of *The Swiss Conspiracy* and his thoughts about it being a well-scripted movie filmed in Switzerland showing the great scenery.

A clip of his film *Once Is Not Enough* which had been released late the prior month was also shown. Dave received a long and loud round of applause from the studio audience.

It was good to see Dave so relaxed, even cracking some light jokes with Johnny Carson. I noted there was no mention of Dani or any other women in his life.

I would not hear from Dave again until five minutes past midnight on Thursday, September 18.

"Good morning, Mike. It's me Dave. I wanted to be the first to wish you a Happy Birthday. Will Rose Marie bake you a cake?"

Dave sounded as if he had already enjoyed a few drinks, but was not too drunk. He had been calling me on my birthday for several years so I thought nothing about it.

"Thanks, Dave! No, I'm taking her out to dinner and I'm going to bake myself a cake - white with chocolate icing. I'll be glad to send you a piece."

"No, that's okay ... make sure you have some ice cream with it ... vanilla, okay? How is everything going with you? How are Rose Marie and Baron?"

"Everything is fine. Rose Marie is doing great; she got a promotion at her job. Baron is doing good. We've been looking at female shepherds ... even though I've been thinking of having him neutered, I'd like him to be a father at least once. What do you think?"

"I think you should. I know it is the right thing to do. I understand having a dog neutered calms them down a little but it would be nice for him to experience fatherhood at least once."

"Good, I'm glad you agree with me. We'll get him a wife this weekend. He will be happy to know you agree with him ... us, I mean. So how is *Harry*? How is Dani? Anything else happening? It has been quite a while since we spoke."

"*Harry's* doing fine; we're back to our shooting schedule. Uh ... uh, I'm getting married!"

"WHAT? WHEN? ARE YOU SERIOUS?"

"Yeah, I'm serious. She set the date for next month, the fourth; it's going to be a small ceremony at a friend's home. I haven't sent out any invitations; she's doing all that stuff. I'd like you to come but I really don't think you'd enjoy it. I'll let you decide; not many of my real friends or even my family will be there."

"Are you for real, Dave? Is this what YOU want? Did you really propose? Are you sure you are ready for this ... commitment?"

"Let's just say it happened ... I can't get out of it. I'll tell you more about it later."

"Okay, Dave ... you're a big boy. You must know what you're doing. I can only wish you the best."

"Say a prayer for me, will ya'?" Dave laughed.

"I'll say a lot of prayers for you, Dave ..."

"Well, I have to get some sleep. We have an early call in the morning. I'll be in touch soon. You enjoy your birthday, give Rose Marie and Baron my best and congratulate Rose Marie on her promotion. Take it easy, okay?"

"I will, Dave ... just make sure you call me when you have everything set for sure."

"I will, Mike. Talk soon," Dave said and hung up his phone.

I had been getting ready to go to bed. Instead I went to the kitchen and made myself a scotch and water. I put a Dionne Warwick album on then went out to sit on the terrace. Taking in the sights of the city as I sipped my scotch, I analyzed my conversation with Dave. I was in total shock.

The way he told me the news, I had the distinct impression he was allowing himself to be trapped. He did not sound as though he was really in love with Dani, that he was enthusiastically looking forward to this union.

He really sounded beaten down, like he was walking into a trap – as if he knew it and the mere thought was depressing him.

It was only a little after nine o'clock in Los Angeles when he called and I could hear background noise that sounded as if he was in a bar ... maybe The Formosa or, perhaps, he had found a bar close to the studios in Burbank. The way he sounded, I was certain he was in a bar. I was also certain he was near his capacity for scotch, or whatever he was imbibing this time.

I concluded Dave was not ready to get married again, even though he had been divorced from Ellie for five years. His divorce was still costing him financially and I felt, emotionally, as well. He sounded very depressed in this call.

I began feeling depressed myself over the fact there was nothing I could do to be of any help to him. I deduced from the way he spoke, I would not expect an invitation and would not go even if I did; maybe I would change my mind if an invitation did show up in my mailbox.

I held onto hope that Dave would call me before October 4 and tell me he had re-considered ... or that he was really getting married because he wanted to.

In assessing what I knew of David Janssen, it just did not make any sense to me at all. Here was a man - handsome, charismatic, multi-talented, a mega-television star, star of the big screen in his own right, possessing fame and fortune ... yet, he continued to be miserable in his personal life.

I knew he had mastered control over his drinking to a point he did not become 'noticeably drunk' in public.

Even so, he never became mean, angry or confrontational with anyone when he had a few too many.

The medically proven fact remained that his overindulgence of alcohol combined with his smoking up to three packs of cigarettes per day was having serious adverse effects on his health.

I had noted over the previous couple of years that Dave was aging physically at a rapid pace. His hair was almost completely grey and the studio make-up could not mask the lines in his face. He was only 44 but, in my eyes, he looked 10 years older. No doubt, this was the result of his years of heavy drinking and smoking. I had never mentioned my opinion of this to him. Perhaps I would if the opportunity were to present itself.

Before I knew it, it was almost three in the morning and I had consumed six scotch and waters. I had fallen into a depressed state of mind, feeling empathy for Dave. I just could not see myself in his situation and had no clue what I could say to him that might help him in resolving his circumstances. I felt certain he had not decided, from his own heart and mind, to marry Dani. I was positive he felt trapped with no way out.

34

Sunday morning, September 28, at 3:45, my phone rang persistently. I had gone to bed just after two and I did not want to answer. I shook my head and grabbed the receiver on the fifth ring.

"Mike, it's me, Dave ... I'm sorry to wake you. Is it okay I woke you?"

"Hi, Dave! Of course! How are you? You don't sound so good." I could tell from his voice he was depressed and drunk.

"I've had a few. I plan on having a few more. I'm okay ... just need to unwind ... get a grip on myself ... you know. I've been working my ass off, non-stop ... and then dealing with all the party bullshit with her ... kind of wears a guy down, you know."

"Is the wedding still on? Are you really going to do it?"

"Yeah ... it's all set ... I have to do it ... no choice ... no turning back now."

"You could still tell her it is not the right time for you. Can't you tell her to wait, at least, a couple more years when you can stop paying Ellie alimony?"

"No, I can't Mike. I've been working. I have money coming in hand-over-fist; money would not be an excuse. I really have no choice ... I have to go through with it."

"Well, tell me, Dave ... it's none of my business but did you at least have your lawyers draw up a prenuptial? I mean, that only makes sense to me after what you went through with Ellie ... what Ellie took from you and all the outrageous lawyers' fees ... did you do that? If not, I strongly urge you to do it. If Dani won't sign, then bingo, there's your out ... if she isn't willing to sign a prenup, then she sure as hell isn't in love with you! She knows what you went through, the costs ... and from what the media said, she made a bundle from divorcing Buddy."

"No ... no prenup ... and I know you're right, but I can't go back now. It's too damn late ... I'm hooked."

"Dave, I really feel bad for you, man. This is no way to start a marriage. IF you are really IN love with her, and she with you, that I could understand but, the way you're talking, I don't think that's the case. It's not too late, Dave. There are plenty of women out there ... just go out and have fun, like you used to ... you don't have to be tied down to one woman. Women change a hell of a lot once they have that ring ... they own you!"

"Yeah, Mike ... don't I know it! I should have learned from my mistake; it's gonna be hell to pay now."

"Dave ... I just don't know what to say. I wish there was something I could do to give you a way out, but we both know there isn't. Why don't you call your lawyers and tell them you want a prenuptial? Have them rush it, present it to Dani the night before your wedding ... maybe that'll work."

"Yeah ... I'll kick that around in my head. I'll call Paul tomorrow and bounce it off him ... see what he says."

"I know you seem to be content with Dani - I mean living together, her cooking and all - but, man, once you say 'I DO' - that's the easy part. Saying 'I DON'T' want it anymore ... that's when all hell breaks loose and the lawyers come busting into your lives."

"Yeah ... yeah ... I know Mike, I know. That's what scares the hell out of me. I just don't have a way out ... too damn late now. Listen, thanks for listening to my bullshit. I'm sorry I woke you up. Get some sleep. I'm going to do that, too. I'll call you later. You take it easy."

"You're not driving are you? I can drive out and take you home; I could be there in three days - just stay where you are. Tell me where you are; I'll leave now," I said and let out a little laugh.

"Yeah, right, Mike! They don't have enough scotch to last me three days. I'm at The Formosa ... I'm not driving, don't worry. I'll be all right," he said and laughed. He hung up.

There was no way I could go back to sleep so I went to the kitchen and turned on the coffee pot.

Dave sounded very drunk and very depressed. I could only hope he would call his lawyers and present Dani with a prenuptial agreement and hope that she did, indeed, love him and sign it or just throw a tantrum and tell him to get out.

It just did not make any sense to me; here is a man who has everything yet he just could not find happiness and fulfilment in his personal life. It was so sad. He had told me on more than one occasion that the only time he was 'happy' was when he finished with the make-up and walked onto the set in the character of his role.

I would not want to be a TV or movie star; I would not want to change places with Dave for all the money in the world.

I recalled the numerous photos of Dave and Dani that had been published over the last couple of years. She was certainly a stunning woman, beautiful with a great smile. She was always holding onto Dave and, from every perspective of the photos, she appeared to be madly in love with him. However, Dave had told me there is the 'public' face and the 'behind closed doors' face of everyone, Dani included.

Dave had said on more than one occasion that he was not an easy man to live with. He knew his faults; he was moody, he was a perfectionist, he wanted his home to be tastefully furnished, spotlessly clean at all times. He worked hard to afford the best of everything and he enjoyed that. When he was working, his role commanded 20 of his waking hours every day.

Dave did confirm what I had come to know about his personality: he was NOT a demanding man to live with. Whatever Ellie, Rosemary or Dani wanted, he gave with a sincere smile. He loved to make people happy and he loved to help people, even total strangers.

Dave had a very unhappy childhood. His first inner feelings of stability came when his mother married Gene Janssen. Mr.

Janssen did all in his power to provide Dave with fatherly attention and love. When his sister Jill was born, Dave was ecstatic at having a little sister. Jill was followed by Teri. Dave loved his sisters and doted on them.

His mother was very strict and HER life and needs came first - before Dave and his sisters' and before her husband. She kept a running account of every dime she loaned Dave in the early years of his career and, while he served in the Army, Dave paid back every dime, and gave much more. He never kept account of what he gave his mother. None of this was published.

When Dave made any disparaging remarks about his mother, she would find a reporter to publish her rebuttal ... saying Dave was lying, making things up. Between my interactions with Ellie and Berniece Janssen and, knowing Dave, I firmly believed Dave. I knew Dave would never lie.

I felt very depressed knowing how depressed Dave was and what he would be enduring over the next week. There was nothing I could do ... nothing anyone could do. I said a silent prayer for him.

35

The week passed with no word from Dave.

I had not seen anything in the New York newspapers, the fan magazines or on television about his wedding - if there had, indeed, been a wedding.

On Monday morning, October 6, my phone rang at 3:30. I was able to grab it on the third ring; I knew it was Dave.

"Mike ... it's me, Dave. I know I woke you again but it's almost time for you to get up anyway. How are you? How's Baron?"

"Good morning, Dave! It's okay you woke me. I've had enough sleep anyway. I'm okay, Baron's okay ... the big question I have is ... are YOU okay? Are you still a bachelor?"

"No ... I'm a married man ... again! It's okay. We didn't consummate the marriage. I got drunk and slept on the couch ... with my clothes on." He laughed.

"Are you serious? So you went through with the wedding?"

"Yeah ... no way around it. I had no choice."

"Did you at least follow my advice and get a prenuptial?"

"No ... it wouldn't have mattered anyway. What's done is done. I just have to learn to live with it."

"Damn, Dave! There goes your career ... think of all the millions of beautiful women fans you'll be losing. You're off the market now; they'll find some other good looking movie star to fall in love with ... think of all those hearts you've broken again," I said, then laughed, trying to bring some levity to the conversation. Dave did not sound drunk or nearly as depressed as he was when we spoke on my birthday.

"Yeah ... I guess it won't be long and I'll be lucky to do commercials." Another laugh.

"I don't think that will happen, although commercials pay pretty well, I hear. So Dave, if you don't mind telling me ... WHY? If you guys have an on-again - off-again relationship, and you don't really feel you are IN love with her, and she with you ... WHY in the hell did you get married without a prenup? You could have just moved out and been a totally free man!"

"Well, Mike, it's a long story. I do love her and I think she loves me, too. To be honest, I fucked up ... big time! You have to understand she is very smart, especially when it comes to managing money.

Anyway, a couple of years ago, she was helping me look over my accounts and she suggested I really didn't need Fred, my business manager. His fees alone were a big chunk of change ... she could take over and save me money. Then she pointed out I really didn't need Frank anymore. The studio could handle publicity for *Harry* and that was a big savings. She could handle my money, investments and we'd be a lot better off - so she has complete control of my money. I get an allowance but she is damn good at it so, IF I didn't marry her, it would cost me ... big time."

"Damn it, Dave! Couldn't you just go to your banks and take her off your accounts? Man ... I really feel bad for you. You lost a lot to Ellie – hell, you're still paying Ellie. You work too damned hard for this to happen. You don't deserve being in this kind of situation.

"I'm sorry. I know it's none of my business and I'm probably saying too much. I obviously don't know what you're going through; I just pray you know what you're doing and can handle it. Dave, keep one thing in mind: IF you can't be 100 percent happy with Dani, money is not worth your happiness ... just walk away! You are a big star; you can always make more money! I can't say anymore."

"I know, Mike. It's my problem. I appreciate you listening to me gripe about it but you're right ... I have to handle it. I'll just have to try and make our marriage one of love and not war. I just have to live with things the way they are. I do keep in mind if it gets bad, I'll walk away, just like I did after four fucking years of hell with Ellie - and I don't care if I'm penniless. As long as I can work, I'll be okay."

"Okay, Dave, you know best. So I guess I'll be seeing some publicity, maybe wedding photos splashed across the newspapers and fan magazines. I can't wait to see them. So tell me, did you get drunk *before* you said 'I DO', or *after*? Where does Dani want to go for your honeymoon?"

"Hell, Mike ... I had to get drunk to even make it in the door!" he answered, then laughed heartily. "No honeymoon now. I have to work! We'll take a little trip when I have a break, probably Mexico. I have to get ready for make-up and wardrobe, Mike. I'll be in touch soon. You take care. Give my best to Rose Marie and a hug for Baron."

"I will, Dave. Keep me up-to-date on *Harry's* cases. Talk later." We ended the call.

It was almost four o'clock so I made it to the kitchen and turned on the coffee pot. Baron followed me to get his morning cookie.

I was astonished at Dave's revelations about his financial arrangement with Dani and his reasoning for getting married ... and without a prenuptial agreement. I felt so much sympathy for him.

I knew he loved Dani and I didn't doubt she loved him. I could only surmise they both were stubborn and set in their ways, which would account for arguments - but just giving her absolute control over his money ... unbelievable!

Dave was a self-taught educated man. He was also a well spoken man; it was seldom that I would hear profanity from Dave. When he used profanity, it was a strong indication of his displeasure over a particular subject. I had the distinct impression Dave was not happy entering his union with Dani.

Throughout the past three years of their relationship, living together, Dave had mentioned a couple of occasions where he had left with no intentions of going back, but he did go back.

I recalled countless interviews and photos of Dave alone, Dani alone and both of them together. In the vast majority, both would be smiling and speaking lovingly of each other - often with Dave inserting his quit wit, bringing laughter to both the interviewer and Dani.

It would appear to anyone who did not know Dave and Dani, personally, that they were the happiest couple in Hollywood. However, they said that about Dave and Ellie all the way up to the date he walked out on their tenth wedding anniversary.

Dave had told me early on: "Don't believe all that crap you see in the papers and magazines ... half of it is pure bullshit ... I just have to go along with it."

I felt so bad for Dave, knowing he felt he was trapped and had to work to make Dani happy and keep peace between them.

I couldn't help but wonder how Dani felt about not rushing off to some exotic place for a honeymoon. After all, a wedding was, typically, planned when both spouses could take time away from work for a honeymoon.

That Dave chose his work over taking time off for a honeymoon did not surprise me. There were over 100 people whose livelihoods depended upon Dave showing up on the set.

The fact the wedding date was selected by Dani, when she knew he would be working on *Harry O*, told me she was more interested in locking Dave into wedded bliss more than taking a fun and love-filled honeymoon away from Hollywood.

36

On Friday, October 10, news of the wedding of David Janssen and Dani Greco was published in the newspapers. I later learned there had been brief articles announcing their nuptials, but somehow I had missed seeing them.

One photo was published showing Dani in a beautiful white dress. Dave was wearing a dark suit, red tie and pocket kerchief. Dani had a radiant smile; she was a very beautiful bride who looked, at least, 10 years younger than Dave, who appeared to be drunk.

The media stated there were over 100 guests, close friends and television executives. There was no mention of Dave's mother or sisters attending. From the photo of the bride and groom, I drew the distinct impression Dave was showing his public face. His smile appeared forced.

Recalling our conversation from just a few days earlier, I felt a pang of sympathy for Dave. I couldn't understand why - even though he had willingly given control of his personal finances to Dani - he would go through with marrying her.

He had said their relationship was 'on again-off again.' He had also told me he loved her but couldn't say, for sure, that he was 'in love' with her. I just felt he was setting himself up for more emotional turmoil and, IF he and Dani could not 'make' their marriage work, he would have another very costly divorce on his hands.

I had to force myself to put the negative thoughts out of my mind, to think positive and wish and hope he and Dani would find happiness. After all, I thought, now that she had him locked into the legal and binding state of matrimony, she would feel more secure and do all she could to be a loving and supporting wife.

I had read in one of her interviews quoting her as saying, "the star always gets top billing." Dani had given up her acting career at a time she was just getting glowing recognition of studio executives, producers and adoration of fans that were growing in numbers. Now, she was 'Mrs. David Janssen', a role that would require her to give an Oscar worthy supporting role.

Dave called me on Sunday, November 30, 1975.

"Mike, it's me, Dave. Good morning ... had your coffee yet?"

"Good morning, Dave. Actually, I'm on my second cup ... how the hell are you? How is married life?"

"Well, glad I didn't wake you ... since this is Sunday. I'm fine ... as for married life, I don't know yet. I've been too busy working to give it much attention." He laughed. "I'm just giving you a quick call to let you know I'll be appearing on Johnny Carson's show this coming Wednesday ... hope you can stay awake and watch it."

"Of course, I will! How is *Harry* doing? We are watching every week, most of the time just Rose Marie and I, but a couple of times we've had friends over. We've gotten a lot of fans for *Harry*. How is everything else going?"

"All is well ... quiet on the home front. We'll be taking a break over the holidays and Dani and I will be going to Acapulco for our honeymoon ... a little delayed, but we're going."

"That sounds nice. I hope you have a really nice honeymoon, filled with love and fun ... with a little relaxation mixed it."

"Yeah, I'm sure it will be. We'll have some friends joining us so there will be some fun, guaranteed," Dave said, then laughed.

"Wait a minute! I've heard of newlyweds taking their mother-in-law on the honeymoon ... but friends? Never heard of that."

"Well, Dani does ... but, then again, we're not really newlyweds; we've been married over a month and a half." He laughed.

"How long will you be down there?"

"About two weeks. I'll have to get back for *Harry* right after New Year's. So how are things with you? How are Rose Marie and *The Bear*?"

"Everything here is good. Rose Marie and I are having dinner tonight. Baron is getting bigger. I'm thinking of moving to Miami; I'm fed up with the cold and snow here."

"Miami? You have snow there?"

"No, not yet, but it will be here before we know it. I haven't fully decided but I'm seriously thinking about it. I have an offer for a pretty good job ... pay is much better and I'm tempted."

"What about Rose Marie ... and you?"

"We'll stay close ... time will tell. Nothing has been decided yet; I'll let you know when I decide. Are you happy with the way *Harry* is going?"

"You definitely have to keep me informed of your plans. Yeah, I'm pleased; all of us are. We have seen a big improvement in scripts, the cast and all ... it's a lot of fun working with the crew. I'll let you go now but I'll give you a call after we are back ... so you and Rose Marie have a really nice Christmas and a safe New Year's Eve, in case we don't speak before then, okay?"

"Okay, Dave, the same to you and Dani - and I wish you both the best for your honeymoon. Look forward to hearing from you."

"All right, Mike ... take it easy." My line went dead.

Dave sounded very upbeat and happy; it was good. I felt, between his work and his marriage, things were progressing smoothly for him and, perhaps, he was wrong in thinking Dani would end up hurting him.

I felt I was wrong in all of my negative assumptions yet, I reminded myself, my assumptions had been made from what he had related to me. It was early in their marriage but Dave sounded really happy for the first time in months.

I had not heard from Dave since the end of November so I assumed he and Dani were having an extended and very happy honeymoon.

37
~1976~

On Saturday morning, January 17, my phone rang around 3:30. I knew it had to be Dave.

"Mike ... sorry, I woke you up ... wanted to give you a call before I went to bed. How are you? Did you and Rose Marie have a good holiday season?"

"Good morning, Dave! It's okay; you know you can call me any time. Yeah, we had a very nice holiday ... how about you and Dani? How was your honeymoon?"

"Our holidays and our honeymoon ended in tragedy. Dani's daughter's home caught fire; her husband and daughter, Dani's granddaughter, died. Debbie, her daughter, is okay; she suffered minor burns and smoke inhalation. It devastated Dani. She had to fly to Florida. It was so sad ... it's going to take Dani quite some time to recover."

"Oh, my God, Dave! I'm so sorry to hear that. I didn't know Dani had a daughter ... a granddaughter. That is really terrible ... so sad. How are you doing ... how is Dani holding up?"

"Debbie is her daughter from her first marriage; Buddy helped raise her. Dani and Debbie are both so devastated ... it's going to take time. They are both very depressed; I'm trying to hold them together. It was such a shock ... to everyone."

"I can imagine! Did they live in Florida or were they on vacation there? How did it happen?"

"No ... uh, they lived there, a suburb of Tampa, really out in the country. We don't really know yet the cause; the fire department suspects it was an electrical fire. We just don't know yet."

"God, Dave, I'm so sorry. Please give Dani and her daughter my condolences."

"I will. I just wanted to give you a call so you'd know why I've been out of touch with you. I'm back to work so I'll give you a call in a few days. Take it easy, okay?"

"All right, Dave! Thanks for calling ... YOU take it easy, too." The call ended.

38

I hung up my phone, went to the kitchen and made myself a scotch. I was totally shocked and felt so bad for Dani and her daughter. I could not imagine the pain they were feeling. Dave sounded very upset and concerned over the tragedy. I did not know, nor ask, if Dave was close to Dani's daughter.

I had seen nothing in the New York newspapers regarding the fire. I had thought since Debbie was Dani's daughter and Dani was now married to Dave, it would be newsworthy. Apparently not! I would continue scanning the newspapers and fan magazines to see if there would be any news articles. Over the next couple of weeks, there was still nothing in the media.

Dave called me on Saturday morning, February 7, 1976, at 11:15.

"Mike, it's me, Dave. Good morning! How are you?"

"Fine, Dave ... how are you, Dani and Debbie?" I asked.

"I'm good. Dani and Debbie are still suffering from shock and depression; it's just taking time ... really a sad situation and nothing I can do to ease their pain. Thanks for your concern; I appreciate that. We wrapped up *Harry* so I'm going to be working on a new film."

"What do you mean you wrapped up *Harry*?"

"We filmed the last episode ... so I have time on my hands. I'll still be working on other projects."

"All right, Dave ... don't keep me in suspense. Will *Harry O* be back next year?"

"I don't really know but, if I were to place a bet, I'd bet against it. The ratings haven't come up to expectations ... there's a chance, but I wouldn't bet on it."

"Damn ... that pisses me off! I like *Harry;* he is so real, down-to-earth ... never gets flustered. I'm going to start a petition to ABC!"

"Don't waste your time, Mike ... they do whatever they want ... so let it be."

"Well ... do you have any idea when you'll know if it will be renewed?"

"Sometime in May, but I'll be working, so relax. I also need a few weeks off to rejuvenate myself. I'll let you know what happens. Don't worry!" he said with a laugh. "So what's going on with you? Have you made any decision about moving to Miami? What does Rose Marie think of your moving; have you talked to her about it?"

"Yeah, I've told Rose Marie I've been thinking about it. She's not too happy about it but she'll go along with it ... if that is what I decide. Baron says he'll go if they have a dog park; if not, I can't go."

Dave laughed. "Well, Mike, Miami is a nice city. You have the beach, sun all the time ... you have to prepare for hurricanes every few years, but it is a fun place. You may like it."

"I'm thinking about it but, then again, I love the city, and the winter season isn't that long ... lots of things to consider ... no rush. I'll take my time."

"What about that job offer? Do you think you'd like it, the work?"

"Yeah, it would be nice. I have some time; the guy I will replace, his contract expires at the end of August. I'm weighing everything. That's the beauty of not being married with kids - there's just Baron and me."

"Well, let me know what you decide. I have to go. I'll keep in touch and you take it easy and give my best to Rose Marie and *The Bear*."

"All right, Dave! Thanks for calling and I hope things will get easier for Dani and Debbie. You take care and keep me up-to-date about *Harry*."

"Okay, Mike ... we'll talk soon." Dave hung up the phone.

Dave sounded upbeat and positive, but he sounded tired. I knew he must be under a lot of pressure and dealing with personal pain as he tried to help Dani and Debbie through the unimaginable suffering they were going through.

Over the ensuing weeks, I carefully perused the newspapers and fan magazines looking for anything about Dani's tragedy, Dave and, especially, news about the prospects for *Harry O*.

Dave's next call came on Monday morning, February 16, just before one o'clock. There was a lot of noise in the background and I got the distinct impression Dave was drinking.

"Hey, Mike! It's me, Dave ... hope I didn't wake you."

"No, you didn't, Dave ... I just got in. How are you? How are Dani and her daughter doing?"

"I'm okay ... they are coming around. I'm doing a film; you may like it. It's called *Two Minute Warning,*" Dave said, his words a little garbled.

"What's it about? Where are you filming it? Who else stars with you?"

"Some psychotic plans to do a mass murder at the Super Bowl ... the cops are tipped off and send the SWAT team. Gena Rowlands, Charlton Heston, John Cassavetes are the main players; hell, there are too many in the cast to name. It's a damn good script, based on a novel. I'm excited about working with Gena and Heston. We'll be filming at the LA Coliseum."

"That's great! I will make sure I take Rose Marie to see it when it comes out. What's the news with *Harry*?"

"I told you we wrapped up the last episode of the season a couple of weeks ago, didn't I? Did I mention Mike Douglas came out from Philadelphia and did an interview on the set? I don't know when it will air, but it's worth watching - a little light comedy in it."

"Yes, you did, but have you heard anything about it being renewed for next season? No, you didn't tell me about Douglas. I'll check *TV Guide* and make sure I see it. I bought a small TV for my office."

"No, we won't know if they are going to pick it up for another season ... probably won't know anything for a couple more months. I'll be sure and give you a holler when I know something. How is everything going with you?"

"Good, Dave ... everything is good. Baron has a new girlfriend; she's a little younger than he but they love each other. First day I left them alone, I came home from the office and my living room was a wreck ... Baron blamed Sherry, that's her name; she denied it."

"Hey, Mike, that's great! I'll look forward to meeting her the next time I'm in New York. I bet your food bill has gone up a lot. How's Rose Marie?"

"She's fine ... she loves watching *Harry* with me. How are things with you and Dani?"

"Things are okay ... mostly. I'm going home to get some sleep. I'll give you a call in a few days, let you know what's going on. You take it easy. Give Rose Marie and your kids my best. We'll talk soon." My phone went dead.

Dave sounded pretty drunk. I had a gut feeling things were not that good at home with Dani. Then again, she was still dealing with her tragedy. I did not know if her daughter was living with them but, if so, I knew Dave would be the perfect and understanding step-father. Still, I was worried that he was back to drinking more and not less.

39

I did not hear from Dave again until Sunday, February 29, 1976.

"Mike ... it's me ... how are you?"

"I'm good, Dave ... what about you?"

"Doing well ... how are Rose Marie, Baron and Sherry? Have you made any decision about your job change, moving to Florida?"

"Rose Marie is good. Baron and Sherry are really great; they have bonded ... act like newlyweds. I can hardly wait for the day I come home and they tell me Sherry is pregnant.

"I haven't made a firm decision on relocating to Florida, although I am about to - it's damn cold here. I'll tell you Dave, the allure of the tropics ... sun every day of the year, the palm trees, the beach ... I'm ready to do it."

"Well, hell, Mike ... sounds like you've made up your mind. What's stopping you? I think it would be good for you but, then again, remember you gave all that up when you moved to New York. We have the sun, the palm trees, the beaches and the balmy nights right here in LA; you gave it all up."

"Yeah, I know, Dave, but you also have the smog and the massive traffic jams, and the main reason for my move was to be close to my soon-to-be ex. I made the right move. If I do take the job in Miami, I think it would be a good move ... cost of living is a lot less than here ... I could get a house with a big yard for the dogs ... I'm leaning towards it. What's up with you?"

"Make sure you let me know if you decide to move. Abby sent me a script for a new TV movie; it's called *Mayday at 40,000 Feet.* I'll play an airline pilot ... some nut-case passenger tries to shoot me but shoots out an engine so I and my co-pilot have to maintain the aircraft until we can find a place to land. I play the hero, of course ... what do you think?"

"Sounds like it will be an exciting movie ... are you going to do it? Who else is in the cast?"

"Yeah, I'm going to do it. I have the time ... waiting on ABC to let us know about *Harry.* We'll be doing some location shooting which is good - gets me out of LA for a couple of weeks. Too many people in the cast to name. A few you may recognize are Don Meredith and Lynda Day George, Ray Milland and Broderick Crawford, to name a few. My ex-brother-in-law, Steve Lodge, will be doing the wardrobe; he worked with me on *Fugitive.* I've worked with a lot of the cast before ... good people so I'm sure we'll have a ton of fun."

"Yeah ... I'm familiar with them. You've worked with Broderick Crawford before, haven't you? Your ex-brother-in-law; do you still get along with him?"

"Oh, yeah! Steve is a great guy ... he was my wardrobe man on *Fugitive* the last two years. He's a very talented guy as an actor, screen-writer ... he does it all. It will be good working with him again; we'll have plenty of time for drinks and talk about old times," he said with a laugh.

"When will you start the filming? When will it air - which network?"

"Starts filming next week; it will be on CBS but I don't know when. I'll let you know when I find out."

"Where will you be on location?"

"In Utah ... just for a couple of weeks. I'm looking forward to it. I taped a show with Bob Hope a few days ago, a spoof on TV detectives; Angie Dickinson, Mike Connors, Telly Savalas, Jim Hutton and Abe Vigoda ... it is really hilarious! Try not to miss it."

"I won't. Do you know when it will be on - what network?"

"Next week – Friday, I think ... check your *TV Guide*. I won't give it away but you'll get a kick out of it. It's on NBC."

"Okay, I will. So how are things with you and Dani? How is her daughter doing?"

"With Dani and me, it's frosty - sort of like Russia and the United States. Debbie is adjusting ... more so than Dani. I'll be away for a couple of weeks or so. Dani and Debbie will have plenty of time together and Dani will have time to think."

"Okay ... enough said. Sorry, Dave! I don't mean to butt into your private life. I just worry about how she treats you, that's all ... just friendly concern."

"Mike, that's fine ... you are one of very few I can talk to openly about these things; you should know that by now. You know I trust you."

"Thanks, Dave. I don't even tell Rose Marie what we talk about, let alone your private life. I do tell Baron but I trust him implicitly," I said and let out a little laugh.

"That's okay, Mike. You can tell Baron anything and I know he won't talk ... I trust him, too."

"Okay, I'll let him know that. You sure are keeping busy, though. Maybe you should take a couple of weeks off after this one, take Dani for a little trip ... just get away by yourselves for some time to decompress ... just be together."

"No, Mike ... not now ... no time for that. I need to work. You know that is when I am happiest ... working keeps my mind busy and off of matters that frustrate me ... things I can't do anything about," he said in a serious tone. "Well, I have to go. Be sure to watch the Bob Hope special. I'll give you a call in a few weeks. Take it easy ... give my best to Rose Marie, Baron and Sherry."

"I will, Dave. Thanks for the call ... I'll make sure Rose Marie and I see the 'Hope' special. You take care and call when you can," I said before hanging up the phone.

I felt from the conversation that Dave was very happy getting one project after another to keep him busy, earning money and, most of all, keeping his mind away from his home life.

I thought back over the nearly five years he and Dani had been together; it seemed to be an on-again-off-again relationship. Now they were married and it seemed to me that Dave was not happy with his situation. It appeared he was more trapped than he was during his last four years with Ellie. I could not understand it; by all the press they had received, they seemed to be very happy - yet I reflected on more than one photo where Dave did not appear happy at all.

I had not met Dani but, apparently, she pursued Dave and finally got the marriage certificate. She 'owned' him. She had by all accounts (including Dave's) given up her career as an actress and was happy being his wife. Yet, she was a star among the Hollywood elite and was drawn to the party circuit; apparently, she loved it. Dave did not, due mainly to his work schedule. He was just plain too tired to go to parties every night of the week.

If Dani finally had what she wanted - which was Dave, and she did have him - then why did she make his life so miserable? Did she even know she was doing it?

Rose Marie came to my apartment from her job Friday, March 5. We went to the A & P Supermarket and bought the ingredients for the only meal she knew how to prepare: her mother's Fettuccini Alfredo with shrimp, a salad and garlic bread. Neither of us were big wine drinkers so we settled on my Brandy Alexanders for drinks.

Dinner was ready as the *Bob Hope Special* began on NBC. It was a hilarious show, just as Dave had promised. The premise was that guests were being murdered in Bob's home so he hires the best detectives available. Then the detectives were becoming victims, too.

Again, Dave's talent for comedy came through like a bright shining star. The studio audience burst into applause and Dave could not help but laugh at the silliness of the whole skit. Bob Hope and his wife were good friends with Dave and he was laughing, too.

Rose Marie loved the show; it was the first time she had prepared dinner in my apartment. I was pleasantly surprised; the dinner was on par with the finest Italian restaurant in the city.

I complimented her and made a mental note to have a dozen roses delivered to her in her office the following Monday. She and her parents were going to a relative's funeral over the weekend so we would not see each other until Monday evening. I drove her home just before midnight.

I reflected on the 'Hope' show. Dave seemed so relaxed and so happy. No fan having watched the show would think Dave had any personal problems; he hid them very well.

A little tidbit

"Michael Phelps once told me that David Janssen's favorite color was blue."

- Norma Budden

40

It was not until Saturday morning, May 8, that Dave called me; it was just before five o'clock. I was already up and fixing my first cup of coffee.

"Good morning! This is Mike ... you must be Dave," I said cheerfully.

"Good morning, Mike ... you're right! How are things?" Dave asked, then laughed. I could tell he had a few drinks but, at least, he seemed to be in a good mood.

"Everything is good here ... how about on your end? Have you finished the film? How is Dani?"

"Yeah, the film is finished ... I'm back home. Dani is getting better, dealing with her sorrow. She's back to her parties which I think is the best therapy for her."

"So have you heard about *Harry*? Will we have another season?"

"No ... we don't have a firm answer yet, but the rumor is we won't be picked-up. I'll call you when I know for certain. I have a lot of irons in the fire so I'll keep busy. How are Rose Marie, Baron and Sherry?"

"I hope like hell they renew *Harry;* we like him. Rose Marie and my kids are doing fine. The weather here is beautiful so I can spend more time with Baron and Sherry in the park. How are you doing? It sounds like you're at The Formosa."

"Actually, I am here at The Formosa ... wish you could be here. I'm doing great ... getting ready to go home and get some sleep. I just wanted to touch base with you, let you know I'm back and things are okay here."

"I'm glad you did ...thanks. Do you know when *Two Minute Warning* and the new one, *Mayday*, will be aired?"

"They will both be out around late October or early November; I don't know exact dates yet. *Two Minute Warning* will be in theatres and *Mayday* will be on CBS. I'll let you know. You may even see it in the papers or *TV Guide* before I know," he said with a slight laugh.

"Wow, Dave! You'll be on the big screen and the little screen at the same time ... that's great! I'll make sure we go see the movie and maybe we'll have a watch party for *Mayday* at my apartment. I just wish it wasn't so long to wait."

"Well, you know it takes time for all the technical work, the editing and all. When I'm done, I put it out of my mind until time to go on the promotion tours. I'll remind you so you don't miss them," he said and laughed again. "Have you thought anymore about moving to Miami?"

"I keep running the pros and cons through my mind - the cons being that I would miss Rose Marie, the vibrant pace and excitement of the city, the architecture, history, friends and co-workers.

"The pros are the year-round great weather, less congestion, beaches ... a new challenge of work and responsibilities, more income and benefits, lower cost of living ... hell, I could use my Veteran's benefits and buy a house. It would be a great place for my dogs. I have a lot to consider."

"Yes, you have a lot to consider ... then again, you could make the move back to Los Angeles, get accustomed to the smog and traffic, get a higher paying job. We could meet for drinks or lunch a few times a week, I could play with Baron and Sherry ... yeah, Mike, you have a lot to consider," Dave said with a laugh.

"Dave, I'd love to be there but I could never acclimate myself to the smog and the traffic. Aside from those cons, having drinks or lunches with you is the only pro I see in living in LA. I think Miami would be the place ... IF I decide to leave the city."

"Mike ... it's your decision. I hope the best for you either way you go. I guess I'll head home and get some sleep. I'll be in touch. You take care. Give my best to Rose Marie and your kids."

"Okay, Dave, thanks for the call and you take it easy. Keep me informed about what you're doing."

"All right, Mike ... talk later." The call ended.

Dave sounded to be in good spirits, except when Dani was mentioned. I felt bad for mentioning her and had the distinct impression things were not as they appeared in public. I had to laugh that Dave had begun referring to Baron and Sherry as my kids. He had earlier started referring to Baron as 'Bear,' which was my nickname for him. I felt Dave wished he could have dogs, which would require far less maintenance and expense than a woman. I knew he loved dogs ... I knew he loved women, too.

Dave was very much a monogamous man. The only infidelity he admitted to while married to Ellie was with Suzanne Pleshette and that did not occur until his marriage had already reached the point of intolerance and he knew he would be seeking a divorce. Still, he held out for almost four more years before he had had enough and left her.

In the three years of his relationship with Rosemary Forsyth, he remained monogamous from the time they had started dating. In the four years prior to their official marriage, Dave had left Dani on, at least, three occasions, yet he remained loyal; he did not revert to his 'playboy' antics of earlier years.

I just could not get it out of my mind the situation Dave currently found himself in. He was a brilliant man, a very successful man and a very compassionate man. I knew for a fact that whatever his lady wanted, she would get it and price was no object.

Ellie had blamed everything that was wrong with their marriage on Dave. She had said on more than one occasion that it all began with his drinking. She seemed to be blind to the fact it was her demands, her treatment of him, which drove him to find his escape in work and alcohol.

I did not hear from Dave again until Sunday morning, June 6. I had been in a sound sleep and may have been groggy when I, finally, answered.

"Good morning, Mike ...it's me, Dave. How are you? Did I wake you?"

"Yeah, Dave ... what time is it? Where are you? Good morning to you, too."

"I'm home ... well, I'm in LA. I'm heading home to get some sleep. How are things with you?"

"They're good, Dave, thanks ... and what about you? I read where they cancelled *Harry O*. I don't know who was more pissed off, me or Rose Marie, but I guess you already knew it, huh," I said. I could tell Dave had been drinking and it sounded as if he was nearing his limit.

"Yeah ... I meant to call you when I heard, but I've been busy. They'll be running the first season in re-runs for the summer; I think the last episode of season two will be aired sometime at the start of the new season. Anyway, Zerbe and I will be on the cover of *TV Guide* next week. Watch for it!

"I had dinner with Susanne and her husband, Tom, and my mother a couple of weeks ago. It was pretty awkward ... I really messed up, Mike. If I had left Ellie, I could be 'Mr. Pleshette.' My mother let it slip that Suzanne and I had an affair and she wished I had divorced Ellie then and married Suzanne."

"WHAT? Your mother actually said that? My God, Dave! What did Suzanne say? How did her husband react?"

"It was okay. Mother is sly; she thought she was letting a black cat out of the bag, but Tom already knew it ... has no problem with it. He knows Suzanne loves him madly and we are just friends. They both reacted with class ... put mother in her place!"

"What did you say? How did you react?"

"I just smiled at both Suzanne and Tom, and reminded my mother that I am also 'happily married' ... of which mother knows nothing about."

"Damn! Well, I won't ask any more ... except, what are you doing? When will the movie be out and when will *Mayday* be aired?"

"I'm relaxing right now. I have several scripts to study - see if there is anything that interests me ... talking with one of the networks about a deal ... nothing set yet. Mike, sorry I woke you, but they're closing the doors. I have to go ... you take it easy. I'll be in touch."

I did not have a chance to respond before the phone went dead.

His reference to Suzanne told me he was not happy.

David Janssen wanted kids but felt he had lots of time. He did worry, though, what it would be like for *his* child growing up, his popularity being what it was.

41

Weeks passed without hearing from Dave. I had been tempted to call and compliment him for the cover of *TV Guide* where he appeared with Anthony Zerbe. The purpose was to promote *Harry O* which gave me a slim hope that ABC would give *Harry O* a third season; that hope was soon dashed when ABC announced their new fall line up.

As I was about to leave my apartment, my phone rang just after nine o'clock on Monday morning, July 5.

"Good morning, Mike ... I know I didn't wake you. How are you? Did you and Rose Marie have a good Fourth of July celebration?"

"I'm good, Dave ... how about you? It's been a while since we talked. Did you and Dani enjoy the Fourth? I have the *TV Guide* cover from a few weeks ago. Congratulations! It's a good photo. I thought maybe the network would reconsider and give you another season. Have you heard anything?"

"No ... it's over, cancelled. It's okay. The crew will pick up other jobs, the regulars will get other roles ... that was my main concern. I'll tell you, Mike, I don't want another series - not for a long time ... if I ever do another one.

"I'm working on a possible project with CBS. If it materializes, it'll be a joint partnership with my own production company so I'll have a lot to say about how it is produced. Dani and I had a relaxing Fourth, went to a couple of parties."

"That's good to hear. What will your project with CBS be about? I thought you just said you don't want to do another series ... will this be a series on CBS?"

"I don't know yet; we are just bouncing around some ideas. I want to have some humor, some comedy in whatever we develop - you know, a combination of comedy and drama - so I have a chance to lighten up a little."

"Well, I think you had a little bit of that in *Harry*, especially when viewers listened to your thoughts. I saw a lot of humor in *Gertrude* and in *Lester*. Julie Sommars was great with her accent and Les Lannom's character was really funny in both. Don't you agree with me on that?"

"Yes, I do agree ... when we had that mix of humor, the drama of the case and the actors who could pull it off ... that was a real blessing, made that week's work really fun."

"So what are you doing now? When will you know anything about your deal with CBS?"

"Abby sent me a couple of scripts so I'm weighing my options, but relaxing a little ... social obligations with Dani, just taking it easy. How about you ... are you staying in the city or moving south? How are Rose Marie and your kids?"

"I'm glad to hear you are relaxing ... you've been working pretty hard and steady lately; you deserve to give your mind and body a rest. You have a TV Movie of the Week and your film, *Two Minute Warning* coming out soon, so your fans won't forget you," I said with a laugh. "I'm going to make the move, Dave ... I think it will be good for me. I haven't told Rose Marie yet, but I will soon. She is fine ... Bear and Sherry are great. Make sure you let me know about anything new you will be doing so I'll be sure not to miss it."

"Have you given notice to your company? When do you plan to make the move? Do you know anything about Miami, other than being a tourist?"

"Yes, I gave my notice and recommended my replacement. My boss said he hated to see me leave, but wished me the best ... and even said I would always have a place to come back to. I've done a good job for them, I think ... from four men, one secretary to three offices, 72 employees in less than three years ... very profitable. I'll be leaving the city at the end of next month. I don't know that much about Miami, but learning it will be half the challenge and fun ... don't you think?"

"I'd say you've accomplished a lot there. Yeah, I agree, you will have a lot of fun there in Miami ... uh ... do you speak Spanish?"

"No, I don't speak Spanish ... why?"

"Miami has a very large Spanish-speaking population ... mostly exiles from Cuba but a lot from Argentina, Columbia, Central and South America. Lots of beautiful women there! I suggest you take a Berlitz course in Spanish," he said with a laugh.

"Yeah ... okay, Dave ... I'll see about that. I'll let you know my address and phone number when I get settled. I'll be staying in a hotel for a couple of weeks while I hunt for a house, if I can find one that will allow Baron and Sherry."

"All right, Mike! Make sure to let me know. You can always give me a call; if I'm not home, Dani will take your message. I'm going to cut this short. I have to go to a meeting so you take it easy. I'm sure we'll talk before you pack up and leave the city."

"Okay, Dave ... I appreciate the call. Please, definitely, give me a call before the end of next month so I'll know what you're up to and won't miss anything."

"I will, Mike. Give Rose Marie and your dogs my best. We'll talk soon."

"Thanks, Dave." I hung up the phone.

Dave sounded rested, relaxed and upbeat. I felt he was happy at this time in his life. He did not sound depressed with the cancellation of *Harry*, as he had earlier. Of course, Dave always worried about the crew of his shows; he had felt he was responsible for them being thrust onto the unemployment rolls.

I did not hear from Dave the rest of July. On Wednesday, August 11, he called me at my office just before five o'clock.

"Mike, it's Dave ... am I interrupting you?"

"Of course not, Dave! How are you? How is everything?"

"All is well here. I just wanted to warn you the last episode of *Harry O* will air tomorrow night."

"I know, Dave ... Rose Marie and I are hosting a watch party. Rose Marie is making lasagna, her mother's recipe; she's never done it before, so she's nervous. We can't wait to see *Harry O.* It will be sad, though."

"Aww, Mike ... it'll probably be on re-runs sooner or later."

"Yeah, but it's not the same, knowing you aren't doing it anymore. How are things going? Do you know when the movie will be out? What about *Mayday*?"

"The movie should be hitting theatres nationwide in early November. The TV movie will be aired pretty close to the same time. I don't have the exact date, but I'll call you when I do."

"How are you doing? How is Dani?"

"Mike, I've met a beautiful woman - very, very talented. I've moved out of the condo again ... situation with Dani has just gotten too hard to handle."

"Is this woman an actress? Would I know her name? I haven't seen anything in the papers or the fan mags. Do you think you'll be heading to divorce court again?" I caught myself peppering him with questions, immediately regretting the last one.

"You probably know her name. She's not an actress; she's a singer and songwriter - Carol Connors. She is beautiful ... a real bubbly personality, smart, very smart ... so much fun to be with. SHE would be worth going through that agony again, not that I'm contemplating it right now. Who knows?"

"Dave, I know who she is. She was the lead of the group, *The Teddy Bears;* she sang *To Know Him Is To Love Him.* I loved that song ... I used to sing it to my high school sweetheart, Donna! She is beautiful ... petite, right?"

"Yes, that's her ... she is like a little doll. Mike, she makes me feel alive ... again. She is so talented; we're going to write some songs together. One thing I know for sure: she doesn't care about my money or my fame ... she has her own, plenty of both!"

"Dave, I am really happy to hear that! Have you taken any precautions - done anything to get back control of your money from Dani? You better talk to your lawyer ... just a friendly suggestion."

"I'm taking steps, Mike. Don't worry! I damn sure will not go through what I did with Ellie. You know, California is a 'community property' state, so she'll get half of what I've earned since our marriage ... but, that's the price I'll have to pay ... if it comes to that."

"Well, Dave, at least you know it upfront and, hey, if that's what you have to pay to be happy, go for it. The money is not worth your happiness. You are still a big star ... you can make more money but, Dave, damn it! IF you get divorced and then get married again, make sure she loves you enough to sign a prenuptial!"

"Yeah, Mike ... I know you are right ... and I will make certain to do that ... if it comes to that. I have to go, but I'll give you a call later. Oh, when are you making your move to Florida?"

"I plan on leaving here August 28; it's a Saturday morning. I already have an apartment in Miami that is dog friendly. I know in what area of the city I will be looking for a home, so I hope to get settled before the end of September or no later than the end of October. I'll be sure to let you know."

"Okay, Mike ... if we don't talk before, you have a safe trip and call me when you have a phone number. Give Rose Marie my best and a hug for your kids."

"Thanks, Dave ... you take it easy, too ... and be careful."

The call ended.

To Dave, the age difference between two members of a couple was nothing but a number.

42

Thursday evening, August 12, I picked Rose Marie up at her office and we went straight to the A&P Supermarket and bought the ingredients for the lasagna and fresh garlic bread. While she prepared the evening meal, I took Baron and Sherry to Riverside Park for their run.

Our guests arrived at 8:30 and we all had a cocktail before dinner. Dinner was absolutely outstanding and everyone was quite complimentary of Rose Marie's culinary talents. A couple more rounds of drinks and it was time to watch the final episode of *Harry O.*

Our group discussion after the show was full of accolades not just for Dave but the script writers, the guest stars and other actors, even the lighting. We were all mutually angry the series had come to an end.

Everyone asked me what Dave would be doing next; of course I told them about the feature film, *Two Minute Warning,* and the upcoming TV Movie of the Week, *Mayday at 40,000 Feet.* It felt good to know I had a small part in Dave gaining at least five fans he had not had when *The Fugitive* was among the top television series' of the mid-sixties.

I had told Rose Marie of my decision to relocate to Miami and we agreed that we would remain close via telephone and my occasional return trips to New York City. I reserved a nice window table at the Rainbow Room for Friday evening, August 27, for our farewell dinner. I hired a limousine, bought her a dozen roses and made it a special night.

It was a wonderful evening, albeit a sad ending when I dropped her off at her parents' home in Queens just after midnight.

The end of August arrived with no call from Dave. I had settled all my affairs in New York, packed Baron and Sherry in my car and headed for Miami just after sunrise on Saturday, August 28, 1976.

We arrived in Miami on Sunday afternoon and I found the apartment building on North Bayshore Drive at North East Seventy-Ninth Street. The building was right on Biscayne Bay with a magnificent view of North Bay Village and Miami Beach.

I contacted the resident manager and was shown the apartment - a two bedroom-two bath on the third floor, facing the bay. I signed the six month lease and paid the balance of my deposit and rent.

I took Baron and Sherry to the apartment; they walked through every room, sniffing it out and approved. My furniture was scheduled to arrive on Monday, August 30. The manager had installed new wall-to-wall carpeting in a bronze color with beige draperies in every room.

I would also have to contact the phone, electric and cable companies on Monday. I would scout the neighborhood for a decent restaurant for take-out food and pick a comfortable place on the master bedroom floor to sleep with Baron and Sherry.

I unpacked my bags and the few personal items I brought with us.

Monday, August 30, was a very busy day. I first contacted my new employer, Count Tassilo Szechenyi, at his Surf Club residence. I arranged for the electric to be transferred into my name; the telephone lines and cable TV would be connected later in the day.

That was a nice welcome to Miami. In New York City, it would have taken a week, at least, to get phone and cable TV.

I had set a meeting with Count Szechenyi for lunch at the Surf Club on Tuesday. By mid-afternoon Monday, my cable and telephone lines were installed.

Mayflower Van Lines arrived with my furniture just before six o'clock. They unpacked my furniture, put my bed together and departed by 7:30, then I spent the next couple of hours arranging everything. Baron and Sherry, finally, felt at home.

I made myself a scotch and water and spent the evening relaxing. There was a vacant lot less than a block from the apartment and it was perfect for Baron and Sherry to run and play. It would work until I could find a fenced dog park. That would become our morning and evening ritual.

Count Tassilo Szechenyi was a Hungarian nobleman. He had served as Deputy Commander of the Royal Hungarian Air Force during World War II. He was fluent in seven languages and had worked as a mechanical engineer since immigrating to the United States in 1960.

Having fled Hungry at the start of the Russian invasion in 1956, he had lived in Switzerland, Cairo, London and Havana, Cuba before his move to the United States. We had met in New York where he worked as Chief Engineer for an aircraft parts manufacturer. His company hired several engineers through my company and he was impressed with our work.

He retired and moved permanently to his winter home in Miami Beach, offering me a position as his Administrative Assistant; the offer was too good to refuse. I would soon learn I'd be putting in a lot more hours than I did at my former job.

Tuesday morning, August 31, at 11:30 EST I called Dave to give him my new telephone number and address. I got the answering machine on the fourth ring; I assumed it was Dani's voice and left the information for Dave.

Saturday, September 18, Dave called as I was about to leave for a luncheon.

"Good morning, Mike ... it's me, Dave. Happy Birthday! How are you? Are you all settled in? Sorry I haven't called before; I got your message but I've been very busy and sometimes I don't want to wake you in the middle of the night there."

"Good morning, Dave. Thank you! Yes, I'm settled in. I have a nice two bedroom apartment with a balcony, right on Biscayne Bay.

"I'm adjusting to the new job and spending my free time house hunting. How are things with you? What are you doing?"

"I just finished a TV movie for NBC; it's called *Farrell*. I'm a Behavioral Psychologist ... a young boy, nine or 10-years-old, was found deep in the woods. He had apparently been abandoned by his mother, or parents, and had been raised by a pack of wild dogs. My team and I have to teach him how to be a human being. It's a little wild, pun intended," he said with a laugh.

"Any idea when it will be on TV? Did you enjoy the role? Who are your co-stars?"

"Trish Van Devere plays 'Maggie'; she's a speech therapist. A couple of brothers, Ben and Joseph Bottoms, play the 'wild boy' that we name 'Cal'. There are not really big names in the cast but I'm sure you'll recognize some of them. I'm not going to give you the whole story, don't want to ruin it for you. I'll let you know when it will be aired as soon as I'm given the date - sometime early fall, I imagine. So how did Rose Marie take it ... your moving to Miami? How are Baron and Sherry adjusting?"

"Rose Marie wasn't too pleased, but she accepted it with class. I took her to the Rainbow Room for a nice farewell dinner the Friday night before I left. I have a six month lease on this apartment, hoping I can find a house before it expires; otherwise, I have the option of renewing it. Baron and Sherry seem to love it. There's a Miami police officer and his wife on the floor above me; they have a German Shepherd so Baron and Sherry have a new friend."

"That's great ... sounds like all three of you are enjoying yourselves. How is your new job? Have you found any good restaurants ... explored the night life yet? Have you met any of those sexy Latinas yet?"

"Yeah, we are enjoying it here a lot. The job is very interesting; I am learning a lot about investments and portfolio management.

"I've been accepted for membership in a couple of the private clubs here - necessary for me to entertain the Count's bankers and lawyers. I think I am going to enjoy the work. I have a lot of responsibility.

"The Count is a fascinating man; I am sure I'll learn a lot from him. How are things going with you and Miss Connors? How is your situation with Dani?"

"Carol and I are really getting to know each other. I'm even toying with writing some lyrics so we're collaborating on writing some songs. She is really a joy to be around, Mike. I wish I had met her a couple of years ago. I would not be married now. The situation with Dani is rough at the present; I don't know how we will end up. I'm doing my best not to think about it."

"Does Dani know about Miss Connors ... your friendship?"

"Oh, yes, she knows it! It's all over town. I've told you before, Mike, this town is full of backbiting, gossip mongers ... anyone here is lucky to claim any real friends. I don't pay any attention to the crap they spread around."

"I'm glad you look at it that way. It's better for your mind than to let it bother you. I hope everything will work out for you, Dave ... whatever you decide. Does Miss Connors seem to have feelings for you? I mean, she's at least 10 years younger than you ... not that age should matter."

"I think we are developing strong feelings for each other and, you're right. Age is not a factor for either of us. All right, Mike, enough about me. I have to go but now I have your new number. I'll be in touch soon ... let you know what's going on."

"Okay, Dave ... I really appreciate the call. You take it easy and be careful."

"Good, Mike. You take it easy, too. Give Baron and Sherry a hug for me. We'll talk later."

We ended the call.

"The only thing I missed about living
in Los Angeles was sharing
drinks with Dave."

- Michael Phelps

43

I was pleased to hear from Dave; at least, I knew he received my message with my new phone number. Dave was in a positive mood and that was good. I sensed he was feeling some serious regrets that he had give Dani control of his finances and felt he had no choice but to go through with their wedding. I could not help but feel his pain and misery.

Sunday morning, September 26, my phone rang at 5:15. I knew instinctively it had to be Dave; I was right, and he was definitely inebriated.

"Mike ... it's me ... how the hell are you? Awake yet? I hope so. How are your kids?"

"I'm awake now, Dave, but it's okay. Baron and Sherry want to go to their park. How the hell are you? Sounds to me like you've had a few ... not driving, are you?"

"Yeah ... Mike, I've had a few ... since you're not here, I had to drink your share, too. No, I'm not driving; you should know better than ask me that. I'm okay ... they're closing up so I wanted to give you a quick call ... see how you're doing."

"I'm doing well. Bear and Sherry are fine ... weather is beautiful ... so, again ... HOW are YOU, really?"

"Health-wise, I'm fine ... work-wise, I'm fine ... personally, things are all screwed up."

"Well, since you know what the problems are, then you are half way there to finding a solution. You know, you are not going to find the answers at the bottom of an empty scotch bottle."

"Damn it, Mike! I know that! That's why I called you ... just needed you to tell me that. I'm just kidding, Mike. I know you are right. I just can't understand why ... everything else is great. I do anything to make her happy and it just seems whatever I do ... it's not enough."

"Who are we talking about, Dave? Dani or Miss Connors?" I was confused for a minute, then realized he had to be talking about Dani.

"Dani ... Mike, I have tried and tried ... with Dani. Mike, it is simple; it's Dani's way or no way! Hell, I work hard ... damn hard ... all I ask is for a little time to relax. I'd much rather come home and have a few drinks and relax in my own environment. Now, I finish work, have a shower, a few drinks in the 'Bullet', head home and realize I want another drink before I get there. Hell, it's just like I'm in the same situation I was the last few years with Ellie.

"I'm considering leaving her ... but then again, there are so many things to consider. I want to make this marriage work; I don't like failure and, if I go through another divorce ... that's double failure ... and, my God ... the COST!"

"Dave, I can imagine how you feel and you have my deepest sympathy, but that is of no help to you. Have you ... this is stupid, but have you sat down with her cold sober and talked - explained your feelings, how tired you are when you come home from work, that all you want to do is relax and spend some quiet time with her?"

"Yeah, Mike ... I've done that ... at least 100 times over. Sometimes I feel everything is my fault ... my moods. Seldom do I lose my temper and get involved in an argument ... but it happens."

"Are you still seeing Miss Connors? Do you think Dani is jealous ... has she said anything?"

"Hell, yes, she's jealous - and she made sure I know it! Yes, I'm still seeing Carol ... with her I can relax and enjoy the time we're together. I don't have to put on a happy face and go party with people I don't care to be around. I can really be myself ... don't have to put on an act. She likes me just the way I am. She even laughs at my jokes."

"Dave, I feel for you ... the only thing I can suggest is you talk to your lawyer before you do anything drastic. The way you sound to me, you would be better off with Carol Connors than you are with your current wife."

"Yeah ... I know, Mike. I'm going to. Enough of that crap. I'll be doing a guest shot on *Dinah's* - you know, *Dinah Shore's Show*. We'll be taping this week; I'll let you know when it is set for airing. Just in case I don't, watch for it, okay?"

"I will, Dave ... thanks for giving me a heads-up. I won't miss it. What else is going on?"

"I'm looking over some scripts Abby sent ... nothing much else is happening. I'm sorry I hit you with this crap about Dani. You may not understand but I feel better just ranting about it sometimes ... at least I can trust you ... and you're a good listener." Dave laughed but I knew he was being sincere.

"Well, Dave ... just be careful. You've worked too hard to just throw everything away. You know ... you can yell at me about this crap anytime you want, for all the good it does you."

"I know, Mike ... thanks. I'll give you a call soon. You take it easy ... a hug for your kids." The line went dead.

I went to the kitchen and turned on the coffee pot. I gave the dogs a morning cookie. They knew we would go to their park after I had my first cup of coffee. I turned the television on for the news.

Dave's call bothered me. He sounded as if he had passed his acknowledged limit of alcohol.

I knew alcohol had the effect of a stimulant in the brain but, at a certain limit, it became a depressant, which could have devastating consequences for one with serious problems he or she was dealing with in life. Dave was again dealing with serious problems in his personal life.

I was in awe at how he could be married to a strikingly beautiful woman, whose flawless skin and curvaceous body could have been the inspiration for the extraordinarily successful Barbie Doll and be having an affair that recently became public knowledge to an equally beautiful, very talented singer and songwriter, yet be miserable!

I could not help but wonder what Dani was thinking ... feeling ... about Dave. I did not doubt she loved him and he loved her but, what their mutual love was based on, escaped me. Dani had legal claim to one of the most recognizable, most bankable, hardest working leading men in Hollywood. WHY could they not be happy together?

In every conversation we had, I never doubted that Dave was a monogamous man; he worked very hard to make his marriage to Ellie succeed, he worked hard on his relationship with Rosemary and I had no doubt he had given his marriage to Dani everything he could. He was scared to death of another divorce ... another point of failure, at least in his mind.

I knew Dave had no other projects he would be starting any time soon. I hoped he would be able to relax, unwind and focus on his personal affairs.

I would hope and I would pray the next time I would speak with him, he would have soothed things over with Dani or made a decision to talk with his lawyers.

44

Sunday morning, October 3, Dave called at 11:15. I had just finished reading *The Miami Herald*.

"Good morning, Mike. It's me, Dave. How are you? How's the weather there?"

"Good, Dave ... everything here is great. The weather is sunny and around 78 degrees right now. How about you? How are things going? I haven't seen anything about you on the *Dinah Shore Show* yet."

"I'm good, Mike ... the weather here is beautiful. The *Dinah* segment hasn't aired; I don't have an exact date yet, but I'll let you know when it will air. I wish you had waited a couple of months before moving to Miami. I'm going to Philadelphia ... co-hosting Mike Douglas' show for a whole week. Now, if you hadn't moved down there, we could have gotten together, had a few drinks, like old times."

"Damn it, Dave! Why couldn't you have done that in August ... before I moved? That really pisses me off! Maybe I can fly up and spend a day or two; I'll check and find out."

"No, Mike ... you don't need to do that. Taking time off from your new job would not look good for you ... and I know you would not want to leave Bear and Sherry in a kennel. It's okay.

"We'll get together when I have reason to be in Miami. I'm looking forward to it, though ... gives me a chance to be away from the rat race here."

"I'm hesitant to ask, Dave, but is everything all right with you and Dani? Have you smoothed things over? What about Carol?"

"I don't know, Mike. I swear, if I didn't know better, I'd think she's bi-polar or something. I never know when I wake up what kind of mood she'll be in; she's like 'Mrs. Jekyll & Mrs. Hyde'. I'm trying, Mike - that's all I can say. As for Carol ... yes, I'm still seeing her. I wish I could spend all of my time with her. If I were not in the situation I am, I would be the happiest man on earth; with her I feel alive again and I feel appreciated!"

"Well, have you done anything to take control of your finances? Have you talked with your lawyers? Actually, before all of that, have YOU made any decision yet? Are you better off with Dani or without her, and are you willing to pay the price for your freedom again?"

"Better off with or without ... that's a tough question, Mike. I don't have the answer ... at least, not yet. Am I willing to pay the price for my freedom again ... tougher question! You know, Dani has so many attributes and talents; she's a great cook, great hostess. She gave up her career, which no doubt would have been terrific; she is a great actress. All her friends are in the business but most are so 'plastic', it's like they are always on stage ... do you understand?"

"Yeah, Dave ... I do understand. I'm not one to give you advice but I can tell you that, with all of your public obligations, all the stress and requirements of your work, you do not need to have your personal emotions going up and down from day to day! It's like you are a yo-yo. Dave, for a man in your shoes, that is no way to live."

"Thanks, Mike! I know what you are saying and I know you are right. I know I have my faults, too. I try my damnedest to keep them in check and I know I can be moody ... really moody, but I try my best not to take my frustrations out on Dani, or anyone.

"I don't expect her or anyone to bow down to me and treat me like a king, but I do want to be treated like a man ... just an ordinary guy."

"Well, let's hope a week in Philadelphia will do you both good; you know what they say, 'absence makes the heart grow fonder.' I hope it does for both of you. Then, you have to give some serious thought about your relationship with Carol. You don't want to mislead or hurt her, I'm sure of that – but as long as you're married to Dani, that sort of leaves Carol twisting in the wind ... and that's not fair to her, or you."

"I know, Mike. I have a lot of introspection to do and it has to be done soon. Oh, after I finish with Douglas, I may be going over to Japan for a few days. Abby is working on a commercial deal for me."

"Japan? A commercial? Is it for Excedrin? I think it's funny; you had never used Excedrin until I told you my secret of never having a hangover ... now you are their best spokesman," I said, then laughed.

"Well, Mike, you were right. I've not had a hangover since I started using them. The commercial in Japan isn't for Excedrin; it's for a men's clothing company."

"Well, let me know. I hope you can have some fun and find time to relax a little while you're doing the Douglas show."

"I will, Mike. So you take it easy and I'll give you a call while I'm in Philadelphia, okay?"

"Thanks for the call, Dave. You take it easy, too ... and give me a call when you can."

"All right! We'll talk soon." The call ended.

I could tell Dave was feeling anger and depression because of his marital discord and, perhaps, pressure he was feeling over his extra-marital relationship with Carol Connors.

I had no doubt he was sincere and felt complete happiness with Carol. She obviously was not with him because of his fame or his fortune.

I do not think the age difference between them mattered to her and Dave was realizing a younger woman could be genuinely attracted to him, both physically and mentally.

There could be no doubt that IF Dave decided to file for a divorce from Dani, it would be costly. However, under the California community property law, he would not be hit as hard as he had been with his divorce from Ellie.

I could not imagine how he could be so miserable when he should be among the happiest men on the planet. In my opinion, David Janssen deserved to be treated like a king by his wife.

45

Dave called me on Sunday, November 7, just as I was going to bed; it was almost one o'clock in the morning.

"Good evening, Mike ... it's me, Dave."

"Hi, Dave! It's good to hear from you ... where are you?"

"I'm back in LA. Did you have a chance to watch any of the Douglas shows?"

"Actually, I'm sorry to say, I didn't. I tried to tape them on my VCR but I don't know how to work it; it didn't work. Do they show them in re-runs? I did see *Stalk the Wild Child* last Wednesday evening. I thought it was great ... the little kid was outstanding. Is it based on a true story?"

"I really don't know; I think it may have been. I think they do re-runs of Mike's shows when he goes on vacation, but I don't know if they will be from my week with him. Anyway, it was fun.

"I went to Japan, did the commercials, had some great food and now I'm back. I'll be a guest on Johnny Carson's show this coming Friday; we'll show a clip of *Two Minute Warning* ... hope you can watch it."

"Oh, that one! You can count on it! As a matter of fact, I'm going to go see it Saturday afternoon. It opens here on Friday but I have a function I have to attend."

"Good ... make sure you give me your objective opinion."

"I will ... you can count on it. So how is everything else going for you? How is your love life?"

"Ah ... sometimes I get lucky. At home it is like being in a cage with a tiger!" Dave said and let out a sincere laugh. I did not want to push the issue but took it to mean he was happy when he was with Carol Connors and guarded when at home.

"So, do you have any other films or television projects coming up?"

"NO ... not until after the first of the year. December is a time for me to unwind ... clear the chaos from my brain. I'm looking at several scripts Abby sent but I'm not really concentrating on making any decisions right now. I'll keep you advised. Don't worry! Do you talk with Rose Marie? I wonder how she is doing ... without you there? How are Bear and Sherry? How is your work; have you taken a good hold of it yet?"

"Well, there are plenty of re-runs on television and, now, the new film ... so your fans won't forget what you look like. Keep me up-to-date when you pick something to do. Yeah, I call Rose Marie and she calls me; I mean we do miss each other, but this opportunity was too good to pass up.

"Bear and Sherry love it down here. I don't have much time to get out and explore the night life but I will in due course. I love the work! The Count is really interesting, a learned man. He has great stories of the war and Europe before, during and after Hitler. I feel blessed and privileged to have met, and now work for, him. His wife, Countess Helene, is a little too pretentious for my taste but that's okay."

"When I have a chance to get down there, I'd enjoy meeting them. I'm going to head home now so you take it easy and we'll talk soon. Don't forget to watch Johnny Carson Friday."

"Okay, Dave. I hope you find a reason to make it to Miami. You would really enjoy meeting the Count and Countess. I don't know about the Countess, but Count Szechenyi is a fan of yours. He loved *The Fugitive* and *Harry O*. I'll see you Friday on *The Tonight Show*. Call when you can." We ended the call.

Dave sounded to be in very good spirits and sounded as though he was taking full advantage of resting and relaxing. He did not go into any detail how his marriage was faring at this time but just his one insinuation about living with a tiger told me that their relationship was still tenuous at best.

I did not hear from Dave again until Sunday morning, December 19. I had read brief articles in the New York newspapers that there was trouble in his marriage.

"Mike, good morning! It's me, Dave. I hope I didn't wake you. How is everything going for you? Did you have a nice Thanksgiving?"

"Everything here is fine. Yes, I had Thanksgiving dinner at the Surf Club with the Count and Countess. How about with you? Did you have a nice Thanksgiving?"

"Not really ... not that it matters. I moved out of the apartment. I'm staying in a hotel for the time being. I think I'm ready to bite the bullet and get out of this trap I put myself in."

"Uh ... I'm sorry to hear that Dave - sorry for the situation you are facing. Have you spoken with your lawyers ... your bankers? If not, you better do it quick - protect as much of your money as you can, legally, I mean. How is Dani reacting?"

"Right now she's being a BITCH! I've been talking with Paul, my lawyer; he is mapping a strategy out ... nothing has been set in stone, as yet. I just need some time and space."

"Well ... uh ... uh are you still seeing Carol?"

"HELL, YES! She is the reason I moved out. Right now, she is keeping me sane ... helping me get through this nightmare."

"Why don't you move in with her? Why stay in a hotel?"

"I learned my lesson. You may recall Ellie named Rosemary as a co-respondent in our divorce - put Rosemary through hell. I will not take the chance and let that happen to Carol. She is too sweet. She doesn't deserve any crap Dani would throw at her. I'm looking for some property to buy - maybe in Malibu ... definitely a house and definitely on the beach."

"But wouldn't that be part of community property, IF you were to get a divorce? Can't you down size a bit and buy *Harry O's* beach house?" I asked, attempting some levity in his untenable situation.

"No, I need more space than *Harry* had and Paul would make certain it would not be community property. Don't get me wrong, Mike! I don't know if I'm going for a divorce yet or not. I just need some time, space ... some peace and solitude!"

"I understand that, Dave. Why don't you just jump on a plane and fly to Miami for a couple of weeks? I have plenty of room ... Bear would love seeing his 'Uncle Dave', and you could meet Sherry, too."

"That's a good idea and I would do it in a New York minute, but I signed on for another television movie of the week and we start filming next month."

"Oh ... that's good to hear. What's it about? Who will be in it with you? By the way, I saw *Mayday at 40,000 Feet* a few weeks ago - terrific movie! Of course, you were great!"

"Thanks, Mike; I'm glad you enjoyed it. The one I just signed on for is about an alcoholic aerospace engineer ... upper middle class, beautiful wife, couple of kids ... he loses his job but hides it from his family ... falls into the bottle and turns into a real son-of-a-bitch ... wife tries to save him from himself ...and save their marriage. That's it in a nutshell."

"That sounds like a very powerful role for you, Dave. Who will be in it with you? Do you play the alcoholic?" I wished I had not asked the last part of my question.

"Yeah, I think I can play a pretty damn good drunk, don't you? Angie Dickinson plays my wife. I don't know who will be playing my sons; they're young kids."

"Angie Dickinson? 'Police Woman'? Wow! I love her! She is a great actress! Man, you are one lucky guy! By the way, I went to see *Two Minute Warning* a few weeks ago ... terrific! I loved it ... just hope there isn't some nut running around LA who will try and do a copycat of the plot. You were great in your character."

"Yeah, I know it too, Mike. Angie is a really fun gal." He laughed. "I'm glad you saw the movie; hey, if there is a nut out there, don't worry, the LAPD will stop him. Okay, Mike, I have to cut this short. I'll give you a call in a few days, when the dust settles. You take care."

"Thanks for the call, Dave. Take it easy and be careful. Don't make any decisions you may regret."

"Yeah, I know. Hey, if we don't talk before, I sure hope you have a very nice Christmas. Talk later."

Dave seemed to be in good spirits, considering what he was going through with Dani. I was certain Carol was helping him feel desired without placing any kind of demands on him. Considering everything he had said about Carol Connors, I was hoping in my mind that he would get a divorce and see where his relationship with Carol Connors would go.

"It's hard to be in a contentious
situation with someone you love,
especially during the holidays."

- Michael Phelps to David Janssen

46

Christmas Day I was surprised to hear from Dave just as I was making my first cup of coffee at a little past five.

"Merry Christmas, Mike! It's me, Dave. I hope you're awake."

"Yes, making my coffee ... Merry Christmas to you, too. How are you? Where are you?" I asked. He sounded as if he was in a bar and close to his self-imposed limit for alcohol.

"I'm in Malibu ... going back to LA in a few hours."

"How are things with you and Dani? What are your plans for the day?"

"I won't be going to the apartment. Mother invited me to a family dinner - not going to do that either. I'm planning to have dinner with Carol. What are your plans?"

"I'll take the kids to the park and then let them open their gifts from the Doggie Santa ... and relax. I'll be taking some people to The Jockey Club for dinner then come home and relax the rest of the evening ... watch some TV. So, have you made any decision about your situation with Dani?"

"Sounds like you will have a nice day. No, I took her to dinner, sort of an early celebration for her birthday; she was icy. I'm not sure what we will be doing. I saw in one of the gossip columns she's telling people she bought me a house in Malibu. That's bullshit! I'M BUYING a beach house ... for ME!"

"Congratulations! At least you will have YOUR OWN place, but doesn't the community property statutes still apply, if you actually get a divorce?"

"Paul will work all of that out; there would be a 'give-and-take' negotiation. I'm sure I would keep the house; she can have the condo. Too soon to even think about that."

"Well, I just hope things will work out for you ... the way that is best for you. I just feel bad for you; it is hard to be in a contentious situation with someone you love, especially during the holidays."

"Yes, it is hell, but I'm just going to put it out of my mind ... let her make the next move. I don't feel I've done anything wrong towards her. I'll enjoy being with Carol."

"I'm glad to hear that you won't be sitting alone in a dark, dingy bar making love to a bottle of scotch," I said, then laughed.

"No, I won't be doing that; you know I don't go to dingy bars, anyway. I'll be with someone I can relax and enjoy my time with. What are your plans for New Year's Eve?"

"I have to go to a gala at The Surf Club with the Count and Countess - about 600 people, black tie affair."

"Sounds like you are being thrust into the kind of upper crust lifestyle ... do you enjoy it?"

"Actually, Dave, I don't. Most of the people are old enough to be my parents or grandparents; they are all what they call here, 'old money' ... a lot of General Motors money. Most seem like nice people but they seem detached from the real world. It seems to me that at all of the charity balls I have to go to with the Count, most of the people make huge donations, but not in a genuine spirit; it depends on their tax situation for the year. That disgusts me!"

"I know exactly what you're saying, Mike. I advise you to just smile and suck it up. Keep in mind, though, some of them may be sincere and genuine in their giving."

"Oh, I know that, Dave. It just seems to me that the parties are for them and the booze flows like coming from a fountain. They usually last about two, maybe two and a half hours and then, when I leave, I stop at my favorite bar and have a couple of drinks to unwind before going home."

"Ah ... I think you learned that from me. I know where you're coming from," Dave said, then laughed.

"YES! I learned that from you, Dave and, finally, I understand. Of course, I don't have a beautiful wife to go home to but Bear and Sherry are happy to see me, especially when I bring them a steak or something." I laughed.

"Yeah, Mike, but you have to remember ... beauty is only skin deep; it's what's inside the person that matters. Have you met anyone ... socially, someone like Rose Marie?"

"Not yet ... haven't had much free time yet. I'm still learning my way around Miami. I will, eventually, I'm sure. I still speak with Rose Marie and I will have business trips up to New York so I am in no rush. When will you start your new TV movie?"

"In a couple of weeks ... I'll let you know. I am looking forward to it; a few weeks of intense work will do wonders for my psyche."

"I bet it will! Make sure you tell Miss Dickinson that I am a huge fan. Hell, I'd give up everything to marry her."

"Yeah ... I know you would! Take my advice: stay where you are! All right, Mike! They're going to throw me out of here. I'll give you a call when I have more time. Happy New Year to you."

"Thanks, Dave ... the same to you ... and be careful."

Dave was going through hell even though he was good at masking it. I really felt bad for him. I hated to see anyone having problems of any kind, especially during this time of the year, and problems with a loved one were the worst imaginable.

He still sounded as though he was following my advice of taking everything in the moment and keeping his mind in a calm state. I was sure Dave had brief moments where he would lose control of his temper but, as he had said, they were very brief and he would leave so as not to make matters worse. I believed him! That was part of his character; Dave was a 'lover - not a fighter.'

David Janssen's name was recognized throughout many parts of the world but it never went to his head. He always appreciated everyone involved in bringing a television show, movie or film to life.

47
~1977~

The year 1977 was welcomed by the entire world with countless millions making resolutions, only to forget them a day or two later; I was one of those people.

January was unusually warm in Miami but, looking at the bitter cold and snow in New York City, I was happy to be here. I saw brief mentions of Dave and Dani and, to my surprise, Dave and Carol in the Miami newspapers and fan magazines. It appeared the consensus had been reached by the media: Dave would be headed for divorce court soon. I would wait to hear the truth from him.

Monday, January 3, was the start of the new year for business in Miami. It promised to be a chaotic day, if judged by the NBC 6 Traffic report. I was leaving my apartment just before nine o'clock when my phone rang.

"Mike, it's me, Dave ... glad I caught you. Happy New Year! How are you doing?"

"Good, Dave ... what's wrong?"

"Nothing ... why?"

"You said you were glad you caught me. I just thought maybe there was something wrong. Happy New Year to you, too ... how are you?"

"No, I'm glad I caught you because I haven't spoken with you for several days and I took the chance to call you before I left for the studio. I just wanted to touch base and see how you're doing."

"That's nice of you, Dave, thanks. I'm good ... just leaving for my office. You're going to the studio? What do you have in the works?"

"We have preliminary run-throughs for *A Sensitive, Passionate Man*. We start production sometime next week."

"That's great! I can't wait to see it ... any idea when it will be on TV?"

"Not yet. It'll take a few months for all the technical stuff, adding the sound track - you know."

"Why does it take so long? You filmed an episode a week for *The Fugitive* and *Harry O* and they were shown almost immediately after filming. This is a TV movie, not for a theatre - seems to me they can have it ready in a week or two. Why does it take months?"

"This will be a two hour movie, a little less actually, but the network has a lot of commercials to insert. While filming, there is no soundtrack for the music; that is all added. They have to edit the film, frame by frame ... all of this takes time."

"Okay, now I understand. I'm glad I am not in your business. I could never grasp all the technical stuff involved. When I see the show on TV, it looks so seamless, as if what you see is happening in an even flow of dialogue, expressions, the scenery ... even when you go from one scene to another. It just looks like you filmed it all in the hour or so it is shown on TV. I guess that's why actors and everyone else involved are paid the big bucks."

"Yeah, finally, you got it. I think you are right though, Mike. I think most people think the same way you do, that we just get on a set and speak the dialogue, have the expressions, the body movements, and we walk off the set and ... bingo ... it's done, finished ... ready for the screen," he said and let out a genuine laugh.

"Now I'm going to have to be careful not to look for flaws when I watch something. I prefer my way of thinking ... of course, keeping in mind, you really do work hard to make it look so real."

"It's not just the actors, Mike. The entire crew - everyone from the director, camera operators, lighting, set decorators, sound people, wardrobe, make-up ... especially the make-up people - they all really work damn hard to make every scene as realistic as possible. One single scene, maybe lasting two minutes, can take several hours to do ... several 'takes' before the director is satisfied.

"He's not only looking at the facial expressions, body movements, listening to how the actor says his or her lines, the right inflections on any given word, the right body movement and facial expressions; he is looking at the lighting, the movement around the set ... everything has to meet his satisfaction before he approves and we move on."

"Yeah, Dave, I know. I got that when I watched you and the rest of the actors on *The Fugitive* set that day. I know it isn't easy for any of the actors ... but YOU always make it look so easy, so real and so natural. I have to compliment you on that point. I know I could never do any of that ... hell, I couldn't even be an 'extra' walking down the street. I'd probably trip and fall," I said. We both laughed.

"Okay, Mike, that's your lesson in film making for the day. I have to run. I'll give you a call later in the week. You take it easy."

"Thanks for the call, Dave. You take it easy and let me know what's going on with you ... before I read some BS in the media."

"I will, Mike ... talk later."

Dave was in a great mood during this conversation. I had no doubt it was because he was starting this new project.

I knew he was always tense a few days before starting work on a new film or television show but, when he moved onto a set, the cameras started rolling and he interacted with the other actors in the scene, his tenseness and fears seemed to disappear.

I think it's because, in his mind, he became the character he was portraying and he, David Janssen, was not even there.

I knew in my mind that I would not be hearing from Dave for a few days.

When Dave started a new project he diverted all his concentration to the project. He left very little time for stopping at a favorite bar for drinks after leaving the studio; he would rather make himself a few drinks in his 'Silver Bullet', sometimes inviting a cast or crew member. He would then study the script for the next day's shooting schedule.

He shunned parties or even relaxing with friends. All that was important to him was being able to give his very best on screen. He always did that for his fans.

On Sunday, February 27, I was surprised at 5:35 in the morning when Dave called.

"Good morning, Mike. I know it's Sunday ... are you awake?"

"Of course, Dave! Baron and Sherry wake me the minute dawn breaks. How are you? Where are you? Did you finish the movie?"

"Yes, our part is finished. I even got Carol some work for the movie. We've had a great time."

"You got Carol a part in the movie?"

"No ... no, WE wrote the title song; it's called *My Sensitive, Passionate Man.* I wrote the lyrics and Carol wrote the music. Wait 'til you hear it! I think it's a beautiful song."

"Whoa! Wait a minute! YOU wrote the song? I didn't know you could write songs. That must be hard as hell."

"No, it isn't, Mike. It is just choosing the right words, string them together ... the hard part is writing the music for the words to make a song."

"Okay, I know you are a multi-talented man. I would not even try to write anything, especially a song. So it will be in the movie? Carol got paid for it?"

"Yes, it will be the theme song for the movie, and yes, we got paid for it," Dave laughed. "We've written a couple of other songs as well. I write the words and Carol writes the music. *A Beagle's Plea for X-Mas* ... you'd like that one."

"Let me get this straight ... YOU and Carol are writing songs? Who will be singing them? Carol?"

"We haven't gotten into that yet ... hey, I can sing! I took lessons," Dave said and let out a hearty laugh. Personally, I felt his voice was very distinct and perfect for a character's speaking voice, but singing? Dave singing? I was amazed and would hold judgment until I actually heard him sing. I admit I was laughing inside; I just could not think of Dave Janssen being a singer.

"All right, Dave! I'll reserve my judgment until I hear you actually sing." I laughed.

"Here, I'll sing you a verse ..."

"NO ... NO ... no, Dave! Not now! It's too early in the morning here. Just let me know when the record comes out ... I'll buy it," I said, then laughed.

"Okay, Mike ... but I can sing. Carol told me I have a great voice, so I must. You will see! I may change my career. Who knows?"

"I just can't see comparing you to Elvis or Frank Sinatra ... maybe Louis Armstrong," I said, joking.

"Yeah ... 'Satchmo' ... thanks. Listen, I have to go. I'll be in touch soon. You take care."

"Okay, Dave ... thanks for the update. Let me know when the movie will air. You take it easy, too."

I felt a little guilty when reflecting on my comments to him about his singing talent. I was impressed when he told me he had actually collaborated with Carol Connors in writing songs and would be anxiously waiting to hear the song in the upcoming NBC movie.

I failed to ask him who would be singing the song in the movie soundtrack; it was obvious by the title it could not be a male singer, so I was left wondering if it would be Carol or Angie Dickinson. I would make a note to ask the next time we spoke. I hoped it would be Carol. I loved her voice!

In the presence of Johnny Carson, David Janssen
could always relax and be himself.

48

Sunday morning, April 3, Dave called me at 4:30.

"Good morning, Mike ... sorry to wake you. It's me, Dave."

"I know, Dave. I can tell by your voice. How are you?"

"I'm okay, and you? I'm sorry if I woke you. I haven't had a chance to call you lately so I decided this would be a good time, before I grab some sleep myself. I know you're always up early anyway. So, is everything okay with you? How are you doing with your job?"

"Good, Dave. Everything is good. What are you doing? Any word on when *A Sensitive, Passionate Man* will be on TV?"

"I don't know yet. I understand everything is finished; they just have to wait on the programming honchos to fit it into their schedule ... a few more weeks, maybe. I'll be going to South Africa soon ... doing a film with Richard Harris and Ann Turkel."

"What is this one about?"

"A luxury cruise ship is hijacked in the middle of the Caribbean, a lot of rich passengers ... then the plot thickens, gets complicated. I'll let you know more when we're finished."

"Will Dani be going with you?"

"No ... are you serious? I need time alone ... this will be all work, no play ... no wives or girlfriends."

"I understand ... how long will you be down there? Have you given anymore thought to what you're going to do about your situation? Have you talked with your lawyers?"

"I'll be there for about a month, give or take a week. Yeah, I've talked with Paul ... no matter what I do, it will cost me a bundle ... that's why I have to work as much as I can. Now I am just taking one day at a time and trying not to think about it. How about you? Have you met anyone you think you'd want to spend the rest of your life with?"

"Not yet - I have time. What about you and Carol? What does she say about your situation with Dani?"

"She is a perfect lady, Mike ... she does not ask any questions. She knows what I am dealing with and she does all she can to keep my mind off it and keep me happy when I'm with her. I like that ... Mike, she is the one woman I really love. I have to do something soon, I know that."

"Well, at least you will have a few weeks away from the pressure. Just take it easy and think. Make sure your plan will work the way you want before you do anything."

"I know, Mike. Don't worry about me! I'm a survivor. So, if you don't hear from me for a while, you know why. I'll touch base with you when I get back. You take it easy and take good care of Bear and Sherry."

"I always do, Dave. You take care and definitely give me a call when you can."

I would not hear from Dave until Sunday afternoon, June 12, 1977.

"Hey, Mike! It's me, Dave. How are you? How are Baron and Sherry?"

"Welcome home, stranger! They're fine. I take it you are back in the good old U. S. of A."

"Yeah, I've been back a few weeks, have been busy as hell. I haven't had time to give you a call ... sorry about that."

"Well, I saw Angie Dickinson on *Good Morning America* a few weeks ago promoting *A Sensitive, Passionate Man.* I thought you would be there. Anyway, I saw the movie on TV and it was mind-blowing! You were unbelievable and Angie was awesome as your wife. The kids were so believable - great little actors."

"Thanks, Mike ... I am glad you liked it. I enjoyed doing it with Angie. Everyone involved was just a great bunch of people to work with."

"I don't know if you saw it; the ratings were outstanding. How in the hell you played some of those scenes ... like throwing Angie in your swimming pool ... the close-ups of your eyes; they looked really bloodshot. You looked really drunk!"

"That's because I was! Don't tell anyone, but I had a few drinks to get me in the mood for some of the scenes ... that way I knew it would be real on film," he said, then laughed.

"All I can say is, you really pulled it off. I think it is one of your best performances."

"Thanks again! Maybe when I'm 70 or 80, they'll cast me as a homeless wino or drunk." He laughed again.

"I don't really see that ever happening ... maybe an alcoholic millionaire banker or something, but not a homeless wino or drunk." I laughed. "So ... should I even ask ... how is the situation with Dani? How is Carol?"

"The situation with Dani ... ah ... we are both working on it. A divorce ... it is out of the question - right now, at least. Carol decided we should back off until I make a final decision; the way it has been, it just isn't fair to her. That is what hurts me most but I know she is right and, for now, at least, I have to try to make this marriage work."

"How is Dani reacting?"

"She is being an angel ... for now. I'm just going to be good and try to make this work out. If it doesn't, for whatever reason, within a year I will make a choice."

"Okay ... so tell me, how did you enjoy making the film in Africa? You had some major stars with you. Richard Harris and Ann Turkel - they are very good actors."

"Yes, it was a pleasure working with both. The film, it was all right; it's called *Golden Rendezvous.* I am glad it's over; I don't want to do it again. Africa is a beautiful country but it's just not for me. I'll let you know when the movie will be in a theatre near you." He laughed at his intended pun.

"I'll definitely go see it and let you know my expert critic's opinion," I responded with a laugh.

"Good, Mike. I appreciate that. Listen, I have to go, but I'll be in touch. Take it easy. Give Bear and Sherry a hug for me."

"Okay, Dave ... thanks for bringing me up to speed. You take it easy and I hope things work out with Dani - although, right now, I am feeling bad for Carol."

"Yeah, I will, Mike. As for Carol, thanks ... I feel the same way but who knows what will happen? We'll talk later."

Dave sounded good, although when he spoke of Carol, I detected an emotion of genuine sorrow. I felt he would much rather be with Carol and divorced from Dani. He gave me the impression that, although Dani was acting like an angel, it was HE who had to do the work to make their marriage work.

49

Sunday, July 3, was a magnificent day in Miami with low humidity and temperatures hovering around 89 degrees. I was surprised Dave called just as I walked in the door from the supermarket.

"Mike, it's me, Dave. Am I interrupting you?"

"No, Dave ... I just got in from the store. How are you doing?"

"I just got out of the hospital a few days ago. I'm fine. How are you doing; how are your kids?"

"Hospital? WHY? Are you sure you are okay? Baron and Sherry are fine. Tell me about YOU!"

"It was nothing. I, finally, had another surgery on my knee; it had really been bothering me and the orthopedic surgeon said it was time to have surgery again, so I did it. It does feel a lot better so I guess the surgery was a success."

"Did Dani visit you in the hospital? How long were you in the hospital?"

"Dani went with me; she stayed there while they did the surgery. I was only in there a couple of days, came home and I'm supposed to stay off my legs for a week or so. Things are going well with Dani and me, I am happy to say."

"That's good to hear! I hope it will be nothing but wedded bliss for you guys from now on. Have you any new films or television shows lined up? When can you go back to work?"

"Actually, I do. I have a guest role on *Police Story*; we'll start shooting next week."

"I love that show ... very realistic, unlike *Dragnet*. Do you play a good guy or a bad guy?"

"I'm a good guy, an LAPD Sergeant ..."

"Don't tell me you're playing a role like Sergeant Joe Friday, working the day shift out of Hollywood Division," I interrupted him. We both laughed.

"No, I'll be a uniformed sergeant. I don't think Joe ever wore a uniform on *Dragnet*. I think you will like the episode. You know a cop isn't supposed to take anything personal – well, I do."

"Okay, Dave ... don't tell me anymore. I want to see it for myself. Do you know when it will air?"

"No ... we haven't even started shooting. I'll let you know. Don't worry! Okay, Mike, I have to go. You take it easy. Give Bear and Sherry a hug for me ... I'll be in touch soon."

"Okay, Dave ... thanks for calling. Stay off your leg and be sure to let me know about *Police Story*. You take it easy, too!"

"Thanks, Mike! I will ... talk later."

I was happy to hear Dave in such a good mood, the way he sounded so positive about Dani. Perhaps his having surgery gave Dani time to think he was an ordinary man and he needed her. I had no doubt Dave loved her and would do anything to please her and make their marriage a happy one. There certainly was no reason it could not be wedded bliss for them.

He was very successful, handsome and charming. She was beautiful, charismatic, intelligent and an excellent housewife with extraordinary cooking and hostess skills.

Most of the marriages that failed were because of infidelity on the part of a spouse or financial problems.

Dave had been monogamous during his marriage; his affair with Carol began *after* he separated from Dani and was seriously contemplating a divorce.

I had the opinion Dave was driven to his brief affair with Susanne Pleshette years earlier by Ellie's insane jealousy and attempts to control every facet of his life. His affair with Carol was perhaps caused by Dani's demands for him to party non-stop as he did in his 'Playboy' years, before he married Ellie.

Perhaps Dani failed to notice or take into consideration how physically and mentally drained he was when he came home from a long day at the studio.

I knew his character was to be faithful to his wife; he viewed divorce as a personal failure. Dave also had made clear he bore his share of responsibility for his marital problems, in both marriages.

David Janssen readily admitted to any faults he had. He always claimed to be a hard man to live with, especially if he wasn't working or didn't enjoy a project he was working on.

50

Dave's next call came on Saturday morning, August 27, at 5:30.

"Mike, it's me, Dave. Good morning ... please tell me I didn't wake you. I'm on my way home - thought I could catch you before you take your kids to the park. How are you?"

He sounded in good spirits and almost completely sober.

"You didn't wake me, Dave. I'm fine ... having coffee before I take them to the park. How are you doing? How is your knee? Did you film the *Police Story* episode? How are you and Dani doing?"

"My knee is still a little sore ... not bad. Yes, we did the *Police Story*, which I'm not too happy about. Dani and I are getting along great. I'll be going on location to New Orleans in a week or so for a movie for television."

"First, I'm happy to hear you and Dani are doing well; second, I'm glad your knee is healing; third, WHY aren't you happy with the *Police Story* episode and, last, what movie are you doing in New Orleans?"

"Well, as for *Police Story*, my knee was really hurting and, not wanting to pop those damn pain pills the doc prescribed for me, I sort of self-medicated in between takes ... maybe a little too much - at least for Jerry, the director. I'm glad it's over. Took a lot longer to shoot it than expected."

"What do you mean you 'self-medicated'? You didn't have a few too many drinks, did you?"

"Let's just say I had a few ... it's finished and, when you see it, you tell me if I look drunk ... okay? I mean, this is the season premier; it's a two hour show ... took a lot of time to get it right. I'll wait for you to see it give me your opinion, okay?"

"Good, Dave ... I won't miss it and I'll be sure to give you my honest opinion of your performance. What is the movie in New Orleans about?"

"It's called *Superdome* ... appropriate enough, since there is a sniper running loose in the Superdome on Super Bowl Sunday."

"Wait a minute, Dave! Didn't you just do that ... *Two Minute Warning,* a sniper in the Los Angeles Coliseum?"

"Yeah ... but that was a feature film; this is a television movie. There are enough differences in the script. Besides, I need to work," he said, then laughed.

"How long will you be in New Orleans? Will Dani be going with you?"

"No, Dani's staying home; I'll only be there for about a week or so."

"Do you have anything lined up after that?"

"I'm looking at a script for a feature film; it'll mean I have to go on location overseas ... Rome, Athens and a few other places. I haven't decided if I will do it ... but the pay is good, so I may just do it."

"Let me know when you decide. What's it about? Who will be your co-stars?"

"Arthur Kennedy and Catherine Bach. You should know her; she was in *Thunderbolt and Lightfoot* with Clint Eastwood. Did you see the movie?"

"Yes, that was a couple of years ago ... it was good. Eastwood is a dynamic actor. I think Beau or Jeff Bridges was in it, too."

"Yeah, it was Jeff Bridges. I think she's a very good, young actress so I'm seriously considering the role. It's a spy movie about a CIA operative who is writing a tell-all book; CIA doesn't want him to do it ... it's a solid script. I like it."

"Well, it seems like, even with a bum knee, you aren't slowing down. So everything is good with you and Dani?"

"Yeah, we're both working hard ... respecting each other;

that's a big part of making a marriage work. Speaking of which ... have you found time to meet someone there in Miami to fill in for Rose Marie?" he asked, then laughed.

"Don't rush me, Dave! Right now I am too busy, but I will soon. I've got plenty of time. I want to take my time and really know the girl first before I make any moves like proposing. I'm not in any rush."

"You're right, Mike. Take your time and make certain you have the right girl, one you'll spend the rest of your life with. Okay, I'm going to get some sleep. We'll talk soon. You take it easy."

"I will, Dave. Thanks for the call and you take it easy on your leg. Call when you can ... and let me know if you're going to do that film."

I was glad to hear Dave in such a good and positive mood. It sounded like he and Dani were happy.

Dave called me on Saturday morning, September 17, as I was leaving to take the dogs to the park.

"Good morning, Mike. It's me, Dave. I'm sure I didn't wake you. I only have a few minutes before I go to make-up. Just wanted to let you know the *Police Story* show will air the end of this month. Check it out in your *TV Guide.* I wouldn't want you to miss it. Hey, Happy Birthday! I have to run ... we'll talk later."

"Okay, Dave, thanks ... and thanks for letting me know about *Police Story*. I won't miss it! I guarantee you."

"Okay, I'll give you a call later," Dave said, then hung up.

I assumed he was in New Orleans filming his new television movie of the week. Dave's next call did not come until Sunday, December 11, just before ten o'clock in the morning.

"Hey, Mike! It's me, Dave. How are you? Sorry I have been out of touch; did you have a good Thanksgiving?"

"Yes, I did, Dave ... how about you and Dani; did you have a nice Thanksgiving? Are you finished with the New Orleans movie?"

"Yeah, we finished that a few weeks ago. I called you from there, don't you remember? Yes, Dani and I had a great Thanksgiving. Did you see the *Police Story* season premier?"

"Yeah, I remember your call but I didn't know you were in New Orleans; you didn't say where you were. I'm glad you and Dani had a nice Thanksgiving. Yes, I saw the *Police Story* ... and I loved it! It is very, very realistic."

"Well, did I look drunk to you?"

"No ... not at all! You actually looked like an LAPD Sergeant ... great action scenes. I thought you were right on point. You did great!"

"Good! I am glad I didn't look drunk; if you couldn't tell, then maybe no one else could either." He laughed. "I wasn't really drunk, but I did have a few drinks to ease the pain in my knee. We did have to do several takes for some of the scenes. I kept fucking up my lines. Anyway, I am glad to hear I pulled it off. Thanks!"

"You are welcome. So what are you doing now? Have you decided on the spy movie; are you going to do it?"

"Yeah, I'm going to do it. I'll be going over to Rome the first week in January. I'll have some downtime until then ... time to relax and keep Dani happy. There are a lot of parties around this time of the year ... so I'll force myself to enjoy them."

"That's good to hear ... just don't drink and drive," I said jokingly.

"Well, I may not have time to call you before, so you have a very Merry Christmas and get Bear and Sherry a steak for Christmas from their Uncle Dave. I'll try to give you a call before but, just in case ... Merry Christmas and a Happy New Year!"

"Thanks, Dave ... and a very Merry Christmas to you and Dani and, of course, your mom and the rest of your family."

"Thanks, Mike ... I'll call you when I have a chance."

Dave ended the call.

51
~1978~

I was quite pleased that everything seemed to be going so well for Dave. From what he told me, he and Dani were getting along very well and he enjoyed being home with her. Professionally, he had one project after another, steady work; his work was the most important aspect of his life. When he was in between projects for a month or two, he was more susceptible to drinking much more than normal.

I did not hear from Dave again until Sunday morning, April 16, 1978. I had just poured my first cup of coffee when the phone rang.

"Good morning, Mike ... how are you?"

"I'm good, Dave ... thanks, and how are you? It's been a while since you called. I know you have been pretty busy. Did you do the film in Italy?"

"Yes, and it was a nightmare! I don't ever want to work with an Italian crew again but, in my humble opinion, the film is pretty damn good! We had to do a lot of filming in Athens, which was a joy compared to shooting in Rome. You'll have to let me know what you think when you see it. How are your kids?"

"They are good. Sherry is still growing ... not pregnant yet. I have four more kids ... real kids."

"What? Did you get married?"

"Hell, no, Dave! I have sort of adopted a Cuban family here in Miami - father, mother, two boys and two girls. They had a very sad situation. One of the girls had been burned in Cuba; she needs plastic surgery. They are having a pretty rough time here. The mother and father both work; the father works two jobs.

"I'm most impressed by the fact the parents would not leave Cuba without all of their kids. I had met Dr. Maxwell Maltz; he's a famous plastic surgeon in New York. I'm taking the little girl (she's nine) and her mother to see him in New York; I hope he can help her. I'm getting close to this family; it's sort of like you when you married Ellie - you had an instant family."

"That's very interesting but, Mike, plastic surgeons can be very expensive. Are you sure you know what you're getting yourself into? How did you meet them?"

"Yes, I know it can be expensive but, hey! It will be money well spent; at least I won't be throwing it away. I met them at the park a few weeks ago; the parents take the kids for a little picnic every Sunday and the kids fell in love with Baron and Sherry.

"The parents speak little English but the kids are pretty good at it. The boys told me what happened to their sister; some kids were playing and a gas can exploded. She has horrible scars on her face and chest."

"When are you taking them to New York?"

"Next Wednesday morning. This is just an exploratory consultation; the doctor isn't charging for it. If he can do the surgery, he'll tell me his fee and all it will take, the hospital and time frame. I feel good about it, Dave. She is a beautiful little girl."

"I have to say, Mike ... that's very commendable of you. You won't regret it and you will make a world of difference in this little girl's life. I hope it all works out for her."

"I'm sure it will. I'll let you know. So, what's next for you? Anything exciting?"

"I start a mini-series for television tomorrow; it's called *The Word*. It's a very interesting story. Some guy finds a book, an eyewitness account of the life of Jesus Christ. He hires me to promote it as the new Bible ... and things get sticky from there. A lot of location filming: London, Amsterdam, Rome, New York and here in Los Angeles."

"What? No filming in Miami? You should get them to film

some scenes in Miami, Dave. You could see Bear, meet Sherry, the Count and Countess and my new family," I said. "I'm just kidding, Dave, but it would be nice to have you come to Miami. You have a lot of fans here, you know." I laughed.

"Yeah, I know, Mike. I'll get down there some day. I like Miami and they do a lot of films there and they are doing more television there as well. However, I'll be off to Europe for a while so Miami will have to wait."

"I know, Dave. I was kidding. Who knows? Maybe we'll be in New York at the same time. We could have a quick drink."

"That would be nice, Mike. We could have several quick drinks. If you don't hear from me for a few weeks, don't worry about it. I will be doing a lot of traveling and a lot of heavy work so you take it easy and I'll call you when I can. I'd be interested to know how it goes with your little girl's operation, if you can swing it. If you need any help, just call; I'll get the message and get right back to you."

"Thanks, Dave! I appreciate that. Just do me a favor and call me when you're back in the States so I know all is well with you."

"I will, Mike ... that's a promise. You take care and we'll talk as soon as I have a chance to call."

"Thanks, Dave! Take it easy and good luck."

"Okay ... bye." Dave hung up.

I took Mrs. Rodez and Guadalupe to New York and had the consultation with the famed Dr. Maxwell Maltz. The doctor said it would be a very complicated surgery and his hands were not as steady, so he called in an associate who agreed to do it. Dr. Maltz would observe and consult his colleague.

Their prognosis was very good and exciting for Mrs. Rodez and her daughter. I decided I could handle the costs and the operation was set for May 1.

We returned to Miami and made plans to return on Sunday, April 30, to check Guadalupe into the hospital. The operation was scheduled for eight o'clock the next morning. I called Rose Marie and we made plans to meet for dinner Monday evening; I was looking forward to it.

The operation was a success. Guadalupe would remain in the hospital for five days and then we would have to return to New York in 45 days for a follow-up appointment.

Rose Marie and I had a very sentimental evening. We both enjoyed being together again and I promised I would make it to the city more often. Still, we would not deter each other from seeing other people. We would let the future evolve naturally.

52

Summer passed with two more trips to New York for follow-ups with the doctors for Guadalupe. She was making remarkable progress and her face was beautiful. She would still have scarring on her chest but the doctors said they would fade over time as she grew.

Her family was ecstatic and I felt so good inside that I had been able to do this for her.

Dave called on Monday morning, September 18, just after five.

"Good morning, Mike! Happy Birthday! It's me, Dave."

"Hi, Dave ... boy, it's good to hear from you! Thank you! You remembered my birthday again. Where are you?"

"I'm here in LA. Did you watch the Emmy Awards last night?"

"No, I had a banquet I had to attend. Did you win?"

"No, I presented an award but, had you seen it, you would know I'm home. Did you do anything with the little girl?"

"Yes, the surgery was done on May 1; it was a great success. We've been back to the doctors for follow-ups twice. It is a remarkable transformation; she is really beautiful!"

"I'm happy to hear that, Mike. You did a very good deed. I'll be here for a few weeks so I'll give you a call later ... now I am exhausted. I have to get some sleep."

"Okay, Dave ... how was your trip overseas ... everything done?"

"It was good ... just plain exhausting. I'll tell you about it later. You take care. I'll call soon."

"All right, Dave! Thanks ... get some sleep." We ended the call.

I was happy to hear from him. He sounded really exhausted but he also sounded a little drunk. He did not mention Dani. It was nice that he remembered and called me on my birthday.

I did not hear from Dave later that week as I had expected. His next call to me came on Sunday, November 12, just before eight o'clock.

"Good morning, Mike ... it's me, Dave."

"Hey, Dave! How the hell are you? You forgot to call me back in September. I was getting worried about you."

"I know, Mike. I'm sorry but, having been gone so long, Dani had us going from one party to another ... and I was trying to get work done. I just did not have time. I'm in Colorado now so I took the chance to call. How are you? How is your 'family', the little girl? How are Bear and Sherry? I meant to ask you, did you see Rose Marie while you were in New York?"

"The 'family' is fine. Guadalupe - that's her name - is really progressing; she gets prettier each day. She – they - are all very happy. I've really gotten close to them. A few weeks ago, the father, Leon, said to me, 'Thanks for all you have done for my family' and the only thing I could say was, 'Thanks, Leon, to you, for sharing your family with me. I am the one blessed.' It was really touching, Dave. I almost cried.

"Yes, I saw Rose Marie; we had dinner a couple of times. That was really nice. Bear and Sherry are doing great. I think Bear has finally realized Sherry's a girl. Hey! I've been watching *Centennial* since the beginning of October; you haven't appeared yet, but it's your voice. I love it - a really great history lesson. *The Word* is premiering tonight; I can't wait to see it! They have really been promoting it. Will you watch it?"

"No, I'll probably still be working. Dani will tape it for me and I'll see it when I get home."

"What are you doing in Colorado?"

"We're shooting the last of the mini-series, *Centennial*, so

I'll be here for a couple of weeks or so. This is the final episode, the one I will appear in. How do you like it so far?"

"As I said, I love it! I can't wait to see the episode you are filming! Did Dani go with you?"

"No ... she has commitments there in LA. I'll be home and then I can relax during the holidays. Listen, I just got a signal. I have to go. I'll call you soon ... if I don't, you have a great Thanksgiving. I'll call when I can."

"Thanks, Dave ... if we don't talk before, you have a Happy Thanksgiving, too." My phone went dead.

Dave sounded as though he was in good spirits. He even sounded as if he was rested. I was looking forward to seeing the mini-series, *The Word*, which would premier tonight and continue through Thursday. I did not have a chance to ask Dave what he thought of it while he was working on it, but I would.

David Janssen had a soft spot for children and single mothers. When they were in distress, he wanted nothing more than to help them.

53

~1979~

    I would not hear from Dave again until Tuesday, January 2. My phone rang at 1:15 in the morning.

    "Happy New Year, Mike! It's me, Dave."

    "Gosh! Happy New Year to you, too ... and Merry Christmas, too! How were your holidays? How is Dani?"

    "The holidays were very hectic, too many damn parties. I couldn't go to them all, no matter how hard Dani tried; she made them all, I think," he said, then laughed. "I have been meaning to call you but, every time I would start, I was interrupted. So, you had nice holidays? Did you spend them with your new family?"

    "Yes, actually, I did! They were fantastic! The kids - there is Roly, Miguel, Guadalupe and Gena. I played Santa Claus big time! It was a lot of fun; it was like I was a kid again. I took the entire family to the Palm Bay Club for Christmas dinner; they were impressed. So you and Dani had a busy time, huh?"

    "Yes, very busy. Everything is going good; Dani is very loving, treating me like a king! How is everything with you?"

    "Good, Dave. I'm still watching *Centennial.* I watched all of *The Word* and I liked it, too. Man, you have been all over television this past couple of months; I bet your fan mail is filling up the whole mail room at the studio there. I'm glad to hear Dani is treating you like you should be treated; that's nice."

    "Yeah, I've been really busy, but the studio has a couple of girls that answer most of the fan mail. I sneak in and grab a few every chance I have. So you like *Centennial*?"

"Yeah, Dave, I like both of them. *The Word* has a very intriguing plot - believable, at least in my mind."

"Well, I wouldn't go that far, Mike. I didn't believe it at all; it's just a television plot, that's all. I read Stone's book and I liked it and, though time prevents telling it the way he wrote it, I like the way we're doing this. Have you read the book?"

"Not yet, but after the series ends, I want to. You know, since I can't sit down and have a few drinks with you every now and then - I mean, since you're a couple thousand miles away - it's good to see you on television so much ... and in what I think are damn good characters."

"Thanks, Mike! I've got another one. I'll be going to San Francisco for a couple of weeks, a TV Movie of the Week. The director is one of my favorites, Walter Grauman from *The Fugitive* days. It's a cop show so I know you'll like it."

"What's it going to be called? Who's in it with you? Will Dani be going with you?"

"No, Dani stays home. It's called *The Golden Gate Murders*. I play a detective ... have to catch me a serial killer. You won't want to miss this one."

"Don't worry! I won't ... but promise you'll give me a heads-up when you know it will be aired."

"I will, Mike. Listen, I have to go and I'll call you later. Take it easy and give your kids a hug for me."

"Thanks, Dave! I appreciate it. You take it easy, too. Stay in touch!"

I was glad to hear from Dave. It had been a long time between calls and, of course, I wondered what was going on with him.

I had seen a few small articles with photos of he and Dani out and about Hollywood. There were several articles promoting both *Centennial* and *The Word* so I knew Dave had been kept very busy.

Dave would be going to San Francisco to film his new TV Movie of the Week, *The Golden Gate Murders*, and had assured me he would give me a call when he had the opportunity.

The remainder of January passed without hearing from

Dave. I was glad when he called on Saturday morning, February 10, 1979.

"Mike, it's me, Dave. Are you awake yet?"

"Good morning! Of course, I'm awake. I was expecting your call," I said, then laughed. "How are you? Where are you?"

"I'm home ... finished the filming in San Francisco and wrapped it up here in the studio.

"I'll be going to London in a couple of weeks to do another television movie, as soon as my beard grows. How is everything with you? How are Baron and Sherry?"

"Everything is good here. Bear and Sherry are fine. You're growing a beard! For what? Hell, it doesn't take two weeks for your beard to grow ... what's the TV movie about?"

"It's the *S.O.S. Titanic.* I play John Jacob Astor, IV. Do you know who he was?"

"Of course, Dave! He built the Waldorf-Astoria and the Astor hotels in New York City. I've been to the cocktail lounges in both ... magnificent hotels. I think he inherited most of his fortune and, yes, I know he died in the Titanic sinking."

"Very good, Mike. You impressed me. I think it's going to be a very good movie."

"Well, you'll be playing one of America's richest men - at least, in that era - and I believe he had a reputation for holding his liquor well, so I'll expect to see you at your best." I laughed. "You'll have to promise to let me know when the filming is over how you feel about the movie. I know it will be several months before it will air but I damn sure do not want to miss it!"

"I know, Mike. I'll give you the inside scoop when we're finished. I'll be out of touch for a while, just wanted to let you know."

"Will Dani be going over with you? How long do you think you'll be in London?"

"No, Dani won't be going. She may come over for a visit - depends on how long I'll be there. Could be a month, maybe six weeks, give or take a few days."

"Do you have an idea when *The Golden Gate Murders* will air?"

"No ... it will be several months. I'll let you know but keep an eye out. *TV Guide* or the newspapers will probably announce it before I even know."

"I will, Dave. Listen! I saw *Centennial: The Scream of Eagles* last week. I thought you were terrific! I thought it was great, the whole series ... now I have to read Stone's book."

"I'm glad you enjoyed it. It's not what I would call my best work but it did well in the ratings, and that's good."

"Yes, the ratings in the New York papers were very good. There were a lot of actors ... famous actors you have worked with in *The Fugitive* and *Harry O.* Did you like working with them again?"

"Oh, yeah! I don't pick the cast but, in a lot of ways, it was like a good family reunion. Good people, that part I enjoy."

"Dave, you are working non-stop since *Harry O.* When are you going to take some time off; don't you feel you need a break?"

"Mike, you know me. I have to work ... I need to work. My wife has expensive tastes and working keeps my mind occupied. I'll take a break when I feel I really need one."

"Okay ... you know what you're doing. One thing is for sure: your fans can see there's more to you than *Richard Kimble* ... and that's good for you, at least, in my opinion."

"Thanks, Mike! I hope you're right. I felt like *The Fugitive* sort of boxed me in ... people couldn't see me doing anything else. Hell! I still look over my shoulder for Lieutenant Gerard." Dave laughed.

"Well, how is everything else going? How are things with you and Dani?"

"Everything is fine ... one day at a time. There are good days and then there are some days I want to skip but, for the most part, things are good.

"Well, I better get going. I'll try to give you a call before I go overseas. You take care and give Bear and Sherry a hug for me."

"All right, Dave! Thanks for the call and you take it easy, too." Dave ended the call.

I looked at my kitchen clock; it was 5:15. I assumed Dave was just going home to get some sleep. He sounded to be in very good spirits and eager to be going overseas to start the new movie. He did not elaborate on the current situation with Dani but, from what he said, I felt things had improved in their marriage.

I expected it would be, at least, a couple of months before he would have a chance to give me a call. I knew there would be some publicity surrounding all of the projects he had recently completed so I would have some idea how things would be going for him while he was in Great Britain.

I was surprised when Dave called me on Saturday evening, February 24, at 6:20.

"Mike, it's me, Dave. How are you doing?"

"Good, Dave. I didn't expect to hear from you until you got back from England. How are you? Where are you?"

"Well, I told you I would try and give you a call before I went to London ... and that's what I'm doing. I'm in LA, getting ready to fly across the Pond," he said, then laughed.

"Thanks! I didn't think you would have the time; I appreciate it. So are you excited about the Titanic movie? I know you like London, so that is good. Will you have time there to relax between filming?"

"Yeah, there will be time to relax, weekends and such. I just wanted to give you a quick call and tell you I was leaving and to remind you to keep any eye on your *TV Guide.* I don't want you to miss any of the programs."

"I don't need reminding. I check *TV Guide* every day. So I guess you are excited about filming this movie in London?"

"Yes, I am, actually; it will give me time to work and a little time to play. I am looking forward to it very much."

"Dani is staying home? Then you better be careful. You know the press will probably be watching your every move."

"Yeah, Dani is staying home. She has a calendar full of party commitments; she may come over for a short visit between parties ... that's still to be determined. Don't worry, Mike! I know the press and paparazzi will be out in full force. I don't do anything that would cause a scandal anyway; you know that," he said with a laugh. "So, you take it easy. Take care of Bear and Sherry and your new family. I'll give you a call as soon as I get back."

"Okay, Dave, and thanks. I really appreciate the call."

"All right, Mike. Talk later." My line went dead.

54

Saturday morning, April 7, I was awakened by the persistent ringing of my phone at 4:50.

"Good morning," I managed.

"Good morning, Mike. It's me, Dave. Did I wake you?"

"Yeah, Dave, but that's okay. How are you? I guess you're back from England."

"Yeah, I've been back a few days. How are you? How's Bear and Sherry? How are you doing with your family?"

"Everything and everyone here is fine. Did you finish the *Titanic* movie; are you going to take a break?"

"We still have some scenes to shoot here ... we'll be doing that on the Queen Mary here in Long Beach in a couple of weeks. Then I'm going to take a little break, take Dani to Palm Springs for a few weeks. How are you doing? How's your job? What's the latest with your little family?"

"I'm glad to hear you're almost through filming and you will take a break! I take it all is going well with you and Dani; that's good to know.

"My job is very interesting. I'm learning a lot about the stock markets, investments. Baron and Sherry are doing great - no puppies yet. The family is great. I spend all my free time with them ... keeps me out of bars and out of trouble," I said with a light laugh.

"That's all good. I'm glad everything is going so well with you. Yes, Dani and I are doing great. We need some time and there's no better place for us than Palm Springs. I've got a few things Abby has sent me so I'll get something going after a few weeks with Dani."

"Dave, I am really happy to hear that ... you need a break. My God, you've worked in what ... five or six films and movies in the last year? YOU need a break!"

"YES, for once, I have to agree with you, Mike. I'm getting a little older and, with age, comes a decline in one's energy. I do need a break ... but a short one," he said and then let out a laugh.

"Yeah, Dave ... speaking of getting a little older, why don't you have your hair stylist put a little more black in your hair? It is really starting to show the grey," I said, then laughed.

"I won't do that, Mike - that's what God has given me, grey hair. If they need to make me a blond for a character role, so be it, but I'm not going to try to look younger than I am. I'm not that vain," he said with a big laugh.

"Okay ... okay! Don't get me wrong but I think you are getting prematurely grey. Then again, as hard as you work, I guess that's one of the prices you pay. Still, grey looks good on you." I laughed.

"All right, wise guy! With that, I've got to go and get some beauty rest ... I'll give you a call later." Dave hung up.

I hoped I had not said anything he took as an offense. I was certain that, of his millions of fans and those who knew him off screen, I was not the only one who had noticed how rapidly he was aging physically. I noted, too, that his voice seemed to be changing, getting deeper and with a pronounced gravelly sound to it.

I concluded a little time alone in Palm Springs with Dani would do Dave a world of good. At least, I would pray for that.

My next call from Dave came on Saturday evening, May 5, just before six o'clock.

"Hey, Mike! It's me, Dave. How are you? Am I interrupting you?"

"Hi, Dave! No, you're not interrupting me. I'm getting ready to go to a charity ball at the Surf Club with the Count and Countess. I'm doing fine. How about you and Dani? Are you still in Palm Springs?"

"We're back home. We had a great time in Palm Springs, a lot of time to relax. I played some golf ... feel like a new man. We finished the *Titanic* film a couple of days ago. I'll be starting a new TV movie in a few weeks; it's called *Panic on Page One*. My character is a washed-up newspaper man trying to reclaim his glory by tracking down a serial killer ... solid script, I like it."

"It sounds intriguing ... do you catch him?"

"I don't know. I haven't read the end of the script yet." He laughed. "Hell, Mike, you know I'm not going to give it away ... spoil it for you ... and then you wouldn't watch it!" He laughed again.

"It sounds to me that you are jumping back into the frying pan ... work ... work and more work."

"Yeah, but I need to, Mike. I have to work ... that's what keeps me young. Even though I don't look as young as *Diamond*, I feel young."

"As long as you're happy ... that's all that really counts, Dave. I suppose Abby has sent you a pile of scripts to go through too, right?"

"Yeah, I have a few ... I asked for them." He laughed.

"That is good, Dave; it will keep your fans happy. You know, I was just thinking. With all your TV series, I and your fans would look forward to seeing you every week, but you were always the same ... just different storylines ... and I know how hard it was on you, physically. Now that *Harry* is no more, you are making so many movies and we get to see how YOU are as a different character. I think that is really good, for you and your fans."

"Hey, you have a good point! I never looked at it that way, but I think you are right. Thanks! I'll take that as a compliment."

"I meant it, Dave. Look back at the different roles you've played. You have taken on so many diverse roles yet, in every one, YOU have brought the character to life and we SEE the character. You make each one seem so real. Not every actor can do that."

"Thanks again, Mike ... I like your observations."

"Well, it's true. Look at John Wayne - he either plays in war movies or westerns. In the war movies, he is always an officer and his lines are almost the same; in westerns, he's the sheriff or marshal, always a good guy and, when he plays a love scene, it is just not believable."

"Yeah, I couldn't agree with you more, but he is a good actor. You have to give him that."

"Okay, I'll give him that, but someone also told me he is an arrogant S.O.B." I laughed.

"I won't deny that; I met him a few times," Dave said, then laughed. "Okay, Mike ... I'll let you get ready for your high brow affair. Good talking with you ... so take it easy and I'll be in touch later."

"Thanks, Dave ... look forward to hearing from you."

Dave sounded relaxed, positive and, for once, really happy. I felt his little vacation with Dani in Palm Springs had done him a world of good. Now he was back to the grind and fully engrossed in his element of 'Lights ... Camera ... Action'!

The new television movie sounded very exciting and a role that sounded to be tailor-made for Dave. I would be anxiously waiting to see it.

Thinking back over the conversation, after telling Dave about his many diverse roles - both in television and theatrical films - I realized that I made this observation to Dave spontaneously, but it definitely had merit.

In his roles, from *A Sensitive, Passionate Man, Covert Action, The Word, Centennial, The Golden Gate Murders, S.O.S. Titanic* and, now, this new production, he had been cast in such a variety of roles playing characters so diverse. I really believed his fans were seeing the immense range of his acting talents. I hoped the major Hollywood studio executives would see them as well, take notice and give Dave a starring role in a major film.

I would continue anxiously waiting for his most recent projects to be aired so I could see the merit I had proclaimed. It would be several weeks before I would hear from him but I knew he was really busy and I felt certain he was happy at this time of his life.

55

I next heard from Dave early Monday morning, May 28, as I was in my kitchen turning on my coffee pot.

"Good morning, Mike. It's me, Dave. Had your coffee yet?"

"Good morning, Dave. As a matter of fact, I just turned the pot on; I knew you'd be calling," I said with a laugh.

"How'd you know? I'm just giving you a wake up call. Your kids need to go to the park. Kidding aside, how are you? Sorry I've been out of touch, busy ... getting ready to start the newspaper film. They changed the title; now it's *City In Fear*. It's an excellent plot, good supporting cast. I'm excited about it."

"Good ... what network? Where will you be filming it?"

"It's for ABC; it will be a three hour movie, including the commercials on air, of course. We'll be filming here in LA. Thankfully, there will be no location shooting."

"I'll be looking forward to seeing it! What else have you got in the works?"

"I'll be going to Washington state, to the mountains. I'll play a mountain ranger, a hero. I rescue a group of climbers trapped on the side of the mountain; it's a good script, but I hate the ending."

"Why ... how does it end?"

"Can't tell you, Mike; it's a secret. You have to watch it, then you'll know."

"Aw ... come on, Dave! Don't do this to me! It'll be months before I get to see it. You always do this to me; it's just not fair. I'm your friend - at least, I thought I was."

"Of course, we're friends - that's why I want you to see it; I don't want to spoil it for you." He laughed. "I think you will like it ... even the ending, it's very well written. Now if I can just get the acting right, it'll be a good movie."

"Okay ... I know better than to push you! When are you going up to Washington? I love that state; it's beautiful."

"After we finish this one. It will be sometime in July, probably mid-July. Okay, sorry to cut this short. I have to get some sleep. You can go back to sleep, if Bear lets you." He laughed.

"All right, Dave! Thanks for the wake-up call. I was already awake; Bear and Sherry woke me. Give me a call when you can. I want to know all you're willing to tell me about this movie."

"Okay, you take it easy and I'll give you a call as soon as we're done." He ended the call.

I did not hear from Dave until Sunday, July 29, at 9:45 in the morning. I was relaxing with my coffee and *The Miami Herald*.

"Mike, good morning. I have a few minutes so I wanted to let you know we finished *City In Fear* and I'm in Washington. We started work on *High Ice*; I had to let my beard grow again."

"Any idea when the *City In Fear* movie will be shown? I don't understand why it takes them so long. When you did your series, you filmed an entire episode in a week or so and it would be shown almost immediately."

"Television movies of the week are usually two hour shows so it's like two episodes and it takes the technical people extra time to do their work. Then the network sales team has to lock in the commercial sponsors and, finally, the network programming people have to decide when to put it into their line up. So now do you understand it?"

"Yeah, I do, Dave. I just wish they would work a little faster," I said with a laugh. "So how is everything on the home front? How is Dani doing? Is she with you? Where will you be filming? Do they have mountains there?"

"Everything is going well ... hold my breath ... at home. No, Dani's not on location with me. We're based in a small town called Darrington? Have you heard of it?"

"No, I haven't. Where is it in proximity to Spokane; do you know?"

"No, it's close to Seattle. We'll be filming on the Cascade Mountains, at least that's what I'm told. It's a really small town so it should be fun. Spokane is in the southeastern part of the state."

"Yes, I bet it will. You and the other actors, with all the film crew and everything, you will be setting the town on fire. People will be calling 'Gerard' to tip him off ... be careful."

"Yeah, right ... that's okay. I really enjoy small towns, getting to see the people. Hopefully, some of my fans live here," he said, then laughed.

"I hope you have fun ... you deserve to. I hope the town has a nice, friendly bar to welcome you." I laughed.

"No, Mike, I'll be doing my drinking in my hotel room. We'll only be here for three or four weeks, give or take a few days. We have been so busy I haven't seen much of the town, met the people yet. I'll give you a call in between ... tell you all about it."

"Good! I love Washington, but I hope they don't expect you to climb the mountain. I don't think you could do it ... unless you had a Saint Bernard with you." I laughed.

"I have to agree with you. It would have to be a very large Saint Bernard with a very large flask. The plan is we will leave the town, travel to the mountain and film the scenes and then we'll all come back to the comfort of the hotel. A lot depends on the weather - which is cooperating, so far."

"I hope you enjoy it. I mean, I know it's hard work but that's what you like and, at least, you are in a good location, not doing it all in a make believe studio in Los Angeles."

"They can do a lot in the studios, Mike, but they can't replicate a real mountain. I am enjoying it ... we have a good cast and outstanding crew. Okay, I have to run; I'll call you when I have a chance. You take it easy."

"Okay, Dave ... thanks for keeping me up-to-date. Enjoy and you take it easy, too."

"I will, Mike ... later."

Dave sounded happy and perfectly sober. I know it's hot in Washington state during July but there is definitely snow on the mountains. I just wondered how far up the mountains they had to go for filming, or whether they make their own snow.

56

Dave called me next on Saturday, August 11.

"Hey, Mike! It's me, Dave. How the heck are you? How's your family?"

"Good morning, Dave ... family's fine, I'm fine ... what about you? Are you still in Washington?"

"No, I'm home; we finished on location, doing some studio work here. I'll be going to South Korea in a couple of weeks or so."

"WHAT? South Korea? Don't tell me you're doing another war movie with your favorite actor, 'the Duke'?"

"HELL, NO! I'll be doing a war movie but with Sir Lawrence Olivier. It's called *Inchon*; it's scripted more like a documentary than a real war movie, the way I read it. Olivier is playing General Douglas MacArthur; are you familiar with the Korean War history?"

"Yeah, Dave ... President Truman fired him because he was allegedly insubordinate. History sort of made MacArthur right, as I recall. Well, are you a Major or a Colonel, at least?"

"No ... you want a laugh? I'm a journalist! Can you believe that?" He laughed hard.

"Well, that's probably because you played such a good journalist in *The Green Berets* and *Shoes of the Fisherman,* they figured you act like a real journalist.

"Hey, don't knock it! You are good in that role ... or maybe I shouldn't say that. I don't want you to feel you are being stereotyped."

"Yeah ... well, I feel I am being stereotyped, but the money's too good to pass up."

"Yeah ... I bet it is ... and, hey! You told me that, years ago when you were in the Army, you would have gone to Korea - so now you're going. Is this a television movie, too?"

"No, this is a major film ... big budget, all star cast."

"Who else is in it?"

"Ben Gazzara, Jacqueline Bisset, several others. I think it will be a good movie, very realistic to how events actually unfolded at Inchon."

"Okay, again I guess I have to wait to see the film, but you've got to tell me some of the details when you get back ... before the movie comes out," I said with a slight laugh.

"Yeah, right Mike ... I'll think about that. So, I'll give you a call when I can ... you take it easy and give Bear and Sherry a hug for me."

"I will, Dave. You be careful and enjoy Korea; at least, they won't be shooting at you."

"Yeah, that's true. I'll call you when I have a chance." The line went dead.

I did not ask Dave how long he would be on location in South Korea or if Dani would be going with him, but then I realized that she most probably would not be going. I would just have to wait until he had the chance to call and ask him if he enjoyed being so close to North Korea, our sworn enemy.

I was very surprised to get a call from Dave at 6:30 on Tuesday evening, September 18, 1979.

"Mike, it's me, Dave ... just wanted to give you a call and wish you a Happy Birthday. How are you?"

"Wow! Dave, that's very nice of you ... thank you! Are you still in Korea?"

"No, I got back a few days ago but still have to go back there; we are still shooting the film. I just didn't want you to think I had forgotten about you. What are your plans?"

"The Rodez family has a little surprise party planned for me, but Miguel told me, so I won't be too surprised!"

"Well, you enjoy your party and I'll give you a call in a few weeks when I'm back in the States, okay?"

"Okay, Dave, and thanks ... thanks a lot for calling. You take it easy, too."

Dave and I had developed the practice of wishing each other birthday wishes but I certainly did not expect him to call as I thought he may still be in Korea. His consideration made me feel good and reinforced what I already knew about Dave: he was a considerate man when it came to those he liked.

I enjoyed a nice celebration with the Rodez family.

Sunday, September 23, *S.O.S. Titanic* began as the ABC Movie of the Week at eight o'clock in the evening. It was an outstanding movie, in my opinion. Dave's portrayal of John Jacob Astor IV was brilliant.

There had been numerous ads in the Miami newspapers promoting the movie, and then promoting *The Golden Gate Murders* which was scheduled to be aired on CBS on Wednesday, October 3. I would be anxiously waiting to see that movie as well. I thought it funny that Dave would be on ABC and then CBS. He had also been prominently aired on NBC in the television movie, *The Word*. Dave was a star!

"Witnessing the friendship unfold between
David Janssen and his friend, Michael Phelps,
was a beautiful experience for which
I will forever be grateful."

- Norma Budden

57

Dave called me on Sunday morning, October 14, at 12:45.

"Mike, Dave ... I hope I didn't wake you."

"You didn't Dave; I just got in ... getting ready for bed. Where are you?"

"I'm home. Well, I'm going home to go to bed. I'm exhausted," Dave said.

He also sounded pretty drunk which, being so early in the evening on the west coast, was unusual for Dave. "You sound it, Dave. You need to take a vacation. You have really been working yourself too hard. Are you finished with *Inchon*?"

"Yeah ... all done ... all wrapped up ... I'm taking a break. I'm going to my beach house for a while ... unwind ... clear my head ... read ... have some peace and quiet. Gonna shut out the world for a few days ... maybe weeks. So, how're you doing, Mike?"

"Fine, Dave ... couldn't be better. How are things with you ... and Dani?"

"All fucked up ... but that's par for the course. It'll work itself out ... in time. I'm just going to go hide at the beach ... let her cool down. Things will get better."

"I take it things aren't going well with you and Dani. You are right; you need some time alone, Dave. You should go to your beach house and have some solitude ... you have worked a hell of a lot this year. Hell, for the last two years, you haven't stopped working.

"You need to rest and you don't need aggravations of any kind from anyone."

I could tell in his voice he was physically and mentally exhausted, completely drained. Having arguments with Dani, or anyone for that matter, was the last thing he needed to deal with.

"I know, Mike ... that's what I'm going to do."

"You're not driving ... are you, Dave?"

"No ... uh ... I'm waiting for my driver. I'm going straight home ... to Malibu and going to sleep. I'll call you in a few days. You take it easy ... we'll talk later."

"Okay, Dave ... don't leave me hanging. I want to tell you my opinion on *S.O.S. Titanic*."

"Oh, yeah! You saw it?"

"Of course! No way I would miss it. You go now and we'll talk about them when you have a chance to call me back."

"All right, Mike ... I'll call you." The phone went dead.

I just could not believe it. He had been working so hard, one project after another. The little 'down-time' he had, he chose to take Dani to Palm Springs for relaxation and some quality time together. I didn't know all the details, I'm sure, but I knew that Dave did not deserve to have the kind of stress she was putting him under.

I knew Dave loved Dani and I wanted to believe she loved him as deeply. I know that every couple had moments of stress, for whatever reasons, and it sometimes led to arguments.

I just couldn't understand what could be the cause of so much dissension between Dave and Dani. They had everything a couple could want, and more. I would say a prayer for Dave - and Dani, too.

Dave called me on Tuesday, October 23, as I walked in the door with Baron and Sherry from their evening run.

"Hey, Mike! How are you?"

"I'm good, Dave, and you? Where are you?"

"I'm still at my beach house. I've been relaxing and reading ... a lot of reading. I take my walks on the beach, very peaceful ... rejuvenating for body and soul."

"I am really glad to hear that. I love walking on the beach

here. I have to ask ... how is Dani? Have you spoken with her? Have things cooled down since we spoke a couple weeks ago?"

"Yeah, she's called a few times ... she's okay. I just told her I needed to stay here awhile ... alone. She's okay with that. I'm going to drive in and bring my mother here tomorrow for lunch. She's never been here."

"That's nice, Dave. I'm sure she will be very happy to see you ... and your house. Are you really taking advantage of this time to rest? You sound a hell of a lot better than last time we talked; you sound rested ... and you really need some rest."

"Yeah, I'm rested, Mike ... and, yes, you are right. I didn't know just how exhausted I was and this time alone has worked wonders on my psyche."

"That's good, Dave. I'm happy for you. Listen, I saw *S.O.S. Titanic* a few weeks ago ... all I can say is you were superb!"

"Gee, thanks Mike! That's good of you to say; I'm glad you liked it! So, how are you doing with your adopted family? How are your kids?"

"Guadalupe has another surgery coming up, the first of the year. The family is all doing well; they are such a close knit family, very well mannered. The parents are learning enough English that we can communicate and I have the kids to translate for us; it's comical, but nice.

"Baron and Sherry are doing great. Now, what about you? Does Abby have anything lined up for you? Are you in any hurry to get back to work? The holidays will be here soon; you don't like working over the holidays ... or would that matter now?"

"Yeah, Abby sent me a script ... based on a true story about a Catholic Priest. He goes to a leper colony and sets up a church ... helps the people. I'm pretty sure I'll do it but it won't start filming until after the first of the year and, the good part - it will be filmed right here in Malibu, just a little ways up the beach from here."

"That sounds interesting, Dave ... you playing a Catholic Priest. That's going to be something I have to see. I just don't see you wearing a collar," I said with a laugh.

"Yeah ... I agree with you, but I'll practice my 'Hail Mary's'. I think I can pull it off."

"Is this going to be a film or a television movie?"

"It's another television Movie of the Week ... that's okay; only take a few weeks of work. I'll let you know if I'm going to do it. So, you take it easy and we'll talk later, okay?"

"Okay, Dave, I'm glad you called. You sound a hell of a lot better ...so, you take it easy, too. Don't let anything or anyone mess with your head."

"I know, Mike ... don't worry! I've got it all under control. We'll talk soon." He ended the call.

I was relieved. Dave sounded like his old, positive, happy self. He sounded completely sober and that was good. I had envisioned him spending his days drinking scotch from the time he awoke until he would pass out several hours later.

58

Dave called just after midnight on Sunday, November 18.

"Mike ... Dave. I know I didn't wake you ... or did I?"

"No, Dave, as a matter of fact, you didn't. How are you? Are you still at your beach house? Did you take your mother to see it?"

"Yeah, I brought her here; she was impressed. I'm back home. I just wanted to give you a quick call and wish you and all your family a Happy Thanksgiving."

"Thanks, Dave ... and I wish you and Dani the same. How is everything with you ... and Dani?"

"Everything is going smooth. I told you she would cool down and everything would get back to normal. We are, finally, getting to the point of establishing a mutual understanding - that is, I don't care how much she spends, how many parties she has or attends - and she doesn't question how much I drink, how hard I work, where I go, who I'm with, and if I tell her I am too tired to attend this party or that, that's the end of the conversation."

"I'll tell you, Dave, I am very relieved to hear that! You've made it four years - I guess almost nine, if you count your years together before you married. You have figured out that communication and respect for each other is a lot of what makes a marriage work.

"To be honest, Dave, I know it's none of my business and I shouldn't - but I do worry about *you* ... not Dani. I just cannot understand why a guy like you ... in your position, as hard as you work ... would have any stress put on you, especially from your wife. I know what you went through the last time; I hate the thought you would be in that position again. I pray for you, Dave ... hope she realizes your love is real."

"I appreciate that, Mike, and believe me! I had a lot of time to think in Malibu. I'm taking some very subtle steps to protect myself - just in case. Okay, I have to get back to the party. Have a Happy Thanksgiving. We'll talk soon."

"Okay, Dave ... call and let me know about your next project."

"I thought I told you; it'll be the Priest TV movie ... starts first of the year. I'll call you." The call ended.

Dave sounded relaxed yet a little guarded in discussing his situation with his wife. I had the distinct impression that he and Dani had come to an agreement, and I had no doubt Dave would keep his end. Would Dani? That was the big question.

Although he sounded rested and calm, there was an underlying tone that he was just waiting for the next uproar from Dani. I just hoped he could get through the holidays in a happy state of mind.

I next heard from Dave on Saturday morning, December 15, at 4:45.

"Good morning," I managed, shaking my head awake.

"Hey, Mike! It's me, Dave. Sorry! I'm sure I woke you ... I just wanted to talk ... are you up to it?"

"Sure, Dave ... how are you? Did you have a nice Thanksgiving? How are things with Dani?"

"Thanksgiving was okay. We had dinner with some friends and it was civil. I'm just trying to get through this month ... Christmas and all. I'll tell you, Mike ... I don't like it, but I think I'm going to have to go through another divorce.

"She's fine for a few days then she treats me like a dog and I think hard, looking for what the hell I did to make her explode at me and, Mike, I haven't done anything. I do not understand it. When she goes off, I just shut up and let her rant and rave ... and that makes it worse."

"Damn it, Dave! What about the mutual understanding she had with you? Have you reminded her? Doesn't it matter to her?"

"Yeah ... it matters if I acquiesce to what she wants the minute she wants it. If I am too tired to go out, that doesn't matter. Mike, I give her everything she wants ... anything she wants ... but I can't continue burning the candle at both ends. I am just too damn tired and she does not accept or she refuses to even try to understand. I work hard! Her only career is to spend my money and be a party princess ... I can't live like this anymore!"

"Well, Dave ... I can only suggest you talk to your lawyer and see what can be worked out. You know you are in great demand. You can always make more money. Damn, if it is only the thought of what a divorce will cost you, to hell with it! Cut your losses and look to the future; you will make it all back!"

"I know! You are 100 percent right! I'm meeting with Paul tomorrow. I have to go to Las Vegas right after Christmas. I don't want to do anything until I'm back. I have the new TV movie starting the first week of February ... there is so much going on. I wish now I had stayed in Malibu a little longer."

"Dave, you have to do what is right for your own peace of mind; that is priceless! To hell with the money! You've been flat broke before and look at you now! You have the looks and the talent to go with them. Do what is the right thing for you!"

"I know, Mike ... I will. Hey, I'm sorry I woke you! I just needed a friend I could vent to. I'll give you a call soon ... when things settle down here. Don't worry about me ... and, hey, I'm not driving!" He laughed - a little faint, but still he laughed. "Listen, Mike! In case I don't have a chance to call you, make sure you and your little family have a very Merry Christmas and the best for the New Year."

"Okay, Dave, thanks ... and I wish you the same. Just take one day at a time and stay calm, okay?"

"Yeah, Mike ... sure," Dave said before hanging up.

Dave was definitely drunk and he was depressed.

Dave had related to me that the first five or six years of his marriage to Ellie were filled with love, fun and mutual respect. When he traveled for film locations or publicity tours for *The Fugitive*, Ellie went with him and he wanted it that way.

He had entrusted the confidence in me to relate the last four years of his marriage with Ellie had gone in an agonizing and fast spiral downward. She was insanely jealous, possessive and controlling. She was even jealous of his female fans.

When Dave first began his relationship with Dani, they were full of fun and growing, mutual attraction and blossoming love. He had said things began to go downhill in the second year, which is the reason he kept evading the issue of marriage each time Dani brought it up - which increased in frequency during their third and fourth years of dating.

Finally, Dave gave in; they were married on October 4, 1975. Their disagreements began immediately and increased in frequency during their time together.

I knew of five separate occasions where Dave left their marital home - once for seven straight months when he even refused to take her calls.

During that period he met Carol Connors, collaborated with her on writing beautiful songs and he fell completely in love with her. He was tormented inside, wanting a divorce from Dani, but fearful of the financial costs.

Of course, there was another reason Dave fought so hard to make his marriage to Dani work, returning to her multiple times: he hated failure. He did not want to fail as a husband.

59
~1980~

On Saturday morning, January 12, 1980, my phone rang at 4:25, waking me from a very sound sleep.

"If this isn't David Janssen ... hang up and call back at noon," I muttered.

"Hey, Mike! Don't hang up ... it's me, Dave."

"I just had a feeling it was you ... how the hell are you? Did you have a decent Christmas?"

"I'm okay, Mike. Christmas was not the best I've had, but I got through it. How are you? Hey, I'm really sorry I woke you. You know what? I'm going to start wearing one of my other wristwatches. I'll keep it on Eastern time so I know when I can call you without waking you. Do you think that's a good idea?" He laughed.

"No, you don't have to do that, Dave. You can call me at any hour - you know that. I know you are busy and I appreciate your calls, when it is convenient for you. I'm a light sleeper," I said. "So, has anything improved at home?"

"No, it's like living on a roller coaster ... except there is no real fun in it anymore. I'm having Paul draw up the papers for divorce; she's driving me crazy! I have the new TV movie starting in a few weeks; I need to be able to concentrate on it and not have this kind of bullshit bouncing around my head."

"I wish I could say I am sorry to hear that - divorce, I mean - but I happen to think it is the best move you can make for yourself. I know it is going to be costly, but take my advice. DO

NOT let it cause anger inside your mind! Stay civil, keep your eye on the prize - your peace of mind and your freedom!"

"Yeah, I agree with you ... that is damn good advice and I will be sure to follow it."

"When things get ugly - and they will, you know that - just take a deep breath and repeat in your mind, 'This too shall pass!' Don't think about the financial costs. YOU WILL make a hell of a lot more ... after your divorce is final."

"I know, Mike. I know. You know, for a young guy, you've got a pretty level head on your shoulders. Do you follow your own advice?"

"Well, I've never been in your shoes, Dave; my divorce cost me very little but, yes, in other matters - business matters, and yes, even personal relationships - if there is a problem I look for the cause of the problem, then I look for a solution. I take a few deep breaths and repeat in my mind, 'This too shall pass!' and, you know what? Within time, the problems are resolved and they pass from my mind." I laughed.

"Yeah ... that's pretty good, Mike ... logical thinking. I knew that. Well, in my case, I know the cause of the problem: it's not me and it's not Dani. It was getting MARRIED that caused this fucking mess ... so now I look for a solution. Bingo! I've got it ... D I V O R C E! You know what, there are seven letters in the word married, and there are seven letters in the word divorce! Figure that one out." He laughed. "Seven is NOT my lucky number."

"So have you given your lawyer the green light to file the papers?"

"He's drawing them up for me to review, but I want to wait until the end of shooting this movie. Then I'll take whatever time off from any new projects to go through this process. I'm filing; there are no girlfriends or mistresses that she can drag into this. She really has no grounds to throw any mud at me - unless my drinking falls into that category, and I don't think it does."

"So, maybe sometime towards the end of next month, the shit will hit the fan and there will be all these nasty stories in all of the fan magazines and newspapers ... worldwide! I think you learned, from past experience, this will not drive your fans away from you. It will draw them closer!

"Hey, you're still a good-looking man. You can have any woman out there; maybe even Carol Connors will still be available! Maybe you might want to have your hair darkened a little ... get rid of some of that premature grey." I laughed.

"Hey, Mike! I think you just might have something there. I hope Carol will still be available. We can pick up where we left off and, who knows? I'm still going to leave my hair the way it is; that's what God has given me. Hell, at least I still have hair." He laughed again.

"When are you going to Las Vegas? Don't tell me you're going to gamble all your money away so Dani won't get any." I laughed.

"No, you know I don't really gamble all that much; I learned my lesson there. I'm going for a celebrity tennis tournament for charity. Milt Berle and his wife invited me. I'm going to have lunch with Diane, Ellie's daughter. I'll only be there three or four days."

"I take it Dani is not going."

"Hell, no! I moved out of the condo; I'm living at my beach house. She's there in LA. She won't even know I'm in Vegas."

"That sounds nice, that you still see Ellie's girl. I'm sure you will have some fun and have some time to relax there. Let me know how you do in the tournament, okay?"

"Yeah, I will. Okay, listen, I'll let you get back to sleep. I am sorry I woke you, but thanks for being there, for listening."

"All right, Dave! You take it easy and, please, give me a call and let me know everything is going okay with you. I know you are a big boy and can take care of yourself, but I have this gnawing problem. I care about my friends and, when they have problems, I worry about them."

"Thanks, Mike ... thanks a lot. We'll talk soon."

"When you have a close friendship with someone like David Janssen, even the trivial conversations are memorable."

- Michael Phelps

60

On Saturday morning, February 9, 1980, Dave called me at eleven o'clock.

"Hey, Mike! It's me, Dave. I know I didn't wake you ... how the hell are you?"

"Good, Dave. Good morning to you, too ... and how the hell are you? How was Las Vegas? Did you win anything - tennis ... at the tables? Did you see Ellie's daughter? Where are you?"

"I'm doing great! No, I lost everything in Vegas! Just kidding. Yeah, I saw Diane; we had dinner at Caesar's with Ruth and Milt. You'll never guess who else I saw at Caesar's."

"Okay, I won't even try to guess. Who did you see?"

"BITCH Number Two! Dani came in to the dining room where we were finishing our dinner. She created a hell of an embarrassing scene – screaming, shouting obscenities.

"I'm sure all of the people there thought I was cheating on Dani with Diane. I mean, Diane is a beautiful young woman and we didn't paste a sign on her saying she's my step-daughter. It was un-fucking-believable!"

"How did she know you were in Vegas? Does she know you are planning to divorce her? Doesn't she know Diane or, at least, what she looks like? How in the hell could she do that to you ... in public?"

"I have no idea how she knew I was in Vegas; very few people in LA knew I was going to the tournament. I don't know IF she has a clue that I'll be filing for divorce; the only people I've told is my lawyer, Paul; Sid Korshak; a good friend, Paul Burke and, in Vegas, after that tirade, I told Diane, Milt and Ruth ... and you! No one else knows!"

"So what happened in the dining room? Didn't hotel security come?"

"No, no security. I asked her to quiet down. She only got louder ... more obscene so I excused myself to the Berles', took Diane and we left. I have no idea where she went."

"Well, where are you ... in LA?"

"No, I'm in Malibu at my house. I start shooting *Father Damien* at six o'clock in the morning."

"So have you told your lawyer to go ahead and file?"

"That will be done the day after we wrap this movie. I'll tell you, Mike ... it's over. I can't live like this; she is hammering my sanity."

"I understand, Dave, and I don't blame you. I think you are taking the right step. You don't deserve this kind of bullshit. So, aside from that ... how do you feel? Are you ready to start this new movie? Do you like the script?"

"Mike, I'll tell you, I feel great! I had my physical a couple of days ago - you know, for the studio's insurance company. I passed it with flying colors. I'm well-rested, have a lot of energy and I'm rearing to go. I won't have any real physical challenges in this film, so it will be easy. I like the script.

"The real guy, he was quite a devoted man ... did a lot of good for people who were shunned and dirt poor. I think you'll like the story when you see the movie."

"I'm sure I will, Dave. I just hope you can get through it without Dani showing up on the set like Ellie did."

"She would not dare do that. Okay, Mike, I have to go so I'll give you a call in a few days, maybe next weekend. You take care. Give Bear and Sherry a hug for me."

"Thanks, Dave. I will. Make sure you let me know when your lawyer files. I want to scan the fan magazines and the newspapers; I don't want to miss any of the fireworks."

"Yeah ... I'll call you the minute I know the papers are filed. Talk later."

Dave ended the call.

Epilogue

I awoke at my usual time of 4:30 in the morning and let Baron and Sherry into the back yard. I turned on my coffee pot and went to the bathroom to brush my teeth.

Afterwards, I turned the television on to the CNN cable news. I fixed the dogs their breakfast and gave them fresh water, then went to the family room to relax with my coffee and watch the news.

After taking my shower and preparing for work, I relaxed with orange juice and fresh coffee while watching *The Today Show* on NBC. My first appointment was at ten o'clock with Count Szechenyi at his Surf Club apartment. I was enjoying my leisure, half-watching television, reading the newspaper, having my coffee and giving Baron and Sherry their morning cookies.

At 8:55, the announcer on *The Today Show* broke into a commercial:

"We have Breaking News from Los Angeles. David Janssen, the tough-talking TV private eye of *Richard Diamond* and *Harry O* and the falsely accused hero of *The Fugitive* died today at age 48. Janssen was pronounced dead at Santa Monica Hospital after suffering an apparent heart attack at his Malibu home."

I slumped into my chair and stared at the television, unable to believe what I just heard. David Janssen - DEAD! I could not bring myself to believe it! Was it a joke? Was it some kind of promotion for one of his films?

NO! I knew it was true. I broke down and cried like a baby!

Dave was a real friend. He was a real man, so much more than a celebrity and actor. David Janssen was an all around, down-to-earth guy.

I cancelled my day at work. I stumbled around my family room, switching the television news channels to find as much information as I could about this unfathomable tragedy.

Dave was so young! I had just spoken with him four days earlier. He was pleased that he had passed his physical - a complete physical required by his studio producing his new TV movie. I just could not believe the news!

My first thought was to get on a plane and fly out to Los Angeles for his services. Reality set in and I knew I would not be able to do this. I also had a feeling I would not be among the 'chosen' to attend his services.

All I could do was watch the television news reports detailing the circumstances surrounding his death. Could there have been an underlying cause of his sudden death ... something even sinister? I dismissed the thought.

How could a man, so young, so strong - with no history of heart problems - pass a complete physical examination and a few days later die of a heart attack? I just could not comprehend it. I learned Dave was pronounced dead at 5:55 AM.

Eight months later, on December 11, 1980 at 7:05 in the morning, I was called by a close friend, Detective Tom Lovell of the Indianapolis Police Department.

He informed me that a close friend and mentor, Detective Sergeant Jack R. Ohrberg - of the Robbery & Homicide unit of the Indianapolis Police Department - had been brutally murdered in a shoot-out with a gang of armed robbery and murder suspects. He died at 5:11 AM, less than an hour before Dave had been pronounced dead eight months earlier. That was a very bad year for me. I lost two close friends.

Years have passed and I have been encouraged, and even inspired, to write this book. This is for Dave's fans ... so they can have an insight into the kind of man he truly was.

The women he married were not his wisest choices. Dave took responsibility for his faults; the women in his life continued to live in denial and placed all the blame on Dave. It simply was not true.

I struggled at first, although I pride myself for having a photographic memory. The only way I found I could write this book was to close my eyes and remember Dave and our conversations. In doing so, I found I could actually HEAR his voice. If it was times we were sitting together, I could actually see his expressions, his laugh and his smiles.

It has been a long, somewhat tedious, journey with a lot of laughs, some fits of anger and depression, but mostly great memories.

In my opinion, David Janssen was a truly kind, sensitive, passionate man who gave his all to provide his fans with real entertainment. It is so sad that such a gifted man who gave so much had to endure such torment in his life.

I have purposely left out many conversations we had discussing his mother and his feelings about her placing him in the McKinley Home for Boys. His three years in the home tormented him the remainder of his life.

When his mother married Eugene Janssen, Dave felt secure and he found a father figure whom he loved. His mother's divorce from Gene Janssen had a tremendous effect on Dave.

No doubt his drinking and smoking contributed to his untimely demise.

I was blessed, honored and privileged that Dave Janssen extended his friendship to me and considered me to be a true friend.

Even 34 years after his death, he is still talked about, written about, remembered and beloved by millions of people. *The Fugitive* is still running on the ME-TV cable network and I am sure in other parts of the world, his films are often aired on television today.

Now, this journey with Dave is complete. I will now prepare myself a J & B Scotch, a splash of water and a lemon wedge, raise my drink in hand: "Here's to you, DAVE! Rest in peace."

***

A gem posted on the Internet

Drinking With David Janssen: The Fugitive
October 30, 2011

In the late 1960s - early 1970s I spent my summer months in Acapulco, Mexico. I was single and teaching American History at Liberty High School in Amite County, Mississippi. I was very wild in those days and spent at least two months of each year South of the Border, mostly in Acapulco.

My first trip was inspired by the old Elvis movie 'Fun in Acapulco' which came out in 1963 and was filmed in Acapulco around the old 'Acapulco Hilton'. I knew when I first saw the film that one day I would swim in that Hilton pool where Elvis was. Thus, my first trip to that city was in 1966. Several years later on one of what would become an annual pilgrimage I met three Canadian guys from Toronto. We became good friends and planned our future trips to that great town.

To make a long story short, and it is a long story, on one trip we had been seeing some stewardesses who worked for Qantas Airlines. They would often fly down from San Francisco on the weekend and spend a few days with us at our 'A' Frame cabin across from the beach.

On a trip to the airport to pick the girls up, David, John, Eugene (my Canadian friends) and I were sitting in the airport lounge waiting for their flight to come in. I looked at a solitary man sitting at the bar and told my friends that was David Janssen - they didn't think so.

I got up and walked over to the man and politely asked him if he was 'David Janssen' and to my surprise he said, 'Yes,' and invited me to sit and have a drink. We had several over about a thirty minute period and then parted company.

YES, I drank with David Janssen. Next week we were back at the airport seeing the girls off and, much to my surprise, Tony Curtis and David were at the bar.

I approached the two and David remembered me, but other than introducing me to Tony, gave me little time. On our return trip to town from the airport we stopped at the PEMEX station to gas up and saw David and Tony with two very young Mexican girls gassing up their van - I knew then why he didn't have time for me at the airport lounge!!!

Strangely, of all the events of the trip - including the many nights at the 'Zona Rojo' - meeting David Janssen and having those drinks with 'The Fugitive' is the one that stands out.

For those not old enough to remember, 'The Fugitive' TV series was the most popular of its day from 1963-'67. The 1993 movie 'The Fugitive' with Harrison Ford and Tommy Lee Jones was based entirely on that series from the 1960s.

And in case you may be wondering how a lowly teacher could afford those months in Mexico - the 'A' Frame cabin on the beach rented for $300 a month - split four ways came out for less than $3 a day for the four of us.

Beer was less than 50 centavos when the rate of exchange was 12.5 pesos to a dollar; that comes out to about 3.04 per beer when purchased at the 'Super-Super', their big supermarket.

And for the cost of certain unnamed products in the 'Zona Rojo' (the 'red light district') I'll leave that to your imagination. And we always avoided the 'Tourista' traps, but occasionally did stumble into that dreaded 'Tourista' baiter known as 'Montezuma's Revenge' - or for you uninformed - 'diarrhea'!

- Courtesy of Mr. Ron Russell.

Author's Note

The experience related by Mr. Ron Russell is only one example of thousands which demonstrate David Janssen's 'down-to-earth, ordinary guy' character.

That is how we met. In a ballroom full of Hollywood celebrities, Captains of Industry and Political figures, he chose to speak with me. Fortunately for me, our friendship developed and lasted for the remainder of his life. I was blessed.

Unfortunately for him, his fame did not allow him to live an ordinary, normal life. That was the price he paid for being such an extraordinary actor. I can attest to the fact that deep inside, David Janssen was an 'ordinary guy' with extraordinary talents. David lived an extraordinary life to the end.

I miss him.

Printed in Great Britain
by Amazon

23712274R00165